The Whiskey Rebellion

Recent Titles in
Contributions in American History
Series Editor: Jon L. Wakelyn

The Whiskey Rebellion

Past and Present Perspectives

Edited by STEVEN R. BOYD

Contributions in American History, Number 109

G P

Greenwood Press
Westport, Connecticut • London, England

Library of Congress Cataloging in Publication Data

Main entry under title:

The Whiskey Rebellion.

 (Contributions in American history, ISSN 0084-9219 ;
no. 109)
  Bibliography: p.
  Includes index.
  1. Whiskey Insurrection, 1794—Addresses, essays,
lectures. I. Boyd, Steven R. II. Series.
E315.W65 1985   973.4'3   84-22437
ISBN 0-313-24534-7 (lib. bdg.)

Library of Congress Catalog Card Number: 84-22437
ISBN 0-313-24534-7
ISSN: 0084-9219

First published in 1985

Greenwood Press
A division of Congressional Information Service, Inc.
88 Post Road West
Westport, Connecticut 06881

Printed in the United States of America

10 9 8 7 6 5 4 3 2 1

Copyright Acknowledgments

Judge Alexander Addison's letter is from the Craig papers of the Carnegie Library of Pittsburgh,
reprinted by permission.

Roland M. Baumann's essay copyright © Historical Society of Pennsylvania, 1982, reprinted by
permission.

Mary K. Bonsteel Tachau's essay excerpted from Mary K. Bonsteel Tachau, *Federal Courts in the
Early Republic: Kentucky, 1789-1816*, copyright © 1978 by Princeton University Press, reprinted
by permission of Princeton University Press.

To
Mary K. Bonsteel Tachau

Contents

Preface

This collection grew out of a request from Roland Baumann, program chair, for me to serve on a panel on the Whiskey Rebellion at the 1976 annual meeting of the Pennsylvania Historical Association. In the process of developing my ideas and presenting the paper I discovered that several people were engaged in research on the rebellion. I also realized that some of them were not aware of the work of others and decided that an anthology chiefly of current essays could serve a useful purpose. This anthology is the result of that idea.

The texts of the documentary chapters in this volume are true to the originals. Minor changes in punctuation, spelling, and the like were made, however, when appropriate to clarify meaning.

In the process of preparing this volume I have accumulated a host of debts. First, I wish to thank the contributors to this volume who have labored with me in its preparation. Second, I wish to thank those who, for reasons of space or time, are not included. Among those, in particular are David Sloan, an associate professor of history at the University of Arkansas and Dodee Fennell, a member of the labor history project at the City University of New York. Third, I want to acknowledge my own and the other contributors' indebtedness to those who preceded us in writing about the Whiskey Rebellion. In particular, I wish to thank David Whitten, a professor of economics at Auburn University, who has offered timely encouragement over the years. Finally, I want to thank Jon Wakelyn, a professor of history at Catholic University and the editor of the series in which this volume appears, for he too has played a key role in its completion.

The dedication is to a person who, by her example, encourages all of us to strive to better understand the past and to communicate that past to the present and future generations.

Chronology

July 16, 1794	100 men attack General Neville at his home
July 17, 1794	500 men attack and destroy General Neville's home
July 23, 1794	Meeting at Mingo Creek Meeting House, Washington County
August 1, 1794	Rebels rendezvous at Braddock's Field
August 2, 1794	Rebels march through Pittsburgh; meeting at President Washington's
August 6, 1794	Governor Mifflin appoints commissioners
August 7, 1794	Washington issues a proclamation
August 8, 1794	Appointment of United States Commissioners
August 14, 1794	Meeting at Parkinson's Ferry; United States Commissioners reach Pittsburgh
August 17, 1794	Pennsylvania Commissioners reach Pittsburgh
August 20–23, 1794	United States and Pennsylvania Commissioners meet with Committee of Twelve
August 28–29, 1794	Committee of Sixty meets at Brownsville and accepts terms negotiated by Committee of Twelve
September 11–12, 1794	Inhabitants of the four counties vote whether or not to submit to the laws of the United States
September 13, 1794	Judges of elections meet to certify and report the vote
October 2, 1794	Second Parkinson Ferry Meeting
October 24, 1794	Army enters Pittsburgh
November 13, 1794	Prisoners marched to Pittsburgh
November 18, 1794	Most troops leave Pittsburgh
May 1795	Trial of the whiskey rebels begins in Philadelphia

The Whiskey Rebellion

JAMES KIRBY MARTIN

Introduction: The Whiskey Rebellion Redivivus

Throughout the history of the United States, violent confrontations have erupted, and some have threatened the nation's political and social fabric. No sequence of events came as close to destroying the republic as the Civil War. Historians have and will continue to debate why that bloody internal holocaust, which cost the nation hundreds of thousands of lives, came about in the first place. Students of the Civil War know what happened. The challenge is to determine why it happened and to comprehend its consequences. And the same is true for another confrontation, much less disastrous but nonetheless significant, known as the Whiskey Rebellion. This insurrection could have resulted in a tragic internal war at the very moment of the nation's birth. It could have suffocated the republican experiment even before the new nation had much of a chance to breathe, let alone experience an independent life. That the Whiskey Rebellion did not result in some form of national self-destruction is of real historical significance. As with the Civil War, the challenge is to determine why the insurrection occurred and to assess its implications with regard to the overall nation-making process.

From the 1790s to our own time, the Whiskey Rebellion has been a fascinating event for study and commentary. The insurrection developed at the very end of the revolutionary period, which was a violent epoch in and of itself. The American Revolution represented a host of confrontations, the most consequential of which was the War for American Independence. During the 1760s and early 1770s, the British government, according to provincial perceptions, seemed bent on a course of tyranny. More and more the colonists perceived that they were becoming entrapped in the chains of political slavery. That threat became too much to bear, and the result was a nasty civil war that forever terminated formal political relations between the British Empire and thirteen of its American provinces. The call word of the Revolutionary Era was *liberty*, and American leaders repeatedly spoke about the need for new governments that would insure the basic rights of citizens. A central objective of the Revolution thus turned into a search for just and evenhanded government. However, the promulgation of state constitutions and a strong national Constitution in 1787 to replace the Articles of Confederation did not necessarily guarantee equitable policymaking for all citizens.

The perception of inequitable policymaking was central to the concerns of those who became the whiskey rebels. In review of their actions, the insurrection represented a clash of wills between backcountry farmers, mostly from Pennsylvania, and Federalist leaders during George Washington's first and second presidential administrations. The source of the controversy may be traced to the whiskey excise tax of 1791, passed by Congress after strong promptings from Treasury Secretary Alexander Hamilton. Hamilton was deeply committed to full funding of the nation's war debt. The new tax on whiskey was one means of paying that debt. However, this type of tax did not please many common citizens, especially those farmers who lived west of the Appalachians and on whom the burden of taxation fell. From their perspective, the excise tax severely threatened any margin of economic solvency that they could expect to enjoy as they wrestled with rocky soil and uncooperative weather in their struggle to provide at least subsistence living conditions for their families and themselves.

The primary economic factor facing these pioneers, besides problems of soil and climate, was the inaccessibility of markets for the modest surpluses they produced. Since the Mississippi River was not open to American commerce, the pattern was to transport farm goods to the East—across the Appalachians. Yet grain was so bulky that the costs of transportation offset potential profits. In response to these circumstances, the custom had become to distill grains into whiskies before hauling the less bulky brew to market. Over time, whiskey had also become an important fiat currency in the barter economy of the backcountry. Hence, an excise tax on whiskey was as threatening as any tax could be, since it fell on an essential trading commodity, one that also served as a medium of exchange in the acquisition of needed supplies to operate homesteads.

The whiskey tax was threatening from other angles as well. First, the excise was to be collected from the farmers themselves rather than from the retailers of their product. Not only would federally appointed tax collectors be combing the countryside and demanding payments, but such a plan also indicated that the tax, set at roughly 25 percent of the market value of a gallon of whiskey, would be collected before farmers realized any gain in the marketplace from their labors. If prices did not rise at market, then the farmers would have to absorb the full brunt of the tax, portending the loss of any margin of gain from operating in the market economy in the first place. The tax thus held out the prospect of economic ruin, especially for those who depended upon the sale of whiskey for supplies to be able to plant next year's crops.

There was also a second factor that incensed the farmers. The original 1791 law specified that individuals charged with evading the tax could be tried only in federal district courts, the closest one being in Philadelphia. This meant that adjudication would be far removed from sympathetic neighbors who could serve as jurors. It also suggested that fines and other court penalties, coming on top of the long journey eastward and lost labor, would be severe enough to cost any alleged violator his home and property.

Despite everything, the West did not explode in responding to the whiskey tax. While there were some ugly individual incidents, serious outbreaks of collective violence did not automatically ensue. Mostly, westerners met and prepared petitions demanding that grievances be redressed. Most hoped that the Washington administration would back down. In turn, Congress adopted modifications of the 1791 law, which included lowering the tax rate and improving collection procedures. The West thus passed through a period of unsteady calm before the storm finally broke in 1794.

And break loose it did. Alexander Hamilton seemed to ignite the charged atmosphere. In early 1794, he called upon Congress to modify the whiskey law so that alleged violators could be tried in state courts if they lived more than fifty miles from meeting sites of federal district courts. This seemed to be an olive branch. But while Congress deliberated, excise collectors went after delinquent farmers with renewed vigor, including some seventy-five men who had avoided paying the tax in 1793. By the time they had received notices to attend court in Philadelphia, the new law was already in effect.

Western Pennsylvanians were pleased with the statutory concession, yet it appeared to many that a few had been selected for a special form of harassment. Among those who ultimately got notices were individuals who had been active in a local Democratic-Republican Society, only one of many such societies formed throughout the states to celebrate the ideals of the American and French Revolutions. Some chapters had been openly critical of Alexander Hamilton in particular and Federalist policies more generally. Washington later acknowledged that he considered these societies as more than putative political arms of the developing Jeffersonian opposition party; he also thought that they were subversive of the national interest. Yet for settlers facing officers of the law handing out writs to appear in Philadelphia, it seemed that they were now being tampered with because of their political views, regardless of whether they had been evading the whiskey tax.

Thus it was that the federal marshal serving such notices ran into serious trouble. On July 15, he rode into Allegheny County, accompanied by John Neville, the excise inspector for the whole region. Before the day was over, the marshal and the inspector had to flee in the face of an armed, hostile party that fired shots at them. The next day, July 16, Neville had to fend off a crowd of some one hundred settlers at his residence. The inspector estimated that at least five protesters were wounded during this brief confrontation. All of this caused the farmers to regroup themselves with greatly expanded numbers. They mounted a much more furious assault the next day. The hastily assembled defenders of Neville's home gave in to superior numbers when it was clear that they would be overrun. Having secured their victory, the protesters torched and burned

Neville's home, one of the most palatial in western Pennsylvania, to the ground. For two more weeks, sporadic protest continued, climaxed by a well-controlled march, as a show of strength, of an estimated 7,000 backcountry inhabitants through Pittsburgh. Little property or personal damage resulted from this show of force. And with that, the insurrection for all practical purposes came to an end.

Just as the western Pennsylvanians were regaining their composure, the Washington administration decided to act. The president met with his advisers the day after the march on Pittsburgh. Not knowing about the demonstration there, they focused in their discussion on the possible spread of turbulence to other backcountry locales, from Maryland to Georgia and as far west as Kentucky. Deeply concerned whether the national government could cope with widespread domestic violence, the president argued for a show of force; his advisers, including Hamilton, agreed. As a result, Washington ordered the states to call out some 15,000 militiamen. That army gathered at Harrisburg during September, with the aging former commander in chief in attendance for a brief period. Under the leadership of the well-known Revolutionary War officer Henry ("Light-Horse Harry") Lee and with Alexander Hamilton accompanying them, the soldiers marched west but could find few, if any, insurrectionists. The fury of the backcountry had long since passed. Before the army disbanded, it rounded up several suspected rebels, twenty of whom were sent to Philadelphia in irons. The federal government charged each with high treason, but only two were convicted. Anticlimactically, President Washington wisely pardoned both men on the grounds that one was insane and the other dimwitted. Such was the inglorious end of the Whiskey Rebellion.

In such a brief description, it is difficult to capture the full flavor of the insurrection. Certainly there was action and drama, heightened by the involvement of such major personalities as George Washington, Alexander Hamilton, Thomas Jefferson, Albert Gallatin, and Hugh Henry Brackenridge, who served as protagonists and antagonists. Yet the rebellion represented much more than good historical theater. Historians have long recognized that the issues and events of the insurrection contain real explanatory power regarding the turbulent course of nation making in late eighteenth-century America. While interpretations have shown a marked variance and in some cases have been highly partisan, all those who reflect on the rebellion soon realize that it does shed meaningful light on the internal struggle to formulate an enduring republican edifice during Revolutionary and post-Revolutionary times.

The essays contained in this anthology represent a judicious mixture of the new and the old. As a group, they suggest how and why historical interpretations have evolved over time—and from that point of view this collection becomes a contribution to changing historiographical sensibilities about the American experience.

The art of historical interpretation is much disputed and debated. At its core is the author's analytical focus and range of concerns. At one time, explanations of the Whiskey Rebellion had a decidedly partisan quality. This is hardly unusual, when interpretations are generated as reminiscences to justify this or to explain away that action. But with the passage of time, more dispassionate commentators have come to the fore and, learning from earlier explanations, have raised more profound questions. Thus, in our own time, historians of the rebellion do not dwell on such matters as whether this person was a potential tyrant or that person was deluding and misleading the people. Rather, they have asked questions like the following: Was the whiskey tax really so unreasonable? If it was, were not these settlers relatively restrained in their defense of individual and community interests? How much did long-standing traditions of rural protest influence the whiskey rebels? Does this indicate that the insurrection was a culminating event of the Revolutionary Era? Given the Federalist perception of 1794 that violence might spread to other localities, did Washington and his advisers overreact to circumstances? Should they have been that worried about the security, strength, and stature of the new national government, or were other matters affecting their decision making? How did the rebellion influence the delicate balance between the use of law relative to force of arms in the young republic? What does the insurrection reveal about attitudes concerning representation and possible restraints on the actions of a new—and more powerful—central government?

Providing answers to such questions requires careful inquiry predicated upon immersion in the sources. And one place to start is with the conflicting testimony of various participants, samples of which are presented in this anthology. Students need to consider and evaluate that evidence if they are to become involved in the art of historical interpretation. That is one purpose of this volume. A second purpose is to present an array of thoughtful recent interpretations that help to draw out meaningful conclusions about the role of the Whiskey Rebellion in American history. In neither respect is this anthology meant to be fully definitive. It does not contain all the possible interpretations. There is too much work left to be done on the rebellion to hope for that. Rather, this anthology is meant as a beginning in support of further historical inquiry. It is to be hoped that it will gain the interest and attention of scholars of the early American experience, as well as their students—and assist in encouraging those students to become involved in the historical enterprise.

The Friends of Liberty, the Friends of Order, and the Whiskey Rebellion: A Historiographical Essay

Liberty must prevail at any price.
—Louis Antoine de Saint-Just, *Institutions*

The Whole World consisting of parts so many, so different, is by this only thing upheld; he which framed them hath set them in order.
—Richard Hooker, *Of the Laws of Ecclesiastical Polity*

Until recently historians of the Whiskey Rebellion asked the same basic questions—who was right, who was wrong? Was the real issue of 1794 the beleaguered liberty of poverty-stricken frontiersmen or the genuine threat to order that tax resistance represented? Was the rebellion a consequence of ideological conflict over the issue of just taxation, over the cash drain that such a tax might inflict on a specie-poor region, and over the threat to commercial activity posed by an excise on settlers' only cash crop and fundamental component of their barter economy? Or had one frontier district among many simply become infested with a high proportion of European ''rabble,'' people with little respect for law and no real stake in American republicanism—violent, uncivilized folk inspired to anarchy by the example of the French Revolution and the connivance of certain ''self-created'' societies, ruthless newspaper editors, and frontier demagogues? Was the suppression of the western Pennsylvania insurrection a crushing blow to the noblest ambitions of American revolutionaries or a preemptive strike for constitutional governance? In other words, whose side should we take,

I gratefully acknowledge the financial support of the Danforth and Whiting Foundations during the period in which this chapter was researched and written. I also thank Steven R. Boyd, Douglas Greenberg, J. William Frost, Stanley N. Katz, Louis P. Masur, and John M. Murrin for their helpful comments on earlier drafts.

Tom the Tinker's or Alexander Hamilton's? Since historians who phrased these questions have usually responded with one of two answers, the historiography divides neatly between what I will call the "friends of liberty" and the "friends of order."

The rebellion has thus been used and abused by its chroniclers to tell and retell stories about the demise of anti-Federalism, the defeat of frontier liberty, or the emergence of a strong and credible national government. The story has been told from the top down, the bottom up, and, alternatively, from eastern and frontier perspectives. This essay tells the tale of the rebellion's historians. It recounts the origins and the contributions and failures of the rebellion's two historiographic schools—the friends of liberty and the friends of order. The essay relates this historiographic saga, and it proposes an agenda for future students of the Whiskey Rebellion.

The rebels have always seemed in the retelling, even by their friends, to have had somewhat overactive imaginations. Their cries of oppression, their caricatures of the threats posed by tax collectors, their nightmares of nakedness, starvation, and abuse of power by national leaders look like exaggerated responses to so inconsequential a tax on whiskey. George Washington has always appeared no less silly squeezing into his old general's uniform, mounting his stallion, and riding off into the sunset at the head of a 15,000-man army— approximating the entire force that battled British troops in the Revolution—to wage war against an ephemeral band of rag-tag farmers and erstwhile laborers hundreds of miles from nowhere, who were armed, in some cases, with nothing more threatening to the nation than sticks and stones. What a joke of an internal war, what an obvious reflection of the "paranoid style" afflicting politics at the time.[1]

The Whiskey Rebellion was more, however, than a comic episode, although the partisan concerns of historians have tended to obscure this point. People on both sides of the rebellion died; others suffered the disease and injury associated with fighting any war in that era. Some lost property, endured the humiliation of defeat, and languished (or died) in jail as a consequence.

These were not all silly, middle-aged men acting out their midlife crises on the sporting fields of a martial campaign. The rebellion was, according to John Marshall, *the* major political confrontation of the republic's first quarter-century. The rebellion marked the first large-scale resistance to a law of the United States under the Constitution. The federal government's response represented the first exercise of the internal police power of a president under the Constitution. There were good reasons to believe that "liberty" and "order" really were at stake here, that a secession crisis or civil war really was in the offing. The rebellion was a standoff between the two regions, the two ideologies, and the two competing interests that defined the poles of mainstream national politics during the Federalist administrations. It was fought over the most divisive issues of domestic politics during the second half of the eighteenth century—the relationship between order and liberty, the center and the periphery, the national and the local, the East and the West. For all these reasons and in all these ways we should take all sides—historical and historiographic—more seriously than they have taken each other. We should aim at modest syntheses that credit contemporary and modern friends of liberty and friends of order with similar insight and blindness to the issues and the stakes of interregional politics during the 1790s. These are the tasks undertaken by contributors to this anthology and the chores that lie ahead for other students of political conflict in the late eighteenth century.

Early accounts of the Whiskey Rebellion came from writers whose role as actors blurred their visions as historians. These were unabashedly partisan defenses of the authors' participation in contemporary events. Hugh Henry Brackenridge, for example, baldly admitted in 1795: "What I write is with a view to explain my own conduct, which has not been understood." Likewise, William Findley published his book only two years after the event, in 1796, in part because Brackenridge's was "chiefly confined to what fell under his own observation," and because others had misrepresented the conduct of Findley and some of his friends.[2]

Relatives of participants wrote the next generation of accounts with the intention of vindicating their progenitors. Neville Craig was scion and literary defender of the John Neville family, whose house the rebels burned in 1794. In his *History of Pittsburgh* (1851), Craig laid down the gauntlet by naming Brackenridge, Findley, and Albert Gallatin as "leading actors," foreigners, and courters of popular favor.[3] Henry Marie Brackenridge, son of Hugh, responded to Craig through nineteen issues of Pittsburgh's *Commercial Journal*. Craig took five issues to rebut. Brackenridge rejoined with another ten articles and, finally, Craig had the last words of this particular exchange with four more responses.

Their venom not yet vitiated, the two septuagenarians each wrote another book on the rebellion. Brackenridge's *History of the Western Insurrection* (1859) appeared because his father "was the object of the most indecent abuse by the scurrilous writer [Neville Craig]."[4] Craig responded in kind with his own short book (1859) which he "intended not as a history of the Insurrection, but as a neutralizer of the influence of the books of the Brackenridges, by exposing a few of the many inconsistencies, contradictions and falsehoods of those books, and thus showing that they are unworthy of credit."[5]

This literary feud between the Nevilles and Brackenridges became, then, along with Findley's account, the primary source for scholars writing about the rebellion. Historians supplemented participants' perspectives with either Alexander Hamilton's Treasury Department records, some of which were ultimately published in the *Pennsylvania Archives* series, or blasts from contemporary newspapers that opposed the Federalist administration. Few ever questioned partisanship as the organizing principle of analysis. Historians now assaulted each other from the same ideological trenches as had the subjects of their study. Liberty, order, patriotism, and the continuing meaning of America's Revolution remained volatile issues among chroniclers of our past. Only poor marksmanship kept historiographic warriors from mortally wounding our potential for understanding this event.

The friends of liberty and the friends of order among historians of the Whiskey Rebellion reveal themselves both by the causes they identify as instrumental in bringing on armed conflict and the historical actors whose roles they choose to defend or attack. Historiographic friends of liberty, like their historical counterparts, also take the grievances of western Pennsylvania's farmers far more seriously than do their opponents.

Hugh Brackenridge, a local attorney and later a judge, thought that the roots of opposition to the excise lay in cultural and economic factors. He viewed the opposition to excisemen as a traditional sentiment among natives of Scotland and Ireland. Since Pennsylvania's four western counties were full of Irish, Scots, and Scots-Irish settlers, he believed the ethnic composition of the area affected the possibility for collecting an excise tax. Of even greater significance in Brackenridge's mind than these "abstract prejudices" were the economic factors that made a tax on whiskey excessively burdensome for the frontier settlers. "The people of the western country not having a market for their grain," he wrote, "had recourse to the distilation of it; and under the acts, all beyond what was for private use, was liable to the duties. Thus it became still more an object to evade the law, or oppose it."[6]

William Findley—weaver, lawyer, and congressman—also believed that the rebels had received a bad press, that their impoverished condition and the other hardships of frontier life made them worthy of sympathetic understanding. Like Brackenridge, Findley believed that economic conditions were a primary cause of resistance to the excise. He wrote:

the people anticipated their experiencing peculiar hardships from the excise. Without money, or the means of procuring it, and consuming their whiskey only in their families or using it as an item of barter, which, though in some respects answered the place of money, yet would not be received in pay for the excise tax, they thought it hard to pay as much tax on what sold with them but at from two shillings and six pence, as they did where it brought double that price. These, and such like arguments were not new. I found them in use against the state excise when I went to reside in that country. They arose from their situation, the simplest person feeling their force, knew how to use them.[7]

Findley identified no other specific grievance that prompted opposition to the excise tax in western Pennsylvania. To him, the economic fact of a barter economy was the fundamental base of resistance. Violence, of course, was not a necessary consequence of opposition. But subsequent acts, Findley argued, rather than grievances, dictated the course of violent protest.

Later accounts identified two additional grievances as causes of the western Pennsylvania excise riots. The Reverend James Carnahan, a student in the Pittsburgh area during the mid-1790s and later president of the College of New Jersey

(Princeton), saw events much as Findley and the elder Brackenridge did. He maintained that economics, culture, and "Whig" traditions all contributed to the settlers' hatred of the excise, and he emphasized the Scottish and Irish origins of the inhabitants of western Pennsylvania even more heavily than Brackenridge. Finally, and uniquely, Carnahan called attention to the rioters' conscious paralleling of their case with that of the Stamp Act rioters in 1765 and the Boston Tea Party "Indians" in 1773. Alone among nineteenth-century chroniclers of the Whiskey Rebellion, Carnahan pointed out:

These people also remembered that resistance to the stamp act and duty on tea at the commencement of the American Revolution began by the destruction of the tea and refusal to use the Royal stamps—That the design was not to break allegiance to the British throne, but to force a repeal of these odious laws.[8]

These same people had, almost to a man, fought against the British army. Now, "they flattered themselves that they were only carrying out Whig principles and following Whig examples in resisting the excise law. These ideas pervading the great body of the people, caused those who were orderly and peaceable citizens to look with an indulgent eye at the first acts of insult and violence to the federal excise officers."[9] Thus, the ideological traditions of frontier Whigs stood high for Carnahan among the factors that governed the course of resistance in western Pennsylvania. Rarely since the 1850s has any historian stressed either the ideological dimension or the conscious link to Stamp and Tea Act resistance. Yet neither have more recent historians developed arguments that contradict Carnahan's observations.

Henry Marie Brackenridge, another friend of liberty, emphasized two reasons for the general hostility to the excise tax in the region of his birth. First, he restated the economic causes for resistance. He believed that lack of marketable crops, distance, and difficulty of transportation made whiskey production an economic necessity. Brackenridge argued, "The still was . . . the necessary appendage of every farm, where the farmer was able to procure it; if not, he was compelled to carry his grain to the more wealthy to be distilled. In fact some of these distilleries on a large scale, were friendly to the excise laws, as it rendered the poorer farmers dependent on them."[10] The novelty of this description of economic conditions lay in the identification of two classes—wealthy and poor—among the distillers. None of the previous accounts contradicted this picture, but neither did they delineate the significance of the class distinction.

Brackenridge also discussed another of the settlers' grievances that other authors neglected to stress. In fact, according to Brackenridge, *the* major cause of *violent* resistance had nothing directly to do with the excise tax itself. Rather, the method of enforcement provoked the rage that turned to violence among the farmers of the Pittsburgh area. Brackenridge thought:

the Western riots, improperly called an insurrection, were not instigated by hostility to the government of the United States, nor did they originate merely on account of the excise on whiskey, but in a more excusable motive the service of process on delinquent distillers, who would in consequence be compelled to attend in Philadelphia, at the sacrifice of their farms and the ruin of their families. . . . The taking persons "beyond the seas for trial," is one of the grievances complained of in the Declaration of Independence, and the idea of trial by the vicinage, is one of the instincts of Saxon and American liberty.[11]

According to Brackenridge, then, the heart of excise resistance was the ruinous expense in time and money required by litigation in a federal court some 300 miles distant. *Any* law placing such an untoward burden upon a class of defendants would probably have met with similar disdain.

All of these accounts—those of the Brackenridges, Findley, Craig, and Carnahan—are essentially primary documents. The personal involvement of the authors or their relatives, their unconcealed wish to defend themselves and/or the whiskey rebel's cause, and their asserted desire to provide first-person versions rather than genuine histories of events, all mark them as being less analytical than is desirable. To note this fact is not to denounce the early writers or to denigrate the value of their contributions. On the contrary, the historian of the Whiskey Rebellion is twice-blessed by the number and the literary quality of first-person accounts. These narratives open several avenues of exploration in search for causes—culture, economics, geography, "Whig" ideology, and the courts all suggest encouraging possibilities for research.

At least four other narratives of the Whiskey Rebellion that belong among the friends of liberty appeared during the nineteenth century. The first, drawn solely from the published accounts discussed above, was in an appendix to Israel Rupp's *Early History of Western Pennsylvania* (1847). This was simply a derivative account summarizing events and defending the rebels as loyal, if sometimes misguided, citizens. Townsend Ward's scholarly study of the rebellion (1858) was, on the other hand, the most judicious, comprehensive, and reliable of the nineteenth-century histories in either historiographic camp. Ward traced the tradition of popular opposition to excises in England from the mid-seventeenth through the eighteenth century. He described the practical and theoretical opposition to excises in the state constitutional ratifying conventions of 1787–1788, in state legislatures, and in Congress itself. Finally, Ward studied life on the frontier and concluded:

However rude the frontier population of Pennsylvania may have been, a thorough examination of all the circumstances connected with the important event of 1794, will, I think, relieve them from the charge of disaffection to the Federal Government, and exhibit some palliation for that lawlessness which has been, not without exaggeration, ascribed to them.[12]

Ward's analysis was more moderate in tone than first-person accounts by other nineteenth-century friends of liberty, but ulitmately his, too, was an apologia for the rebels and an indictment of Federalist excesses.

One historian carried the banner of the Whiskey Rebellion's friends of liberty into the twentieth century. Leland D. Baldwin's *Whiskey Rebels* (1939) was the only book-length treatment of the event published since the mid-nineteenth century. Its focus was entirely local—the causes, courses of events, and results of resistance to the excise in western Pennsylvania. At the time Baldwin wrote, he noted, there were "great gaps in the materials bearing on the Whiskey Insurrection, particularly on the military and statistical aspects, and on the motivations of the Federalist party."[13] As a result, Baldwin's work is a one-sided and, given the sources he relied on, a predictably partisan account of the Whiskey Rebellion as seen through the eyes of western Pennsylvanians. Baldwin's major, though not exclusive, sources for the bulk of his narrative were Findley and H. H. Brackenridge. He also incorporated, uncritically, the accounts and arguments of Carnahan and the younger Brackenridge.

Thus, on the question of causes, Baldwin's book was a reprise of the entire litany of the friends of liberty. According to Baldwin, "The heredity, the psychology, and the situation of the Monongahela farmer all conspired to make him an enemy of the excise. The expanse of transportation to distant markets reduced the profit on the product of his still to a scant margin. . . . Heredity, convenience, and habit made whiskey his characteristic tipple as well as the most acceptable article for barter."[14] Finally, Baldwin asserted that the frontiersmen's sense of honor and their distance from Philadelphia courts combined to assure staunch resistance to the tax:

The Monongahela countryman's pride made him resent, almost hysterically, the inquisitorialness of excise officers with their searches and seizures, their markings with paint and branding irons. "What was it caused the Revolution, if it was not this?" the westerner asked, and refused to be convinced that such actions from a government seated in Philadelphia were any less dangerous to liberty than from one seated in London. Some of the more radical Presbyterians also found an additional fault in the fact that the law required them to make oath, for this was a violation of their conscientious scruples.—It is possible that the westerner would have submitted to these conditions, galling as they were, had not one other circumstance added to insult and injury what he regarded as certain ruin. This was the provision for trial of excise cases arising in Pennsylvania in the federal court in Philadelphia.[15]

What Baldwin's narrative lacked was a critical analysis that would allow us to weigh the significance of these "causal" factors. What is the evidence for each, other than the assertions of Findley or Brackenridge? Are these the only causes or merely the most important ones? Upon which issues did the mass of participants focus? Finally, what motivated the friends of order to deny the cultural, economic, geographic, and ideological arguments of the friends of liberty? Baldwin's narrative offered answers to none of these questions. Because he ignored government records and official justifications for action, the picture Baldwin painted was one-dimensional, a portrait that lacked perspective and therefore distorted the events it sought to clarify. The friends of liberty thus remain inviting targets for the barbed arrows of the rebellion's law-and-order historians.

Since the Whiskey Rebellion, friends of order have addressed each of the causes outlined above and found each wanting. In turn, the authoritarian historians of the rebellion have offered their own set of explanations for the behavior of the rebels. A discussion of these views may assist us in sorting through the contradictory wisdom accumulated by the two camps. Only then can we proceed to examine the assumptions and attitudes underlying previous histories of the whiskey rebels and the champions of order.

Typically, the friends of order dismiss out-of-hand their opponents' sympathies for the rebel's cause. To Neville Craig, the rebels were clearly "lawless men, ruffians who burnt their neighbors' property." He considered them dregs of society who "had no scruples about attempting to commit murder, and actually committing arson."[16] The rebels were simply a lawless band of malcontents, encouraged by unscrupulous leaders like Brackenridge, Findley, and Albert Gallatin, egged on by the frenchified rhetoric of the Democratic Societies and persons with foreign ideas and loyalties. Craig ignored all rebel grievances, reasoning that the carpings of these low-life types were nothing more than the ravings of criminals elevated by the rhetoric of ambitious and traitorous lawyers.

In truth, Craig paraphrased or borrowed verbatim most of his narrative from Richard Hildreth's *History of the United States of America* (1851). Among the most vituperative assaults upon the rebels ever to appear in print, Hildreth's *History* never mentioned any of the grievances of the rebels. The causes of the rebellion were clear to Hildreth; the western region of Pennsylvania was settled mainly by Scots-Irish Presbyterians, who were, he wrote, "a race of men of great energy and decision, but never distinguished for quiet or subordination, and whose hasty and ferocious temper had already more than once stained the history of Pennsylvania with blood." Had they acted alone, the Scots-Irish rabble of the western counties would have proved a very minor threat to order outside of their immediate environs. But, wrote Hildreth, "so far from being confined to a few obscure or directly interested persons, as had been the case elsewhere, this opposition was encouraged and inflamed by many of the most influential and intelligent of the inhabitants."[17] In sum, the discontent and unruliness in the region were not much more than would ordinarily be expected among the sort of people who lived there. According to Hildreth's account, the crucial difference that made western Pennsylvania unique was the unconscionable participation and encouragement of mob action by members of the local elite.

Other nineteenth-century historians who sided with the forces of order in the Whiskey Rebellion shared a disdain for the rebel's grievances and never questioned the taxation policy or the methods used by the federal government. The rebels acted unreasonably and unlawfully. Implicit (and sometimes explicit) in this interpretation is the belief that in a republic citizens abdicate all lawful right to resist the edicts of government. Elections mean that all are represented. When represented, one must abide by a government's decisions. Historians sharing this view during the nineteenth century differed only in the tone they used to denounce participants in the rebellion.

The most emotional attacks on the whiskey rebels came, not surprisingly, within the first twenty-five years after the event. Among these writers, John Marshall (1807) and David Ramsay (1818), two of the staunchest defenders of the federal regime, were especially unsympathetic to the rebel cause. Marshall took perhaps the hardest line of all. To him no grievance seemed worthy of comment, no reason lay on the insurgents' side, all opposers of the law were motivated solely by "a spirit of disorder." The western Pennsylvanians had always opposed the national government. Marshall observed:

The constitution itself had experienced the most decided opposition; and that early enmity to the government, which had exerted every faculty to prevent its adoption, had sustained no abatement. . . . With these dispositions, a tax law, the operation of which had extended to them could not be favourably received, however general might be the support it should experience from other parts of the Union.[18]

To Marshall, then, the Whiskey Rebellion was yet another incident in the continuing attempt by the anti-Federalists to destroy the union. Fomented by French Jacobinism and its agents in America, the Democratic-Republican Societies, the violent actions of malcontents bore no real relation to actions of the government. The opposition was entirely negative in character, bent upon testing the power and resolve of the federal government at every turn. Under these conditions it was inevitable and necessary that President Washington forcefully suppress the unlawful supporters of anti-Federalism—if not in western Pennsylvania at relatively little cost in blood and money, then later, perhaps somewhere else, and perhaps at the cost of many lives and the destruction of much property.

Other friends of order in the early nineteenth century deviated little from Marshall's vision of the struggle between the government and a lawless faction of anti-Federalists. David Ramsay believed that successful persons under the new government were the subjects of envy. The moral level of national character during the revolutionary years had declined, and the "high reputation which the citizens had acquired . . . in their country's cause, was tarnished," leaving disgruntled office-seekers who had opposed the Constitution hostile to both the new government and its system of finance. Among the followers of this disgruntled elite, "The principle of excise, and not the detail of its execution was the object of hostility," Ramsay believed. As a result, "The government had no choice, but to subdue, or submit to the insurgents. . . . [Only] the greatness of the force, sent against the insurgents, by rendering resistance desperate, prevented the effusion of blood."[19]

Ramsay was virtually silent about the westerners' grievances, although he did grant that the frontier farmers found distillation of grain "convenient and profitable." It is clear from Ramsay's choice of words, as well as from his argument, however, that he did not believe the rebels acted to salvage a "convenient" marketing enterprise. Jealousy, local prejudices against all forms of taxation, and a rebellious spirit of opposition to the government seemed to Ramsay the motivating forces behind the insurgency.

Washington Irving's *Life of George Washington* (1859) lacked the intensely emotional disdain for the rebels displayed in earlier works. Nonetheless, Irving never questioned or deviated from the version of events provided by Washington himself. Citing Washington as his source for every observation about the rebellion, Irving seldom elaborated and never criticized. No notice of grievances appeared in these pages. Following Washington, Irving believed that the inhabitants of western Pennsylvania had been unreasonable. If laws could be trampled with impunity, he argued, a minority would soon overthrow the government. Inspired by an anti-Federalist faction and the Democratic Societies, the challenge to order could only be quieted by the application of overwhelming force. Washington and his biographer agreed that the rebellion and its resolution were "fortunate" occurrences. They agreed that the opportunity to display the ability of the government to enforce its laws was important and necessary.[20]

The Civil War put a real damper on interest in the Whiskey Rebellion. The latter event paled by comparison to the violent threat to national union posed by the war between the states. The lessons of the Civil War—from either side—were even clearer, even more horrible, and even more conclusive than those of the earlier episode. As a consequence, Whiskey Rebellion historiography entered a long postwar hiatus that was in large part a reflection of an anachronistic conviction that the union was secure, that interregional tensions could be suppressed by force if necessary, and that the contest between local and central control, although not conclusively resolved, was not threatening to the nation's survival. Those historians who bothered to consider the rebellion at all in the century after 1860 could imagine it as a "charmingly benign episode," significant only within the context of western Pennsylvania's local history.[21]

The 1960s brought something of a revival of interest in the rebellion from a law-and-order perspective. Perhaps historians of several different political stripes united, at least subconsciously, in response to civil rights protests, struggles between local and national authorities in the South, and crowd protests against the Vietnam War. For whatever reasons, historians began to consider the rebellion anew, and virtually all of them defended the actions of President Washington's Federalist administration and denounced those contemporary actors and subsequent historians that I have labeled friends of liberty.

Several scholars devoted their energies to redeeming the name of Alexander Hamilton. Indeed, the line of argument first developed by John Marshall and David Ramsay has most clearly descended through recent biographies of Hamilton. One historian has gone so far as to argue that "the only major historiographic controversy [about the Whiskey Rebellion] has been over whether Hamilton provoked the rebellion in order to enhance the government's stature with a show of military power."[22]

Perhaps Robert Hendrickson (1976) and Forrest McDonald (1979) are the two most apparent heirs of this historiographic tradition. Hendrickson, like Hamilton, condemned the protestors against the excise as "Shaysites." Hendrickson's evidence for dismissing out-of-hand the voiced grievances of the whiskey rebels was the testimony of Hamilton himself. According to this biographer, "A reading of Hamilton's report . . . tends to confirm his judgement that objections to the tax on whiskey were largely a cover or focal point for general rebellion against all federal authority."[23] He consulted no other evidence to verify this opinion.

Hendrickson's implicit argument seems to be that because Hamilton was a great man, there is no reason to test the veracity of his statements. One side—Hamilton's—monopolized truth and justice in the rebellion. Therefore, no evidence is superior to Hamilton's official report; there is no reason to explore other government records and certainly no cause to test the contentions of self-interested criminals like Brackenridge, Findley, and Gallatin. Western Pennsylvania was simply "a center of terrorism under the guiding hand of Albert Gallatin." The government's forceful response was not only reasonable, but necessary. According to Hendrickson:

The house burnings, seizures, woundings, and killings of federal officers reliably reported by Neville, Mentges, and others, egged on by local newspapermen and community leaders like Hugh Brackenridge; formal actions like the Mingo Creek resolutions to form a new government; and threats to Fort Fayette, the last remaining outpost of federal authority in the area, meant that at least one-sixteenth of the nation had accomplished a de facto secession from the Constitutional union. Contemporary academics who are inclined to ridicule Washington's and Hamilton's resort to military measures, after three years of patience and under judicial authority, as overreaction might consider what the response of a contemporary American president to formal and warlike secession on such a scale might be.[24]

In truth only one house burned, not several, as Hendrickson intimated. There were no "seizures" except for one batch of local mail. Actually, excise rioters never killed federal officials (although one soldier perhaps died defending the Neville home), and "woundings" were largely limited to the clothing and pride of excisemen. Hendrickson's rhetoric, then, both exaggerated and misrepresented the nature of the excise resistance. His analysis was less reasoned, less accurate, and less reliable than the first-person accounts of Neville and Hamilton.

Forrest McDonald adhered to the general line of thought outlined above. He supplemented this view, however, with even more inflamed rhetoric and a rabid intolerance for alien cultures, opposition to government, and "liberal" historians. McDonald adopted Crèvecoeur's description of the western Pennsylvania settlers as "uncouth, drunken, lazy, brutal, wasteful, and contentious, 'no better than carnivorous animals of a superior rank.' " He dismissed Findley, Gallatin, Brackenridge, and other community leaders as "a new group of office-hungry demagogues" and described the entire populace summarily as "lawless hotheads."[25]

McDonald discussed the economic grievances of the western Pennsylvanians in a footnote. The "myth" that whiskey was a "cash crop," according to McDonald, apparently originated with Henry M. Brackenridge and has simply been uncritically repeated by every subsequent historian down to Leland Baldwin. Since McDonald studied "prices current" lists in Philadelphia newspapers for the 1790s and never saw whiskey listed, he argued, there remains no reason to accept Brackenridge's second-hand and unverifiable contention.[26]

McDonald's condemnation of historians' "uncritical" adoption of arguments must be applauded. But his attribution of the economic grievance argument to Henry M. Brackenridge and his own research leave much to be desired. The economic argument did not originate with the second-generation account of Brackenridge. It appeared, among other places, in the *Pittsburgh Gazette* at least as early as 1792, in the resolutions and petitions of western Pennsylvanians from 1792 to 1794, and in the first-generation accounts of William Findley and Hugh Brackenridge.

Furthermore, McDonald was wrong about the absence of whiskey from Philadelphia "prices current" lists. He simply looked in the wrong places. The newspaper notations of commodity prices were abbreviated versions of much longer lists which themselves circulated as independent newspapers. The short lists contained only those items that had the most widely fluctuating prices. Whiskey was clearly a staple commodity with a comparatively stable range of prices. As such, its variations are chronicled in such publications as the *Philadelphia Price Current, Pelosi's Marine List*, the *Weekly Price Current*, and *Relf's Philadelphia Prices Current*, rather than in the newspapers examined by McDonald.[27]

The strictly quantitative method of research advocated by McDonald would not be entirely satisfactory even if he had been right about the insignificance of western whiskey to Philadelphia's economy. One would still have to examine price currents in Pittsburgh and New Orleans as well as Philadelphia. Distillers' records from western Pennsylvania and other distilling areas would also have to be consulted to give the Pennsylvania evidence an essential comparative dimension.

After the months or years of research necessary to address the economic argument in a quantifiably verifiable manner, however, the argument still could not be clinched for either side. Ultimately, although the statistical information would be valuable and possibly very interesting, what seems most important here is the perceptual question. What we wish to know is whether the western Pennsylvanians' actions were rooted in their own perceptions of economic distress and oppression. This argument, if it can be resolved at all, can be based only in literary evidence—newspapers, resolutions, petitions, correspondence, and first-person narratives of events. Actions, as McDonald should know, are based not on "reality" but on actors' perceptions of "reality."[28]

Nor has the cause of understanding been advanced by the blanket assertion by the friends of order from Marshall and Ramsay down to Hendrickson and McDonald that the fundamental division among the rioters and friends of order was anti-Federalist *versus* Federalist. Such a categorization, however attractive it might be, simply does not hold up under even the most cursory examination. Most of the "leaders" of the insurrection were Federalists at the time of the Constitution's adoption.[29]

In sum, there is no readily discernible pattern to the way Federalists and anti-Federalists divided on the excise issue in western Pennsylvania. To assert, therefore, that the rebellion was yet another incident in a chronic attempt by anti-Federalists to destroy the union is misleading. The belief that the leaders of the rebellion were merely a cynical opposition bent upon resistance to every act of the new government, that so-called grievances were simply dishonest attempts to arouse the peasants, is not so obvious as these historians have believed.

Two other historians have contributed extremely valuable essays on the Whiskey Rebellion that place them among the friends of order. In a statement epitomizing his stance as a friend of order, Richard H. Kohn argued in 1972 that historians have ignored the most important issue about the insurrection. The Whiskey Rebellion, Kohn wrote, was "a clear-cut case of the failure of law and the necessity for coercion."[30] The question facing the government was not whether to suppress the rebellion, but how.

Kohn offers easily the best existing account of the federal government's suppression of the Whiskey Rebellion. And, to be fair to Kohn, he was not seeking in this article to explain the causes of the rebellion. By ignoring the motives of the rioters, however, and the course of events from the passage of the excise tax in 1791 to the burning of excise inspector Neville's house in July 1794, he ended up defending the actions of the government without ever seriously considering the rioters' side. Implicit in such an interpretation is the apparent conviction that political violence against the American government in 1794, whatever its grievances, could not have been just. It implies that the government's response was rational and the opposition irrational. This assumption, which Kohn appears to share with all friends of order, dictated the course of his research and rendered examiniation of the distillers' grievances irrelevant.

A final modern friend of order, and perhaps the most sophisticated in his argument and use of evidence, is Jacob E. Cooke. Cooke wrote in 1964 that the previous half-century of scholarship on the Whiskey Rebellion had been dominated by historians with Jeffersonian-Republican prejudices. He recognized that the only other existing tradition was that of the Hamiltonian-Federalist camp. Instead of launching a new historiographical "school," however, Cooke chose to blast the "Jeffersonian" line of Brackenridge, Findley, and Leland Baldwin. He adopted a Namierist-style analysis, an internal study of western Pennsylvania politics, in a short article whose approach no sympathetic follower has ever carried forward.[31]

Cooke argued that a satisfying explanation of the causes of the rebellion would have to ask and answer two questions: (1) Why only in western Pennsylvania did the whiskey tax result in violence? (2) Why in western Pennsylvania was Washington County the seat of the most active opposition? Answers provided

by Baldwin and others failed to satisfy Cooke because none of the causes identified by "Republican" historians was unique to the area that revolted. There
were Scots-Irish settlers in other regions; other places shared a "revolutionary
tradition"; the western Pennsylvanians were not the only Americans who lived
far from a federal court; and the economic hardships, which have never been
convincingly demonstrated, could not have been unique to the four western
Pennsylvania counties. Finally, the contention that Alexander Hamilton provoked
the rebellion for his own reasons seemed ridiculous to Cooke, since Hamilton
never ran the government and Washington's statements were much more bellicose
than Hamilton's throughout the period of excise resistance.[32]

In addition, every cause identified by the Jeffersonian historians ignored the
one most often mentioned by participants themselves. "Time and again," Cooke
observed, "their remonstrances emphasized the same point: excise taxes were
inimical to the freedom which should characterize a free society. . . . Many of
the protestants were using the whiskey tax as a club to strike a blow at all taxes,
indeed, at all governmental restraint."[33] Although he did not use the word then,
Cooke identified the fundamental conflict of the rebellion as involving a radi-
calized vision of liberty *versus* the government stance for law and order. Unfortunately, he did not recognize that the same ideological rift separates the two
historiographical schools that he identified. He did not see that his own research
remained just as deeply embroiled in this same ideological controversy.

Cooke's examination of the internal political arena in western Pennsylvania
did, however, contribute a significant and unique perspective on events. The
most important actor in the rebellion, according to Cooke, was not Washington
or Hamilton, and not Brackenridge, Findley or Gallatin, as others have argued;
rather it was General John Neville, inspector of the excise. "If one man was
responsible for the whiskey insurrection," Cooke wrote, "it was John Neville."
It was Neville's appointment that disrupted the political balance in western
Pennsylvania and provided his opponents with an issue on which to challenge
his position in the community. Three factions dominated western Pennsylvania
politics in 1794: (1) the "Neville connection"; (2) "state or local righters"
without connections (that is, Findley, Gallatin, and Brackenridge); and (3) those
who broke with Neville on the excise after he accepted the inspectorship. Ideology, then, according to Cooke, was not a significant issue. What separated
the leaders of the insurrection from other members of the elite was a factional
political struggle, not their love for liberty. "The Whiskey Insurrection," he
argued:

was not the spontaneous uprising of an oppressed people shaking off the burden of a
crushing tax imposed by an unfriendly government. It was rather the result of an unfortunately literal reading of the Revolutionary creed which equated government with oppression, order with tyranny, rulers, even popularly elected ones, with despots. Its leaders
were not tribunes of the people, courageously leading a crusade of embattled farmers

against a capitalist-dominated government. They were rather self-seeking politicians who hoped to ride the waves of popular discontent to the secure shore of political office.[34]

Cooke's Namierist-style analysis of western Pennsylvania politics provided valuable information and was far superior to the traditional Federalist *versus* anti-Federalist dichotomy described by many friends of order. There are two problems with his argument, however. First, the persons he named, particularly Findley and Gallatin, were not really the leaders of the insurrection; rather, they were sympathetic elites who took an ambivalent stance on resistance, but who never supported violent opposition. Both Gallatin and Findley advocated compliance with the excise coupled with petitions and other nonviolent attempts to secure amendment or repeal of the law. None of the men Cooke named was prosecuted for his leadership of the rebellion, and for good reason. All were instrumental in the nonviolent resolution of a near-bloody civil war. None supported secession from the union. None was a political outsider. Cooke's characterization confused leaders and sympathizers, fomenters and ambivalent courters of popular favor.

Second, Cooke's analysis, even if it holds for the real leaders of the violent resistance, would not explain away the ideological, economic, or cultural opposition of the masses who participated in the protest. Even if we found that the leaders were cynical politicos who chose this issue simply for its potential to advance their political careers, we would still want to know why they chose the rhetoric of liberty and why the farmers found that rhetoric inspiring. While offering one potentially valuable avenue for research, Cooke has not demonstrated the irrelevance of other approaches. In sum, his personal commitment to defending Alexander Hamilton's version of social order caused him to underestimate the possible veracity of friends of liberty and the potential validity of grievances expressed by opposition groups.

Finally, Cooke's argument exhibited a convincing internal coherence; if we accept his premises, his conclusions necessarily follow. But western Pennsylvania was not, as Cooke asserted, the only seat of violent opposition to the excise. Similar violent resistance marked attempted enforcement in Maryland, Kentucky, Virginia, North Carolina, South Carolina, and Georgia. Although historians have not taken these riots seriously, until recently, and hence few secondary accounts of them exist, it seems possible that the four western Pennsylvania counties were not the heart of excise opposition until the officers of the federal government described them as such. If this is so, the critical question must become: why did the federal government choose western Pennsylvania as the place to demonstrate its commitment to law and order?

Friends of order seldom ask whether the government's belief that it must exert force in western Pennsylvania is an attitude requiring examination. They do not entertain the notion that "the necessity for coercion" itself may constitute *prima facie* evidence of the government's failure to represent the interests and needs of many citizens. They do not ask whether the forced recruitment, arming, and marching of 15,000 men was an appropriate response to the burning of one tax man's house in the hinterlands of Pennsylvania. They do not wonder why, in the face of other incidents of similar violence elsewhere in the states, the government chose the fall of 1794 and western Pennsylvania as the stage on which to act out its power play.

In sum, the modern friends of order are plagued by the same limitation that has afflicted the friends of liberty throughout the history of writing about the Whiskey Rebellion. Modern friends of order, some of them perhaps reacting to the tumults of the 1960s, seem to assume that law enforcement has a timeless nature. Ultimately, these historians simply wish to demonstrate that given the existence of an excise law, conditions in western Pennsylvania, the extant relations between the federal government and the state of Pennsylvania, and the attitudes and perceptions of the Washington administration, the use of force by the federal government to quell social protest in western Pennsylvania was inevitable, whether or not Alexander Hamilton was secretary of the treasury. Unfortunately, by adopting such a vision of the Whiskey Rebellion, they ignore the contexts—political, social, economic, ideological, and international—that give any such event its meaning. Also unfortunately, few historians of the rebellion—from either camp—have meaningfully explored those dimensions of the conflict accepted by the friends of order as established fact. When friends-of-order historians uncritically endorse the government's stance and cite as evidence for the motives of Washington and Hamilton their own correspondence and public proclamations, they do not offer a convincing internal analysis of the very texts upon which they rely. Theirs becomes a story without a context, a study of consequences without causes, a tail without a head.

There are strong reasons, then, to call for a new approach to the study of the Whiskey Rebellion. It was an event perceived by contemporaries on both sides to be of the highest significance. From a historiographic perspective, it has much to offer students of the American Revolution and the early national period of United States history. It reveals a great deal about conflicting ideas, economies, and cultures during the 1780s and 1790s. Its nature as a precedent-setting event offers unique perspectives on the establishment of constitutional, military, and political precedents in the young republic. And so many of these contexts that contribute to making events comprehensible remain unexplored today.

In addition to the essays here in this anthology, several studies have recently appeared that transcend the more narrowly focused research discussed above. Barbara Karsky's essay, ''Agrarian Radicalism in the Late Revolutionary Period,'' took an enlightening step toward understanding the Whiskey Rebellion within a larger context of eighteenth-century protest and revolt.[35] Although she focused on comparisons and contrasts between Shays' Rebellion and the Whiskey Rebellion, Karsky also noted parallels between these two revolts and the New Jersey tenant riots (1745–1754), the Carolina regulators (1765–1771), the New York antirent wars (1750s–1770s), and the New Hampshire Grants conflicts

(1769–1791). In this short article she also hypothesized about the influence of the American Revolution on the nature of rural violence and on the "modernization" of protest from the earlier limitations on a specific target or figure to a generalized protest in the name of a cause.

On the theoretical level, then, Karsky has made a major contribution to our reconceptualization of the Whiskey Rebellion.[36] Her study should be only the beginning, however, for students of the Whiskey Rebellion. What about the violent episodes that wracked every single American state with a western frontier during the 1780s? Never has the Whiskey Rebellion been seen and studied as a part of this general phenomenon of East-West conflict, urban-rural struggle, cosmopolitan-localist combat during the decade following the American Revolution.[37] There was discontent everywhere on the frontier dating from independent statehood petitions—Transylvania, Westylvania, Watauga, Vermont, Kentucky, Franklin, and Maine—during the Revolution. There were numerous episodes of rural violence during the 1780s and 1790s in each of these frontier regions, to secure redress of the very same kinds of grievances articulated by the whiskey rebels. There was, as in the Whiskey Rebellion, widespread discontent leading in some cases to the genuine possibility of secession, civil war, and frontier union with Spain or reunion with Great Britain. Karsky's essay should be, then, an inspiration to pursue similar lines of research for other times and places. It should suggest other similar points of comparison and contrast.

Similarly, Mary K. Bonsteel Tachau's superb chapter on the enforcement of internal revenue laws in Kentucky is the first serious study of excise tax resistance outside of western Pennsylvania. How better to test the federal government's and Jacob Cooke's contention that antiexcise violence was limited to the four western counties than to explore a similar resistance elsewhere? Again, however, Tachau's work must not be seen as an end, but rather a beginning for a whole new line of Whiskey Rebellion research. Excise protestors built liberty poles, confronted and abused tax collectors, and petitioned for redress in numerous other communities. Every state south of New York experienced public protest of a nature similar to that in western Pennsylvania and Kentucky. Until Tachau, however, no one had discussed the wider significance of such protest and undertaken the research necessary for its illumination.[38]

The Whiskey Rebellion was also a battle over the nature of representative government, over the appropriate channels for expression of public opinion in a democratic republic. James Roger Sharp's chapter in this collection highlights this conflict and emphasizes the continuing polarity of both political theory and practice following ratification of the Constitution. There was no consensus, Sharp convincingly argues, on the role of public opinion and the appropriate avenues for its expression. George Washington and many others believed that voting was the only legitimate method of expressing public opinion. Many others continued to believe, however, that political societies, parades, demonstrations, liberty-pole raisings, and the burning of politicians in effigy were an important part of the political process. The controversy did not die with the Whiskey Rebellion, although the federal administration strongly made its point about the limitations on expressions of the public will.

We also need, for example, a deeper understanding of life on the western Pennsylvania frontier. We must begin to incorporate creatively the work of historical geographers, anthropologists, and social and economic historians to understand better the local contexts of rural violence in the western country. Until doctoral dissertations by Robert Eugene Harper and Dodee Fennell, no serious studies of the social structure of postrevolutionary western Pennsylvania had appeared. Until Fennel's dissertation, no historian of the Whiskey Rebellion since James Carnahan and Henry Marie Brackenridge had stressed the significance of conflicting interests between large and small distillers in western Pennsylvania. And no historian before Fennell had convincingly demonstrated the genuine economic distress created by the excise for small distillers in the West.[39]

Other dimensions of life in the rebellious regions should also be incorporated into studies of the Whiskey Rebellion. Recurrent Indian wars were at the heart of frontier experience during the late eighteenth century. Where is the recognition of the role played by protracted warfare, fear, and the resulting economic deprivation in the region of protest? How can we ever understand the ardor of excise tax resistance before we explore the connections between ethnicity and rebellion in the West? Contemporaries saw these issues as instrumental in all that occurred. Traveler's accounts, local newspapers, private correspondence, and court testimony are only a few of the available sources for exploring western society and the frontier worldview.[40]

Only the willingness to examine both sides, to study critically and sympathetically documents relating both to life and ideals on the frontier and those emanating from government officials in Philadelphia, can begin to resolve the continuing problem of Whiskey Rebellion historiography. Until now, the historiographical battle over the Whiskey Rebellion has stood as a classic case of hostile ships passing in the night, firing blindly but seldom hitting a mark. The friends of liberty—the Brackenridges, Findley, Carnahan, and Baldwin—accepted without critical analysis the legitimacy of every grievance cited by the insurgents and shared the rebels' frustration with the federal government. The early accounts of Hugh Bracenridge and Findley, of course, forthrightly defended the actions of the authors and explained sympathetically the actions of the excise resisters. None of the friends of liberty had access to the records of the federal government. All remained, therefore, ignorant of the government's perceptions and justifications for its actions. All remained suspicious of the motives and actions of Hamilton and Washington. All exalted the revolutionary ideal of liberty as *the* fundamental principle of civil governance.

The friends of liberty, while maintaining an ambivalent or disapproving stance on political violence, endorsed all attempts short of violence to secure redress and remained sympathetic to the frustration of the aggrieved in western Pennsylvania, whose remonstrances were ignored by the federal government. Friends of liberty have believed that Brackenridge, Findley, and Gallatin were men of integrity torn between the justice of their fellow citizens' cause and their own dedication to peaceful democratic rule. Without the wise and temporizing efforts of these men, the friends of liberty have argued, the Whiskey Rebellion would certainly have become a bloodbath. It was Washington and Hamilton who misunderstood the cultural, economic, and political conditions of the western region and it was they, rather than the settlers, who deliberately escalated rather minor incidents into a "rebellion." The processes of law had not broken down in Pennsylvania, they argued. The federal government, for whatever reason, simply chose to see it that way.

The friends of order, on the other hand, have never seriously examined the grievances of the western Pennsylvania settlers. Some historians, notably Marshall, Ramsay, Craig, Hildreth, and McDonald, simply refused to take seriously any statements made by what they saw as a lawless rabble and an unscrupulous group of ambitious, malcontented lawyers. Others—Kohn and Cooke—believed the grievances irrelevant to the portion of the story they chose to tell, whether sincerely espoused by the rebels or not. Not one of the grievances distinguished the rebellious area from the rest of the nation, Cooke argued. Under the circumstances, whatever the reasons for the rebels' actions, Kohn implied, the federal government had no choice but to uphold law and order with force.

Friends of order asserted that the restoration of peace at such a minimal cost in lives and property must be attributed to the decisive yet restrained response of George Washington. Alexander Hamilton's organizational leadership skills also proved instrumental, but there is no telling, argue the friends of order, how much higher the price of stability might have been without the indispensable presence and prestige of our first president. Government records, they argued, not what they interpreted as the ravings of misguided rebels, are the only valid sources for studying the rebellion. The law seemed clear to friends of order. They thought that anyone can see in Hamilton's report and in Washington's proclamations that they took the only appropriate course under the circumstances.

Perhaps this anthology can serve as an additional step toward overcoming such historiographic simplicity. Perhaps historians can begin anew to weigh equally the perceptions and misperceptions that drove Americans into such a frenzy of interregional distrust in the 1790s. Historical objectivity is, of course, not a possibility, but awareness of the political prejudices that shape our views of the past is a major step forward. Willingness to disengage ourselves from both character assassination and hero worship are essential preconditions for more enlightened analysis. This quest will not lead historians to consensus about the past or the present, nor should we try to hide the chasms of class, politics, ethnicity, and philosophy that divide the profession. It might lead, though, to more sophisticated analyses of events such as the one discussed here.

NOTES

1. James H. Hutson, "The Origins of 'The Paranoid Style in American Politics': Public Jealousy from the Age of Walpole to the Age of Jackson," in David Hall, John

M. Murrin, and Thad W. Tate, eds., *Saints and Revolutionaries: Essays on Early American History* (New York: Norton, 1984), 332–372.

2. Hugh Henry Brackenridge, *Incidents of the Insurrection in the Western Parts of Pennsylvania, in the Year 1794* (Philadelphia, 1795), p. 5. William Findley, *History of the Insurrection in the Four Western Counties of Pennsylvania in the Year MDCCXCIV* (Philadelphia, 1796), pp. x–xi.

3. Neville B. Craig, *The History of Pittsburgh* (Pittsburgh, 1851), p. 273 and *passim*. Craig's account is drawn directly from Richard Hildreth, *The History of the United States of America* (New York, 1851; rev. ed., 1879), vol. 4.

4. Henry Marie Brackenridge, *History of the Western Insurrection in Western Pennsylvania, Commonly Called the Whiskey Insurrection* (Pittsburgh, 1859), pp. v–vi.

5. Neville B. Craig, *Exposure of a Few of the Many Misstatements in H. M. Brackenridge's History of the Whiskey Insurrection* (Pittsburgh, 1859), p. v.

6. H. H. Brackenridge, *Incidents of the Insurrection* 3: 6.

7. Findley, *History of the Insurrection*, pp. 17, 41.

8. Rev. James Carnahan, D. D., "The Pennsylvania Insurrection of 1794, Commonly Called the 'Whiskey Insurrection,' " *Proceedings of the New Jersey Historical Society*, ser. 1, 6, no. 3 (1852): 118.

9. *Ibid.*, pp. 119–120.

10. H. M. Brackenridge, *History of the Western Insurrection*, pp. 17–18.

11. *Ibid.*, p. 30.

12. Israel Rupp, *Early History of Western Pennsylvania, and of the West* (Pittsburgh: Daniel W. Kaufman, 1847); Townshend Ward, "The Insurrection of the Year 1794, in the Western Counties of Pennsylvania," Historical Society of Pennsylvania, *Contributions to American History, 1858*, pp. 181–182. At least one other first-person narrative, unremarkable in its perspective or detail, appeared in print during the author's lifetime. James Elliot's account was included in *The Poetical and Miscellaneous Works of James Elliot* (Philadelphia, 1798). Finally, the *Pennsylvania Law Journal* carried an article on the rebellion in 1847. The article was sympathetic to the rebels, but ultimately concluded that the victory of the government was an important occasion in the nation's history. [J. J. Robbins] "The Whiskey Insurrection," *Pennsylvania Law Journal* 6 (January 1847): 109–120.

13. Leland D. Baldwin, *Whiskey Rebels: The Story of a Frontier Uprising* (Pittsburgh: University of Pittsburgh Press, 1939), foreword.

14. *Ibid.*, p. 69.

15. *Ibid.*, p. 71.

16. Craig, *Exposure of a Few of the Many Misstatements*, pp. 58, 71.

17. Hildreth, *History of the United States*, 4: 373.

18. John Marshall, *The Life of George Washington* (London, 1807), 5: 425.

19. David Ramsay, *History of the United States* (Philadelphia, 1818), 3: 73–78. Ramsay does not even mention the Whiskey Rebellion in *The Life of George Washington* (London, 1807), pp. 75, 78.

20. Washington Irving, *Life of George Washington* (New York, 1859), 5: 130, 131, 196–204.

21. Richard Hofstadter, "Reflections on Violence in the United States," in Richard Hofstadter and Michael Wallace, eds., *American Violence, A Documentary History* (New York: Random House, 1970), p. 10.

22. Richard H. Kohn, "The Washington Administration's Decision to Crush the Whiskey Rebellion," *JAH* 59 (December 1972): 567.

23. Robert Hendrickson, *Hamilton II (1789–1804)* (New York: Mason-Charter, 1976), p. 290.

24. *Ibid.*, pp. 296, 299.

25. Forrest McDonald, *Alexander Hamilton: A Biography* (New York: Norton, 1979), pp. 297, 298.

26. *Ibid.*, pp. 430–431, n. 26.

27. I am indebted to Professor John J. McCusker of the University of Maryland, College Park, for my knowledge about the Philadelphia price currents. All of the ones mentioned here and others are listed in Clarence Saunders Brigham, *History and Bibliography of American Newspapers, 1690–1820*, 2 vols. (Worcester, Mass.: American Antiquarian Society, 1947).

28. David O. Whitten, "An Economic Inquiry Into the Whiskey Rebellion of 1794," *Agricultural History* 49 (July 1975), offered a sophisticated and reliable assessment of the economic impact of the whiskey excise on producers in western Pennsylvania. He concluded that "the collection of taxes at the still required the payment of levies prior to the sale of the liquor, more than a minor inconvenience for frontier farmers with limited sources of cash," (p. 493). Whitten recognized, however, that one must seek the causes of the insurrection in rebels' perceptions rather than in quantifiable economic realities of the insurgents. "The rebellion may be attributed to the economic ignorance of the insurgents or noneconomic stimuli," Whitten concluded, "but not to a cash-loss burden on the frontier farmer" (p. 504).

29. Among those termed "leaders" of the Whiskey Rebellion, Bradford, Brackenridge, and Parkinson had strongly and openly supported adoption of the federal Constitution, while Findley, Gallatin, and Smiley were dedicated anti-Federalists.

30. Kohn, "The Washington Administration's Decision," p. 567.

31. Forrest McDonald, cited in note 25, praised Cooke's article highly, but did not contribute to the line of research begun by Cooke.

32. Jacob E. Cooke, "The Whiskey Insurrection: A Re-Evaluation," *Pennsylvania History* 30 (July 1963): 320–321.

33. *Ibid.*, p. 335.

34. *Ibid.*, pp. 336, 345.

35. Barbara Karsky, "Agrarian Radicalism in the Late Revolutionary Period (1780–1795)," in Erich Angermann, Marie-Luise Frings, and Hermann Wellenreuther, eds., *New Wine in Old Skins: A Comparative View of Socio-Political Structures and Values Affecting the American Revolution* (Stuttgart: Ernst Klett Verlag, 1976), pp. 87–114. See also Richard Maxwell Brown, "Back Country Rebellions and the Homestead Ethic in America, 1740–1799," in Richard Maxwell Brown and Don E. Fehrenbacher, eds., *Tradition, Conflict, and Modernization: Perspectives on the American Revolution* (New York: Academic Press, 1977); John R. Howe, Jr., "Republican Thought and the Political Violence of the 1790's," *American Quarterly* 19 (Summer 1967): 147–165; Peter Levine, "The Fries Rebellion: Social Violence and the Politics of the New Nation," *Pennsylvania History* 40 (July 1973): 241–258; Richard B. Morris, "Insurrection in Massachusetts," in Daniel Aaron, ed., *America in Crisis* (New York: Knopf, 1952); J. R. Pole, "Shays' Rebellion: A Political Interpretation," in *Political Representation in England and the Origins of the American Republic* (New York: St. Martin's Press, 1966), pp. 227–244; David Szatmary, *Shay's Rebellion: The Making of an Agrarian Insurrection* (Amherst:

University of Massachusetts Press, 1980); and Neville Meaney, "The Trial of Popular Sovereignty in Post-Revolutionary America: The Case of Shays' Rebellion," in Neville Meaney, ed., *Studies on the American Revolution* (Melbourne: Macmillan, 1976), pp. 151–175.

36. See also Pauline Maier, *From Resistance to Revolution: Colonial Radicals and the Development of American Opposition to Britain, 1765–1776* (New York: Random House, 1972); "Popular Uprisings and Civil Authority in Eighteenth-Century America" *WMQ* 27 (January 1970): 3–35; "The Charleston Mob and the Evolution of Popular Politics in Revolutionary South Carolina," *Perspectives in American History* 4 (1970): 173–196; Gordon S. Wood, "A Note on Mobs in the American Revolution," *WMQ* 23 (October 1966): 635–642; and Edward Countryman, "The Problem of the Early American Crowd," *Journal of American Studies* 7 (1973): 77–90. See also Charles Tilly, "Collective Action in England and America, 1765–1775," in Brown and Fehrenbacher, eds., *Tradition, Conflict, and Modernization*, pp. 45–72; John Howe, "Attitudes Toward Violence in the Pre-War Period," in John Parker and Carol Urness, eds., *The American Revolution: A Heritage of Change* (Minneapolis: James Ford Bell Library, 1975); Richard Maxwell Brown, "The American Vigilante Tradition," in Hugh Davis Graham and Ted Robert Gurr, eds., *Violence in America: Historical and Comparative Perspectives* (New York: New American Library, 1969); "Historical Patterns of Violence in America," in ibid.; Arthur M. Schlesinger, "Political Mobs and the American Revolution, 1765–1776," in *Proceedings of the American Philosophical Society* 99 (1955).

37. The Terms "cosmopolitan" and "localist" are taken from Jackson Turner Main, *Political Parties Before the Constitution* (Chapel Hill: University of North Carolina Press, 1973).

38. Mary K. Bonsteel Tauchau, "The Whiskey Rebellion in Kentucky: A Forgotten Episode of Civil Disobedience," *Journal of the Early Republic* 2 (Fall 1982): 239–259; *Federal Courts in the Early Republic: Kentucky, 1789–1816* (Princeton, N.J.: Princeton University Press, 1978), ch. 5.

39. Robert Eugene Harper, "The Class Structure of Western Pennsylvania in the late Eighteenth Century," Ph.D. diss., University of Pittsburgh, 1969; Dorothy Elaine Fennell, "From Rebelliousness to Insurrection: A Social History of the Whiskey Rebellion, 1765–1802," Ph.D. diss., University of Pittsburgh, 1981. See also Jackson Turner Main, *The Social Structure of Revolutionary America* (Princeton, N.J.: Princeton University Press, 1965).

40. Alfred P. James, "A Political Interpretation of the Whiskey Insurrection," *Western Pennsylvania Historical Magazine*, 33 (September–December 1950): 90–101, made several of the same lamentations about Whiskey Rebellion literature and offered some of the same suggestions mentioned above. See also James, "Western Pennsylvania, the Military School of George Washington," *WPHM* 32 (March–June 1949): 1–10; Edward Everett, "John Smilie, Forgotten Champion of Early Western Pennsylvania," *WPHM* 33 (September–December 1950): 77–89; Samuel Wilkeson, "The Whiskey Insurrection," *Buffalo Historical Society Publications* 5 (1902): 163–176; and "List of References on the Whiskey Insurrection in Western Pennsylvania in 1794," *Monthly Bulletin of the Carnegie Library of Pittsburgh* 11 (July 1906): 344–352.

Alexander Hamilton to George Washington, Report on the Western Country, August 5, 1794

Although not near the scene until after the fact, Alexander Hamilton remains a central figure in the Whiskey Rebellion. The reasons for that are clear. As secretary of the treasury in the Washington administration, Hamilton had played a key role in the adoption of the excise tax of 1791. It was more, however, than merely his role in persuading Congress to approve the excise. Hamilton also assumed a prominent role in the administration's decision to respond with vigor to the challenge posed by the whiskey rebels. As early as 1792 he had called for stern measures to strike back at the critics of administration taxing policies. He did so again, with greater success, in 1794. Hamilton, moreover, unlike other members of the administration, made public his support for strong military measures to crush the rebels. He also published his views on the origins and nature of the rebellion and of the character of those involved in it. That, coupled with his direct participation in the march to Pittsburgh, made Hamilton susceptible to criticism even as it assured his interpretation of the rebellion a place in history.

Hamilton's letter to President Washington, like the three documents that follow it, is a source that must be considered carefully. William Findley, for example, while acknowledging that he relied on the document in writing his own history of the rebellion, also insisted that there were errors of fact in it. Some historians too have found Hamilton's interpretation of the origins of the rebellion dubious. On the other hand, the document provides a clear narrative of the events leading to the assault on General Neville's home. The document also represents the information on which the administration acted when it decided to call up troops to crush the rebellion.

The day after he wrote it, Hamilton asked permission of President Washington to publish the letter. That permission was granted and the letter appeared in *Dunlap and Claypooles American Daily Advertiser* on August 21, 1794. In preparing the letter for publication, Hamilton made various revisions. Those revisions, as well as others in the original manuscript, are noted in Harold Syrett, et al., eds., *The Papers of Alexander Hamilton* (New York, Columbia University Press) 17: 24-58.[1]

The disagreeable crisis at which matters have lately arrived in some of the Western counties of Pennsylvania, with regard to the laws laying duties on spirits distilled within the United States and on stills, seems to render proper a review of the circumstances which have attended those laws in that scene, from their commencement to the present time, and of the conduct which has hitherto been observed on the part of the government, its motives and effect; in order to a better judgment of the measures necessary to be pursued in the existing emergency.

The opposition to those laws in the four most western counties of Pennsylvania (Alleghany, Washington, Fayette and Westmoreland) commenced as early as they were known to have been passed. It has continued, with different degrees of violence, in the different counties, and at different periods. But Washington has uniformly distinguished its resistance by a more excessive spirit, than has appeared in the other counties & seems to have been chiefly instrumental in kindling and keeping alive the flame.

The opposition first manifested itself in the milder shape of the circulation of opinions unfavourable to the law & calculated by the influence of public disesteem to discourage the accepting or holding of offices under it or the complying with it, by those who might be so disposed; to which was added the show of a discontinuance of the business of distilling. These expedients were shortly after succeeded by private associations to *forbear* compliances with the law. But it was not long before these more negative modes of opposition were perceived to be likely to prove ineffectual. And in proportion as this was the case and as the means of introducing the laws into operation were put into execution, the disposition to resistance became more turbulent and more inclined to adopt and practice violent expedients.

The officers now began to experience marks of contempt and insult. Threats against them became frequent and loud; and after some time, these threats were ripened into acts of ill-treatment and outrage.

These acts of violence were preceded by certain meetings of malcontent persons who entered into resolutions calculated at once to confirm inflame and systematize the spirit of opposition.

The first of these meetings was holden at a place called Red Stone Old Fort [Brownsville], on the 27 of July 1791 where it was concerted that county committees should be convened in the four counties at the respective seats of justice therein.[2] On the 23 day of August following one of these committees assembled in the county of Washington consisting (as appears by their proceedings published in the *Pittsburgh Gazette*)[3] among others of James Marshall, Register and Recorder of the County—David Bradford, Deputy Attorney General for the State—Henry Taylor & James Edgar, now Associate Judges—Thomas Crooks & William Parker then or shortly before magistrates & militia officers, Thomas Sedgwick and Alexander Wright, Magistrates and Peter Kidd, an officer of the militia.[4]

This meeting passed some intemperate resolutions, which were afterwards printed in the *Pittsburgh Gazette*, containing a strong censure on the law, declaring that any person *who had accepted or might accept an office under Congress in order to carry it into effect should be considered as inimical to the interests of the Country; and recommending to the citizens of Washington County to treat every person who had accepted or might thereafter accept any such office with contempt, and absolutely to refuse all kind of communication or intercourse with the officers and to withold from them all aid support or comfort.*

Not content with this vindictive proscription of those, who might esteem it their duty, in the capacity of officers, to aid in the execution of the constitutional laws of the land—the meeting proceeded to pass another resolution on a matter essentially foreign to the object, which had brought them together, namely the salaries & compensations allowed by Congress to the officers of government generally, which they represent as enormous; manifesting by their zeal, to accumulate topics of censure that they were actuated not merely by the dislike of a particular law, but by a disposition to render the government itself unpopular and odious.

This meeting in further prosecution of their plan deputed three of their members to meet delegates from the counties of Westmoreland, Fayette, and Alleghany on the first Tuesday of September following for the purpose of expressing the sense of the people of those counties, in an address to the legislature of the United States, upon the subject of the excise law and *other grievances;* naming for that purpose James Marshall, David Bradford & David Philips.

Another meeting accordingly took place on the 7th of September 1791 at Pittsburgh in the county of Alleghany, at which there appeared persons in character of delegates from the four western counties; from Westmoreland, Nehemiah Stokely & John Young, from Fayette, Edward Cook, Nathaniel Breaden & John Oliphant, from Alleghany, Thomas Moreton, John Woods & William Plume, from Washington, the three persons above named.

This meeting entered into resolutions more comprehensive in their objects & not less inflammatory in their tendency, than those which had before passed the meeting in Washington. Their resolutions contained severe censures not only on the law which was the immediate subject of objection; but upon what they termed the exorbitant salaries of officers, the unreasonable interest of the public debt, the want of discrimination between original holders & transferrees and the institution of a national bank. The same unfriendly temper towards the government of the United States which had led out of their way the meeting at Washington produced a similar wandering in that at Pittsburgh.

A representation to Congress and a remonstrance to the legislature of Pennsylvania against the law more particularly complained of were prepared by this meeting—published together with their other proceedings in the *Pittsburgh Gazette* & afterwards presented to the respective bodies to whom they were addressed.[5]

These meetings composed of very influential individuals and conducted without moderation or prudence are justly chargeable with the excesses, which have been from time to time committed; serving to give consistency to an opposition which has at length matured to a point, that threatens the foundations of the government & of the Union; unless speedily & effectually subdued.

On the 6th of the same month of September, the opposition broke out in an act of violence upon the person & property of Robert Johnson collector of the revenue for the counties of Alleghany & Washington.

A party of men armed and disguised way-laid him at a place on Pidgeon Creek in Washington County—seized, tarred and feathered him cut off his hair and deprived him of his horse, obliging him to travel on foot a considerable distance in that mortifying and painful situation.

The case was brought before the District Court of Pennsylvania out of which processes issued against John Robertson, John Hamilton & Thomas McComb: three of the persons concerned in the outrage.

The serving of these processes was confided by the then Marshall Clement Biddle to his deputy, Joseph Fox, who in the month of October went into Alleghany County for the purpose of serving them.

The appearances & circumstances which Mr. Fox observed himself in the course of his journey, & learnt afterwards upon his arrival at Pittsburgh, had the effect of deterring him from the service of the processes and unfortunately led to adopting the injudicious and fruitless expedient of sending them to the parties by a private messenger under cover.

The deputy's report to the Marshall states a number of particulars evincing a considerable fermentation in the part of the country to which he was sent, and inducing a belief on his part that he could not with safety have executed the processes. The Marshall transmitting this report to the District Attorney makes the following observations upon it, "I am sorry to add that he (the deputy) found the people in general in the western part of the state, and particularly beyond the Alleghany Mountain, in such a ferment, on account of the act of Congress for laying a duty on distilled spirits & so much opposed to the execution of the said act, and from a variety of threats to himself personally, although he took the utmost precaution to conceal his errand, that he was not only convinced of the impossibility of serving the process, but that any attempt to effect it would have occasionned the most violent opposition from the greater part of the inhabitants, & he declares that if he had attempted it, he believes he should not have returned alive. I spared no expence nor pains to have the process of the court executed & have not the least doubt that my deputy would have accomplished it, if it could have been done."

The reality of the danger to the deputy was countenanced by the opinion of General [John] Neville, the Inspector of the Revenue, a man who before had given & since has given numerous proofs of a steady and firm temper. And what followed, announced in a letter of that officer of the 27th of October 1791, is a further confirmation of it. The person who had been sent with the processes was seized, whipped, tarred & feathered, and after having his money & horse taken from him, was blind folded and tied in the woods, in which condition he remained for five hours.

Very serious reflections naturally occurred upon this occasion. It seemed highly probable, from the issue of the experiment, which had been made, that the ordinary course of civil process would be ineffectual for enforcing the execution of the law in the scene in question—and that a perserverance in this course might lead to a serious concussion. The law itself was still in the infancy of its operation and far from established in other important portions of the Union. Prejudices against it had been industriously disseminated—misrepresentations diffused, misconceptions fostered. The legislature of the United States had not yet organised the means by which the executive could come in aid of the judiciary, when found incompetent to the execution of the laws.[6] If neither of these impediments to a decisive exertion had existed, it was desireable, especially in a republican government, to avoid what is in such cases the ultimate resort, till all the milder means had been tried without success.

Under the united influence of these considerations, it appeared adviseable to forbear urging coercive measures, 'till the law had gone into more extensive operation, till further time for reflection & experience of its operation had served to correct false impressions and inspire greater moderation, and till the legislature had had an opportunity, by a revision of the law to remove as far as possible objections, and to reinforce the provisions for securing its execution.

Other incidents occurred from time to time, which are further proofs of the very improper temper that prevailed among the inhabitants of the refractory counties. Mr. Johnson was not the only officer who about the same period experienced outrage. Mr. Wells, collector of the revenue for Westmoreland & Fayette was also illtreated at Greensburgh & Union Town.[7] Nor were the outrages perpetrated confined to the officers. They extended to private citizens, who only dared to shew their respect for the laws of their country.

Sometime in October 1791 an unhappy man of the name of Wilson, a stranger in the county, and manifestly disordered in his intellects imagining himself to be a collector of the revenue, or invested with some trust in relation to it, was so unlucky as to make inquiries concerning the distillers who had entered their stills; giving out that he was to travel through the United States to ascertain & report to Congress the number of stills &c. This man was pursued by a party in disguise, taken out of his bed, carried about five miles back to a smith's shop, stripped of his cloaths which were afterwards burnt, and after having been himself inhumanly burnt in several places with a heated iron was tarred and feathered—and about day light dismissed—naked, wounded and otherwise in a very suffering condition. These particulars are communicated in a letter from the Inspector of the Revenue [John Neville] of the 17th of November, who declares that he had then himself seen the unfortunate maniac, the abuse of whom, as he expresses it, exceeded description and was sufficient to make human nature shudder. The affair is the more extraordinary, as persons of weight and consideration in that country are understood to have been actors in it, and as the symptoms of insanity were, during the whole time of inflicting the punishment apparent—the unhappy sufferer displaying the heroic fortitude of a man, who conceived himself to be a martyr to discharge of some duty.

Not long after a person of the name of Roseberry underwent the humiliating punishment of tarring & feathering with some aggravations; for having in conversation hazarded the very natural and just, but unpalatable remark, that the inhabitants of that county could not reasonably expect protection from a government, whose laws they so strenuously opposed.

The audacity of the perpetrators of these excesses was so great that (as appears by a letter from Mr. Neville of the 22 of December) an armed banditti ventured to seize and carry off two persons, who were witnesses against the rioters in the case of Wilson; in order, as was inferred, to prevent their giving testimony of the riot to a court then sitting or about to sit.

Designs of personal violence against the Inspector of the Revenue himself, to force him to a resignation, were repeatedly attempted to be put in execution by armed parties, but by different circumstances were frustrated.

In the session of Congress, which commenced in October 1791, the law laying a duty on distilled spirits and on stills came under the revision of Congress as had been anticipated. By an act passed the 8th of May 1792,[8] during that session, material alterations were made in it. Among these, the duty was reduced to a rate so moderate, as to have silenced complaint on that head—and a new and very favourable alternative was given to the distiller, that of paying a monthly, instead a yearly rate, according to the capacity of his still, with liberty to take a license for the precise term which he should intend to work it, and to renew that license for a further term or terms.[9]

This amending act, in its progress through the legislature, engaged the particular attention of members who themselves were interested in distilleries, and of others who represented parts of the country in which the business of distilling was extensively carried on. Objections were well considered and great pains taken to obviate all such as had the semblance of reasonableness.

The effect has in a great measure corresponded with the views of the legislature. Opposition has subsided in several districts where it before prevailed; and it was natural to entertain and not easy to abandon a hope that the same thing would by degrees have taken place in the four western counties of this state.[10]

But notwithstanding some flattering appearances at particular junctures, and infinite pains by various expedients to produce the desireable issue, the hope entertained has never been realized, and is now at an end, as far as the ordinary means of executing laws are concerned.

The first law had left the number of positions of the offices of inspection, which were to be established in each district for receiving entries of stills, to the discretion of the Supervisor. The second, to secure a due accommodation to distillers, provides peremptorily that there shall be one in each county.

The idea was immediately embraced, that it was a very important point in the scheme of opposition to the law to prevent the establishment of offices in the respective counties. For this purpose, the intimidation of well disposed inhabitants was added to the plan of molesting and obstructing the officers by force or otherwise, as might be necessary. So effectually was the first point carried, (the certain destruction of property and the peril of life being involved) that it became almost impracticable to obtain suitable places for offices in some of the counties—and when obtained, it was found a matter of necessity in almost every instance to abandon them.

After much effort the Inspector of the Revenue succeeded in procuring the house of William Faulkner, a captain in the army, for an office of inspection in the County of Washington. This took place in August 1792. The office was attended by the Inspector of the Revenue in person, till prevented by the following incidents.

Captain Faulkner, being in pursuit of some deserters from the troops, was encountered by a number of people in the same neighborhood where Mr. Johnson had been ill treated the preceding year, who reproached him with letting his house for an office of inspection—drew a knife upon him, threatened to scalp him, tar and feather him, and reduce his house and property to ashes, if he did not solemnly promise to prevent the further use of his house for an office.

Capt. Faulkner was induced to make the promise exacted—and in consequence of the circumstance wrote a letter to the inspector dated the 20th of August countermanding the permission for using his house—and the day following gave a public notice in the *Pittsburgh Gazette* that the office of inspection should be no longer kept there.

At the same time, another engine of opposition was in operation. Agreeable to a previous notification, there met at Pittsburgh on the 21st of August a number of persons stiling themselves "A Meeting of sundry Inhabitants of the Western Counties of Pennsylvania" who appointed JOHN CANON Chairman and AL-BERT GALLATIN clerk.

This meeting entered into resolutions not less exceptionable than those of its predecessors. The preamble suggested that a tax on *spirituous liquors* is unjust in itself and oppressive upon the poor—that *internal taxes upon consumption* must in the end destroy the liberties of every country in which they are introduced—that the law in question, from certain local circumstances which are specified, would bring immediate distress & ruin upon the western country, and concludes with the sentiment, that they think it their duty to persist in remonstrances to Congress, and in every other LEGAL measure, that may *obstruct* the *operation* of the LAW.

The resolutions then proceed, first, to appoint a committee to prepare and cause to be presented to Congress an address, stating objections to the law and praying for its repeal—secondly to appoint committees of correspondence for Washington, Fayette, and Alleghany, charged to correspond together and with such committee as should be appointed for the same purpose in the County of

Westmoreland, or with any committees of a similar nature, that might be appointed in other parts of the United States, and also if found necessary to call together either general meetings of the people, in their respective counties, or conferences of the several committees: And lastly to declare, that they will in future consider those who hold offices for the collection of the duty as unworthy of their friendship, that they will have no *intercourse nor dealings with them, will withdraw from them every assistance, withhold all the comforts of life which depend upon those duties that as men and fellow Citizens we owe to each other, and will upon all occasions treat them with contempt; earnestly RECOMMENDING IT TO THE PEOPLE AT LARGE TO FOLLOW THE SAME LINE OF CONDUCT TOWARDS THEM.*[11]

The idea of pursuing *legal* measures to *obstruct* the *operation* of a *Law* needs little comment. Legal measures may be pursued to procure the repeal of a law, but to *obstruct its operation* presents a contradiction in terms. The *operation,* or what is the same thing, the *execution* of a *law,* cannot be *obstructed,* after it has been constitutionally enacted, without illegality and crime. The expression quoted is one of those phrases which can only be used to conceal a disorderly & culpable intention under forms that may escape the hold of the law.[12]

Neither was it difficult to perceive that the anathema pronounced against the officers of the revenue placed them in a state of virtual outlawry, and operated as a signal to all those who were bold enough to encounter the guilt and the danger to violate both their lives and their properties.

The foregoing proceedings as soon as known were reported by the Secretary of the Treasury to the President. The President on the 15th of September, 1792 issued a proclamation[13] and likewise directed that prosecutions might be instituted against the offenders, in the cases in which the laws would support and the requisite evidence could be obtained.

Pursuant to these instructions, the Attorney General in cooperation with the Attorney of the district attended a circuit court which was holden at York Town in October 1792 for the purpose of bringing forward prosecutions in the proper cases.

Collateral measures were taken to procure for this purpose the necessary evidence.

The Supervisor of the Revenue was sent into the opposing survey to ascertain the real state of that survey—to obtain evidence of the persons who were concerned in the riot in Faulkeners case—and of those who composed the meeting at Pittsburgh—to uphold the confidence and encourage the perseverance of the officers acting under the law—and to induce if possible the inhabitants of that part of the survey, which appeared least disinclined, to come voluntarily into the law, by arguments addressed to their sense of duty and exhibiting the eventual dangers and mischiefs of resistance.

The mission of the Supervisor had no other fruit than that of obtaining evidence of the persons who composed the meeting at Pittsburgh—and of two who were understood to be concerned in the riot [Alexander Berr and William Kerr]—and a confirmation of the enmity, which certain active and designing leaders had industriously infused into a large proportion of the inhabitants, not against the particular laws, in question, only, but of a more antient date, against the government of the United States itself.

The then Attorney General [Edmund Randolph] being of opinion, that it was at best a doubtful point, whether the proceedings of the meeting at Pittsburgh contained indictable matter, no prosecution was attempted against those who composed it; though if the ground for proceeding against them had appeared to be firm, it is presumed, that the truest policy would have dictated that course.

Indictments were preferred to the circuit court and found against the two persons understood to have been concerned in the riot, & the usual measures were taken for carrying them into effect.

But it appearing afterwards from various representations supported by satisfactory testimony, that there had been some mistake as to the persons accused—justice and policy demanded that the prosecutions should be discontinued, which was accordingly done.

This issue of the business unavoidably defeated the attempt to establish examples of the punishment of persons who engaged in a violent resistance to the laws—and left the officers to struggle against the stream of resistance, without the advantage of such examples.

The following plan, afterwards successively put in execution, was about this time digested for carrying if possible the laws into effect, without the necessity of recurring to force.

1) To prosecute delinquents in the cases in which it could be clearly done for non compliances with the laws 2) to intercept the markets for the surplus produce of the distilleries of the non complying counties, by seizing the spirits in their way to those markets, in places where it could be effected without opposition 3) by purchases through agents for the government for the use of the army (instead of deriving the supply through contractors as formerly) confining them to spirits in respect to which there had been a compliance with the laws.

The motives to this plan speak for themselves. It aimed, besides the influence of penalties on delinquents, at making it the general interest of the distillers to comply with the laws, by interrupting the market for a very considerable surplus, and by, at the same time, confining the benefit of the large demand for public service, to those who did their duty to the public, and furnishing through the means of payments in cash that medium for paying the duties, the want of which, it was alleged, was a great difficulty in the way of compliance.[14]

But two circumstances conspired to counteract the success of this plan—one, the necessity towards incurring the penalties of non compliance of there being an office of inspection in each county, which was prevented in some of the counties by the means of intimidation practiced for that purpose—another, the non extension of the law to the territory north west of the Ohio—into which a large proportion of the surplus beforementioned was sent.

A cure for these defects could only come from the legislature. Accordingly in the session which began in November 1792, measures were taken for procuring a further revision of the laws. A bill containing amendments of these defects was brought in; but it so happened that this object, by reason of more urgent business, was deferred 'till towards the close of the session and finally went off, through the hurry of that period.

The continuance of the embarrassments incident to this state of things naturally tended to diminish much the efficacy of the plan which had been devised. Yet it was resolved as far as legal provisions would bear out the officers to pursue it with perseverance. There was ground to entertain hopes of its good effect— and it was certainly the most likely course which could have been adopted, towards obtaining the object of the laws by means short of force; evincing unequivocally the sincere disposition to avoid this painful resort and the steady moderation, which have characterised the measures of the government.

In pursuance of this plan, prosecutions were occasionally instituted in the mildest forms—seizures were made as opportunities occurred—and purchases on public account were carried on. It may be incidentally remarked, that these purchases were extended to other places, where though the same disorders did not exist, it appeared adviseable to facilitate the payment of the duties by this species of accommodation.

Nor was this plan, notwithstanding the deficiencies of legal provision, which impeded its full execution, without corresponding effects. Symptoms from time to time appeared which authorised expectation, that with the aid, at another sesssion, of the desired supplementary provisions, it was capable of accomplishing its end, if no extraordinary events occurred.

The opponents of the laws, not insensible of the tendency of that plan, nor of the defects in the laws which interfered with it, did not fail from time to time to pursue analogous modes of counteraction. The effort to frustrate the establishment of offices of inspection in particular was persisted in and even increased. Means of intimidating officers and others continued to be exerted.

In April, 1793 a party of armed men in disguise made an attack in the night upon the house of a collector of the revenue [Benjamin Wells], who resided in Fayette County, but he happening to be from home, they contented themselves with breaking open his house, threatening, terrifying and abusing his family.

Warrants were issued for apprehending some of the rioters upon this occasion by Isaac M[e]ason and James Findley assistant judges of Fayette County, which were delivered to the Sheriff [Joseph Hutson] of that county who it seems refused to execute them, for which he has been since indicted.

This is at once an example of a disposition to support the laws of the Union and of an opposite one in the local officers of Pennsylvania within the disaffected scene. But it is a truth too important to be unnoticed and too injurious not to be lamented, that the prevailing spirit of those officers has been either hostile or lukewarm to the execution of those laws—and that the weight of an unfriendly official influence has been one of the most serious obstacles with which they have had to struggle.

In June following, the Inspector of the Revenue [General Neville] was burnt in effigy in Alleghany County at a place & on a day of some public election with much display, in the presence & without interruption from magistrates and other public officers.

On the night of the 22d. of November, another party of men, some of them armed and all in disguise, went to the house of the same collector of Fayette [Benjamin Wells] which had been visited in April—broke and entered it and demanded a surrender of the officer's commission and official books. Upon his refusing to deliver them up, they presented pistols at him, and swore that if he did not comply they would instantly put him to death. At length, a surrender of the commission & books was enforced. But not content with this, the rioters before they departed required of the officer, that he should within two weeks publish his resignation, on pain of another visit & the destruction of his house.

Notwithstanding these excesses, the laws appeared, during the latter periods of this year, to be rather gaining ground. Several principal distillers, who had formerly held out, complied; and others discovered a disposition to comply, which was only restrained by the fear of violence.

But these favourable circumstances served to beget alarm, among those who were determined at all events to prevent the quiet establishment of the laws. It soon appeared, that they meditated by fresh and greater excesses to aim a still more effectual blow at them—to subdue the growing spirit of compliance, and to destroy entirely the organs of the laws, within that part of the country, by compelling all the officers to renounce their offices.

The last proceeding in the case of the collector of Fayette was in this spirit. In January of the present year further violences appear to have been perpetrated. William Richmond, who had given information against some of the rioters in the affair of Wilson, had his barn burnt with all the grain & hay which it contained—and the same thing happened to Robert Shawhan, a distiller who had been among the first to comply with the law and who had always spoken favourably of it. But in neither of these instances (which happened in the County of Alleghany) though the presumptions were violent was any positive proof obtained.

The Inspector of the Revenue in a letter of the 27 of February writes, that he had received information that persons living near the dividing line of Alleghany & Washington had thrown out threats of tarring and feathering one William Coughran, a complying distiller, and of burning his distillery—and that it had also been given out, that in three weeks there would not be a house standing in Alleghany County of any person who had complied with the laws; in consequence of which he had been induced to pay a visit to several leading individuals in that quarter, as well to ascertain the truth of the information as to endeavour to avert the attempt to execute such threats.

It appeared afterwards, that on his return home, he had been pursued by a collection of disorderly persons threatening, as they went along, vengeance against him. In their way, these men called at the house of James Kiddoe, who had recently complied with the laws, broke into his still-house, fired several balls under his still and scattered fire over and about the house.

Letters from the inspector in March announce an increased activity in promoting opposition to the laws—frequent meetings to cement and extend the combinations against it—and among other means for this purpose a plan of collecting a force to seize him, compel him to resign his commission and detain him prisoner—probably as a hostage.

In May and June, new violences were comitted. James Kiddoe the person abovementioned, & William Coughran, another complying distiller, met with repeated injury to their property. Kiddoe had parts of his grist mill at different times carried away, and Coughran suffered more material injuries. His still was destroyed, his saw mill rendered useless by the taking away of the saw and his grist mill so inujured as to require to be repaired at considerable expence. At the last visit, a note in writing was left, requiring him to publish what he had suffered in the *Pittsburgh Gazette,* on pain of another visit in which he is threatened, in figurative but intelligble terms, with the destruction of his property by fire; thus adding to the profligacy of doing wanton injuries to a fellow citizen, the tyranny of compelling him to be the publisher of his own wrongs.

June being the month for receiving annual entries of stills, endeavours were used to open offices in Westmoreland & Washington, where it had been hitherto found impracticable. With much pains and difficulty places were procured for the purpose.

That, in Westmoreland, was repeatedly attacked in the night by armed men, who frequently fired upon it, but according to a report which has been made to this department it was defended with so much courage and perseverance by John Wells, an auxiliary officer, & Philip R[e]agan, the owner of the house—as to have been maintained during the remainder of the month.

That, in Washington, after repeated attempts was suppressed. The first attempt was confined to pulling down the signs of the office & threats of future destruction. The second effected the object in the following mode. About twelve persons armed & painted black, in the night of the 6th of June, broke into the house of John Lynn, where the office was kept, and after having treacherously seduced him to come down stairs & put himself in their power, by a promise of safety to himself and his house—they seized and tied him, threatened to hang him—took him to a retired spot in the neighbouring wood & there after cutting off his hair, tarring and feathering him, swore him never again to allow the use of his house for an office, never to disclose their names and never again to have any sort of agency in aid of the excise; having done which, they bound him naked to a tree and left him in that situation 'till morning when he succeeded in extricating himself. Not content with this, the malcontents some days after made him another visit, pulled down part of his house—and put him in a situation to be obliged to become an exile from his own home & to find an asylum elsewhere.[15]

During this time several of the distillers who had made entries & benefitted by them refused the payment of the duties; actuated no doubt by various motives.

Indications of a plan to proceed against the Inspector of the Revenue in the manner which has been beforementioned continued. In a letter from him of the 10 of July he observed that the threatened visit had not yet been made, though he had still reason to expect it.

In the session of Congress which began in December, 1793 a bill for making the amendments in the laws, which had been for sometime desired, was brought in, and on the 5th of June last became a law.[16]

It is not to be doubted, that the different stages of this business were regularly notified to the malcontents, and that a conviction of the tendency of the amendments contemplated to effectuate the execution of the law had matured the resolution to bring matters to a violent crisis.[17]

The increasing energy of the opposition rendered it indispensable to meet the evil with proportionable decision. The idea of giving time for the law to extend itself in scenes, where the disatisfaction with it was the effect not of an improper spirit, but of causes which were of a nature to yield to reason reflection & experience (which had constantly weighed in the estimate of the measures proper to be pursued) had had its effect, in an extensive degree. The experiment too had been long enough tried to ascertain, that where resistance continued the root of the evil lay deep; and required measures of greater efficacy than had been pursued. The laws had undergone repeated revisions of the legislative representatives of the Union; & had virtually received their repeated sanction, with none or very feeble attempts to effect their repeal; affording an evidence of the general sense of the community in their favour. Complaints began to be loud from complying quarters, against the impropriety & injustice of suffering the laws to remain unexecuted in others.

Under the united influence of these considerations, there was no choice but to try the efficiency of the laws in prosecuting with vigour delinquents and offenders.

Processes issued against a number of non complying distillers in the counties of Fayette & Alleghany; and indictments having been found at a circuit court holden at Philadelphia in July last against Robert Smilie & John McCulloch, two of the rioters in the attack which in November preceding had been made upon the house of a collector of the revenue in Fayette County, processes issued against them, also, to bring them to trial and if guilty to punishment. The marshall of the district [David Lenox] went in person to serve these processes. He executed his trust without interruption, though under many discouraging circumstances, in Fayette County; but while he was in the execution of it in Alleghany County, being then accompanied by the Inspector of the Revenue, (to wit) on the 15th of July last he was beset on the road by a party of from thirty to forty armed men who after much previous irregularity of conduct finally fired upon him as it happened without injury either to him or the inspector.

This attempt on the marshall was but the prelude of greater excesses.

About break of day the 16th of July, in conformity with a plan which seems to have been for some time entertained, and which probably was only accelerated by the coming of the marshall into the survey, an attack by about 100 persons armed with guns & other weapons was made upon the house of the inspector in the vicinity of Pittsburgh. The inspector, though alone, vigorously defended himself against the assailants and obliged them to retreat without accomplishing their purpose.

Apprehending that the business would not terminate here, he made application by letter to the judges, generals of militia & sheriff of the county for protection. A reply to his application from John Wilkins, Junior & John Gibson, magistrates & militia officers informed him, that the laws could not be executed, so as to afford him the protection to which he was intitled, owing to the too general combination of the people in that part of Pennsylvania to oppose the revenue law; adding that they would take every step in their power to bring the rioters to justice & would be glad to receive information of the individuals concerned in the attack upon his house, that prosecutions might be commenced against them and expressing their sorrow, that should the POSSE COMITATUS of the county be ordered out in support of the civil authority, very few could be gotten who were not of the party of the rioters.

The day following, the insurgents reassembled with a considerable augmentation of numbers amounting as has been computed to at least 500 and on the 17th of July renewed their attack upon the house of the inspector; who in the interval had taken the precaution of calling to his aid a small detachment from the garrison of Fort Pitt, which at the time of this attack consisted of 11 men, who had been joined by Major Abraham Kirkpatrick, a friend & connection of the inspector.

There being scarcely a prospect of effectual defence against so large a body, as then appeared, and as the inspector had every thing to apprehend for his person, if taken, it was judged adviseable that he should withdraw from the house to a place of concealment—Major Kirkpatrick generously agreeing to remain with the 11 men, in the intention, if practicable to make a capitulation in favour of the property; if not, to defend it as long as possible.

A parley took place, under cover of a flag, which was sent by the insurgents to the house to demand, that the inspector should come forth, renounce his office and stipulate never again to accept an office under the same laws. To this it was replied, that the inspector had left the house upon their first approach, and that the place to which he had retired was unknown. They then declared that they must have whatever related to his office. They were answered that they might send persons not exceeding six to search the house and take away whatever papers they could find appertaining to the office. But not satisfied with this, they insisted unconditionally, that the armed men who were in the house for its defence should march out & ground their arms; which Major Kirkpatrick peremptorily refused; considering it and representing it to them as a proof of a design to destroy the property. This refusal put an end to the parley.

A brisk firing then ensued between the insurgents and those in the house, which it is said lasted for near an hour; 'till the assailants having set fire to all the neighbouring & adjacent buildings, eight in number, the intenseness of the heat & the danger of an immediate communication of the fire to the house obliged Major Kirkpatrick & his small party to come out & surrender themselves. In the course of the firing, one of the insurgents was killed & several wounded and three of the persons in the house were also wounded. The person killed is understood to have been the leader of the party of the name of James McFarlane, then a major in the militia, formerly a lieutenant in the Pennsylvania line.

The dwelling house after the surrender shared the fate of the other buildings the whole having been consumed to the ground. The loss of property to the inspector upon this occasion; is estimated and as is believed with great moderation at not less than 3000 pounds.

The Marshall, Colonel Presley Neville & several others were taken by the insurgents going to the inspectors' house. All except the marshall and Colonel Neville soon made their escape; but these were carried off some distance from the place, where the affray had happened, and detained till one or two o'clock the next morning. In the course of their detention, the marshall in particular suffered very severe and humiliating treatment—and was frequently in imminent danger of his life. Several of the party repeatedly presented their pieces at him, with every appearance of a design to assassinate, from which they were with difficulty restrained by the efforts of a few more humane & more prudent.

Nor could he obtain safety or liberty, but upon the condition of a promise guaranteed by Colonel Neville, that he would serve no other process on the west side of the Alleghany Mountain. The alternative being immediate death extorted from the marshall a compliance with this condition; notwithstanding the just sense of official dignity and the firmness of character, which were witnessed by his conduct throughout the trying scenes he had experienced.

The insurgents on the 18th sent a deputation of two of their number (one a Justice of the Peace) [David Hamilton and John Black] to Pittsburgh to require of the marshall a surrender of the processes in his possession, intimating that his compliance would satisfy the people & *add to his safety*—and also to demand of General Neville in peremptory terms the resignation of his office, threatening in case of refusal to attack the place & take him by force: demands which both these officers did not hesitate to reject as alike incompatible with their honor & their duty.

As it was well ascertained, that no protection was to be expected from the magistrates or inhabitants of Pittsburgh, it became necessary to the safety both of the inspector & the marshall to quit the place—and as it was known that all the usual routes to Philadelphia were beset by the insurgents, those officers concluded to descend the Ohio & proceed by a circuitous route to the seat of government, which they began to put in execution on the night of the 19th of July.

Information has also been received of a meeting of a considerable number of persons at a place called Mingo Creek meeting house in the county of Washington, to consult about the further measures which it might be adviseable to pursue; that at this meeting a motion was made to approve and agree to support the proceedings which had taken place, until the excise law was repealed and an act of oblivion passed. But that instead of this it had been agreed, that the four western counties of Pennsylvania & the neighbouring counties of Virginia should be invited to meet in a convention of Delegates on the 14th of the present month, at Parkinson's on Mingo Creek in the county of Washington, to take into consideration the situation of the Western Country & concert such measures as should appear suited to this occasion.[18]

It appears moreover that on the 26 of July last the mail of the United States on the road from Pittsburgh to Philadelphia was stopped by two armed men, who cut it open & took out all the letters, except those contained in one packet. These armed men, from all the circumstances which occurred, were manifestly acting on the part of the insurgents.

The declared object of the foregoing proceedings is to obstruct the execution and compel a repeal of the laws laying duties upon spirits distilled within the United States and upon stills. There is just cause to believe that this is connected with an indisposition too general in that quarter to share in the common burthens of the community—and with a wish among some persons of influence to embarrass the government. It is a fact of notoriety, that the revenue laws of the state itself have always been either resisted or defectively complied with in the same quarter.[19]

NOTES

1. Printed in Harold C. Syrett, et al., eds., *The Papers of Alexander Hamilton* (New York, 1972), 17: 24–58. Hamilton subsequently asked Washington for permission to publish this letter, permission which Washington granted on August 19. The revisions in the text of the letter as it was edited for publication are noted by Syrett, as are various deletions which Hamilton made in the original draft. For more details on the background to this letter and its contents see Syrett.

2. William Findley in his *History of the Insurrection* (see chapter 5) objected to Hamilton's criticism of the Brownsville meeting: "How this meeting could have been ranked by the secretary of the treasury, in his report to the President, preparatory to calling out the militia, among the causes of the insurrection, and given as one of the instances of unlawful combination, I know not. Surely such a meeting may be held, and such resolves passed, in Great Britain, even after the sedition bills, which have thrown that nation into such a flame, are enacted into laws. I never knew that a meeting to petition government respectfully, was esteemed criminal in any country that had the least pretensions to freedom."

3. Printed in Syrett et al., eds., *Papers of Hamilton*, n. 6. pp. 28–29.

4. Biographical sketches of these men are most readily available in Leland Baldwin, *Whiskey Rebels* rev. ed. (Pittsburgh, 1962).

5. The resolutions are printed in John B. Linn and Wm. H. Egle, eds., *Pennsylvania Archives*, 2d ser. (Harrisburg, 1876), 4: 20–22.

6. A bill to remedy this situation, "An Act to provide for calling for the Militia to execute the laws of the Union, suppress insurrections and repel invasions," was enacted,

May 5, 1792. Richard Peters, ed., *The Public Statutes at Large of the United States of America, 1789–1873* (Boston: Little, Brown, 1850-1873), 1:264–5 (hereafter cited as 1 *Stat*).

7. Cf. Findley's analysis of this incident in chapter 5.

8. "An Act Concerning the Duties on Spirits Distilled within the United States," 1 *Statutes*, pp. 267–71.

9. Dodee Fennell argues the burden of the tax fell disproportionately upon the small producer. See her "By Calculation Oppressed . . . ," unpublished manuscript in the possession of the editor.

10. Cf. Mary K. Bonsteel Tachau, "A New Look at The Whiskey Rebellion," in chapter 6.

11. The resolutions are printed in *Pennsylvania Archives*, 2d ser., 4:30–31.

12. For evidence that Westerners believed just the opposite, see Brackenridge, *Incidents*, p. 89; and Findley, *History*, p. 43.

13. Printed in *Pennsylvania Archives*, 2d ser., 4:32–33.

14. On this matter see Dodee Fennell, "By Calculation Oppressed."

15. James Carnahan, a local Presbyterian minister described this incident quite differently: "About the last of June or first of July, 1794, John Lyn, a deputy inspector, residing in Canonsburg, Washington county, was taken from his bed, carried into the woods and received a coat of tar and feathers, and he was left tied to a tree but so loosely that he could easily extricate himself. He returned to his house, and after undergoing an ablution with grease and soap and sand and water, he exhibited himself to the boys in the academy and others, and laughed and made sport of the whole matter" ("The Pennsylvania Insurrection of 1794, Commonly Called the Whiskey Insurrection," *Proceedings of the New Jersey Historical Society* 6 [1853], 120).

16. "An Act making further provision for securing and collecting the Duties on foreign and domestic distilled Spirits, Stills, Wines and Teas," 1 *Statutes*, pp. 378–81.

17. Cf. Brackenridge and Findley who both interpret the violence as precipitated by the failure of the government to serve processes under this new act, which allowed trial in local courts, rather than necessitate a trip to Philadelphia for trial.

18. The resolutions of that meeting are printed in *Pennsylvania Archives*, 2d ser. 4:159–61.

19. In the draft Hamilton wrote and then crossed out five additional paragraphs. They are printed in Syrett et al., eds., *Papers of Hamilton*, 17:58.

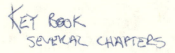

KEY BOOK
SEVERAL CHAPTERS

Judge Alexander Addison on the Origin and History of the Whiskey Rebellion

In late November 1794, as the militia army was withdrawing from the Pittsburgh area, Judge Alexander Addison sat down to write out his opinion of the origin and history of the Whiskey Rebellion. The commander of the army, Virginia Governor Henry Lee, had asked Addison for his "opinion of the late insurrection, the measures taken by government for its suppression, and the effects to be expected from those measures on the people" of western Pennsylvania.[1] Perhaps Lee, hurrying to withdraw the army before winter set in, but worried about whether the rebellion was entirely suppressed, wanted assurances from the chief local judicial officer that the whiskey tax would be obeyed, especially if Lee intended to issue a general pardon to the inhabitants for their acts of rebellion or treason. Perhaps Lee wanted Addison's assurance that the detachment of soldiers to be left for the winter, under General Daniel Morgan, would be sufficient to keep the peace, and that Addison, himself under some suspicion of abetting the rebellion, would not only call them out if necessary, but see in general that the whiskey excise would now be enforced.[2]

Whatever Lee's motives, Alexander Addison knew the inner history of the Whiskey Rebellion as well as anyone. Born in Scotland in 1759, educated at Aberdeen University and an ordained Presbyterian minister, Addison had come to Washington County in 1785 and applied to the local presbytery for a license to preach. When his license was delayed, he shifted to law and after reading with attorney David Redick, he was admitted to practice in 1787. Addison served in the Pennsylvania Constitutional Convention of 1789–1790, then in 1791 was appointed presiding judge of the fifth jucidical district of Pennsylvania, which included the four counties in the Pittsburgh region. As a witness to the opposition to the federal whiskey tax which gathered force between 1791 and 1794, and as a legal official who opposed both the tax and violent or illegal resistance to it, Addison was in a unique position to provide a balanced, objective view. He was a Federalist, but a moderate and something of a reformer on such issues as slavery and penal reform. Apparently he maintained a relationship with the Nevilles, who controlled Federalist politics in western Pennsylvania, and at the same time maintained friendly relations with many of the men who took leading roles in the rebellion. Unlike many prominent men in the area caught in the middle, Addison was not at this stage in his career particularly partisan or extreme in his views, either in local politics or in the increasingly bitter national party division.[3]

The importance of Addison's interpretation, therefore, was its objectivity and credibility. Unlike virtually every other participant or observer, Addison had no apparent personal or partisan axe to grind. (Although he was a judge, he was not responsible for enforcing the excise, which depended on federal tax and legal officers operating in the federal courts.) He questioned the contention, widespread among Federalists, that a long-standing conspiracy against the national government lay at the root of the rebellion; the most prominent Jeffersonains in western Pennsylvania, accused by Federalists of complicity, had always counseled moderation.[4] Addison believed the rebellion grew from diverse sources, as distant as the historic hostility to excise taxes in England and Ireland, and as basic as the "natural *untamedness*" of a frontier inhabited by people "but little accustomed to the subordination of regular government." Through opposition and intimidation, the Pennsylvania excise had been rendered "a mere dead letter." The same methods defeated the federal excise "and impunity produced boldness and perseverence." Eventually the mob action led to the destruction of John Neville's estate.

At this point, "blindly," the rebellion began. It was no conspiracy, but a kind of snowball process fed by variety of motives and encouraged by "a total contempt of the powers of the government." Unlike Jeffersonians William Findley and Albert Gallatin, Addison labeled subsequent events— the robbing of the mail, the calling out of the militia, the meeting at Parkinson's Ferry—a real rebellion, one "which aimed at resistance to government, in all its parts, and open war."[5] Yet once the government responded forcefully, the rebellion immediately began to unravel. The momentum was reversed. The "awakened spirit of publick exertion" checked "the spirit of revolution" in western Pennsylvania and elsewhere. The appointment of federal peace negotiators heartened moderates and divided the insurgents; "the approach of an army" overpowering in strength "altogether broke their resolution." Addison supported the advance of the troops, because many westerners thought that with the difficulties of weather and logistics, the government would not be able actually to send an army over the mountains and sustain it in the western country. And a few, some "unaccustomed to a regular industry and trained to a rambling life," others "turbulent spirits," calculated that they could escape from the area until the army left, then return "without fear of punishment" to renew the rebellion. In a sense, Addison blamed no one for the insurrection; it was the product of the peculiar history and sociology of the western Pennsylvania region, and of passion, delusion, and misperception. The ultimate solution, he concluded, was for "the people of this country" to "acquire the habit of aiding and obeying public authority."

Addison's letter is in the Carnegie Library of Pittsburgh in the papers of Isaac Craig, an early Pittsburgh entrepreneur who came to the area in 1780 as an officer in the Continental Army, stayed and married John Neville's daughter, and during the early 1790s served as deputy quartermaster for the army under Wayne on the frontier and as military storekeeper in Pittsburgh.[6] The document is an unsigned copy; the handwriting is not recognizable, but is apparently not that either of Addison or Craig.[7] The authenticity of the letter rests almost entirely on the word of Craig's oldest child, Neville B. Craig. (The title "Judge Addison's Letter" at the top of the first page of the manuscript is in Neville Craig's handwriting.)[8] Born in 1787, a graduate of Princeton, Craig read law with Addison in 1807, the last year of the judge's life, and practiced in Pittsburgh for the half century after admission to the bar in 1810. He served as city solicitor from 1821 to 1829, then owned and edited the *Pittsburgh Gazette* from 1829 to 1841. After he sold his interest in the paper, Craig devoted considerable time and effort to local history, publishing a monthly magazine called *The Olden Time* in 1846 and 1847, and a history of Pittsburgh in 1851. The latter sparked a fierce battle with Henry Marie Brackenridge, the son of the Pittsburgh lawyer accused by the Nevilles of helping to lead the rebellion. For nearly a decade in the 1850s, the two old lawyers, son and grandson of protagonists during the insurrection, bloodied each other publicly over the events of sixty years earlier, first in the pages of a local newspaper and then in book form. At one point Craig mentioned "a copy of a letter...by Judge Addison to General Henry Lee on the 23rd of November...written at the time."[9]

No other copy of the letter has been discovered, or the original, or any reference to the document in any contemporary source.[10] But while Neville Craig's statements are the only direct verification, in tone and in interpretation the letter fits with Addison's statements at the time, and is compatible with what is known of Addison's opinions and action during the early 1790s, before and during the rebellion.[11]

To His Excellency General Lee, Commander in Chief of the Militia Army

Sir,

You desired me to state to you my opinion of the late insurrection, the measures taken by government for its suppression, and the effects to be expected from those measures on the people of this country. I undertook to do so, at the same time cautioning you, that [12] you were to consider what I should say not so much as facts, or a solid system, as a mere opinion, though certainly a sincere one.

It is not uncommon to trace the origin of this unfortunate business to speculations on the subject of the Excise law, and on the administration of government in general; and to meetings and resolutions at various and distant times on these subjects; and these have not only been considered as having prepared the minds of the people of this country for the outrages which they afterwards committed, but as evidence of a deep and long formed plot, contrived by men who kept themselves out of view in its execution, to resist the excise system, and the government itself, by violence.

Without undertaking to examine or contradict this opinion, I shall content myself with observing, that I think it may well be said of it, that at least more stress has been laid on it than it will bear.

In all countries, the introduction of the Excise has been odious, and its officers have been held contemptable. Even in Britain, at this day, though wealth and little immediate connexion with the people cover the higher officers, yet the inferior are seldom respectable.[13] In Ireland, its introduction was later; of course, the original prejudices are more strong. Many now in the country talk of their having seen the riots and resistance against the excise in Ireland. In Ireland, the ordinary power of government seems incompetent to suppress riots, which have perpetual existence, from successive and varying causes. This country is in a great measure settled from Ireland.[14] Being but a new settlement, and a frontier settlement, harrassed by the danger, distress and ravage of an Indian war, did not consider itself, and was not considered, as a proper [object] for even equal taxation. Every frontier settlement, at a distance from the seat of government hardly weaned from the [territory] state, and in some degree composed of fugitives from justice civil or criminal, must be supposed to be but little accustomed to the subordination of regular government. This natural *untamedness* of temper was increased by the peculiar circumstances of this country. The clashing jurisdictions of Virginia and Pennsylvania excited animosities in the minds of the advocates of each state hardly yet healed by the mutual concessions of both, and an opposition to the government of Pennsylvania hardly yet overcome by the experience of its authority.[15] The idea of a new state, on this side of the mountains, became so prevalent that an act of the Assembly declared it high treason to propose it.[16] Under all these circumstances, an attempt was made to carry into execution the Excise law of Pennsylvania.[17] The officer, in his progress through Washington County, was seized by a number of rioters, collected from different quarters.[18] His hair was cut off from one half of his head. His papers were taken from him, and he was made to tear his commission, and tread it under his feet. They then in a body, gathering size as it proceeded, conducted him out of the county, with every possible mark of contumely to him and the government, and threats of death if he returned.[19] The same object, the removal of an excise officer from the country, was accomplished here, as in the [case] of General Neville. If the violence and enormity was less, it was because more was not necessary to accomplish their object. If their madness had been excited by resistance, and if burning houses, or even murder, had then been necessary to suspend the operation of the law, I now believe they would have thought the crimes sanctioned by the cause. Yet there were then no men of great influence or passion for office or popularity, who, for their selfish purposes, inflamed the minds of the people against the excise law; nor could the destruction of the federal government been then in view; for the confederation was not interested in the law, and the constitution of the United States did not then exist. The Excise law of Pennsylvania continued, as to this county, to be a mere dead letter.

When the Excise law of the United States came into operation,[20] those people, who, without reasoning, and merely from prejudice, were its greatest enemies, supposed that it possessed all the evils which they had ever heard ascribed to any excise law; and, without reflecting on the difference of Circumstances, supposed its operation might be defeated by the same means by which they had defeated the operation of the Excise law of Pennsylvania. Accordingly they had recourse to riots, tarring and feathering, and carrying off papers. These things were done in Washington County and Fayette County.[21] Unfortunately, the prosecutor for the state in Washington County was David Bradford whose disposition inclined him to omit all prosecution of such offences.[22] In Fayette County industry to collect testimony was wanting. The Agents of the United States choose to bring all their complaints into the Federal courts. The difficulties in the way of the Marshall, a stranger in the country, were inevitably great.[23] And there must have been an indisposition in the people of this country, hitherto accustomed to trials in all cases in their own counties, without evident necesity, to aid a jurisdiction which drew them for trial three hundred miles from home.[24] These circumstances contributed to impunity in delinquency and outrage; and impunity produced boldness and perseverance. Animated by their hatred to the law, and their past experience of success, and wanting prudence to forsee the consequences, they imagined that they could compell the excise officer of the United States, as they had compelled the Excise officer of Pennsylvania, to surrender his Commission; and thus reduce the excise law of the United States, as they had reduced the excise law of Pennsylvania, as to them, to a dead letter. With this view, they proceeded to General Nevill's to call for a surrender of his[25] commission and papers; and, that they might accomplish all their objects at once as to past and future, a surrender also of the papers of the Marshall. Probably they presumed their numbers sufficient to extort by fear alone, without actual force, a ready compliance. Irritated by refusal, resistance and repulse, and too deeply engaged to retreat, in their frenzy they drew into their guilt all within reach of their terror, and proceeded to the extremity of burning the house.[26]

Yet here perhaps they might have stopped, and the rioters in this case, like the rioters in the case of the excise law of Pennsylvania, might have been prosecuted and convicted. But they unhappily mistook, in their objects and their means, and blindly rushed into measures that involved the whole country. Those subsequent measures I consider as really the insurrection of this country, and the authors of them, whoever they may be, as really the authors of this insurrection. From the ancient aversion of some to the government of Pennsylvania, perhaps some remains of the idea of a new state, which had long ago existed, yet continued to exist, in this Country. Perhaps the distinction between a separation from the state and from the United States was not attended to. Perhaps even this last, a seizure of the Western lands, an union with Kentucky, the

The rebels were getting confident

navigation of the Mississippi, and a connection with Great Britain were thought of. Perhaps they never extended their reflections to any system or distant object, but acted from the blind impulse of the moment. Whatever might have been their ideas, measures were determined on, which aimed at resistance to government, in all its parts, and open war. The public post was robbed of the mail, the militia of the country was called out, for the purpose of seizing the garrison of Pittsburgh, and possessing themselves of the arms and ammunition there.[27] To obey this call many were compelled by fear; many were induced by usefulness in preventing mischief; many were seduced by wanton curiosity and many were instigated by love of plunder and destruction. The appearance of their strength added ferocity to the ruffians, and a total contempt of the powers of the government, and a general anarchy and confusion pervaded the whole country.

I shall here remark, that none of those men whom I have heard considered as the distant and secret authors of those acts of violence, seem to have been at all consulted in their contrivance or execution, or to have possessed any confidence of those who perpetrated them.[28] All reprobated them, and one (I mean Mr Gallatin) was the foremost, at the public meetings, to step forward to stem the torrent of popular rage, openly, and at great peril, to resist their mad delusions, and by arguments and eloquence, the most ingenious and impressive, to expose to them the danger and effects of their conduct, and the vanity and impracticability of their schemes. Whether any, and what conclusion is to be drawn from this, I submit to you.

To quell the disturbances in this country, and restore it to peace and government, the measures taken by the President were, in my opinion, the most prudent that could have been devised, and they seem to have been executed with a correspondent propriety and effect: The appointment of Commissioners, by shewing the awakened spirit of publick exertion gave a check to the spirit of revolution in this country, and to the progress of disorder into other parts of the Union. A fair opportunity was given to men of sense and virtue here, who, to guide the current, had seemed to run with it, to step out, and change its course. And it gave a rallying point to all well disposed men to flock to. The confidence, arising from their supposed strength, now began to abandon the violent; jealousy and distrust crept in among them; and the approach of an army, far superior to all remaining idea of resistance, altogether broke their resolutions, and, as it advanced, subdued their temper.

Previous to the advance of the army into the country, some attempts were made to stop its progress. At that time the temper of the country was materially changed. The well disposed were recovering spirit and consistency; and they possessed the disposition, and they believed the strength, of gradually restoring energy to the laws, and peace and subordination to the country. They knew the expense of maintaining the army was great, and, more than that, they regarded the labour and fatigue of their patriotic brethren, who, with the sacrifice of domestick interest and enjoyment, at the approach of an inclement season, had undertaken to traverse deep swamps, and vast and rugged mountains, to relieve them from anarchy, and restore them to safety and peace. They blushed for an armed force entering their country, to enforce submission to the laws. They feared also something for themselves; there were still among them disorderly men, who talked wildly. These, without property to secure their attachment to the government or the country, unaccustomed to a regular industry, and trained to a rambling life, had the arms in their hands, were known and associated to each other, and could, without any sacrifice, remove to wherever they pleased. It was this kind of men that were the great terrors during all the troubles, and now only remained to keep those troubles alive. The well disposed were more inclined to quiet, were not generally armed, and had as yet no compleat system to bind them together. They believed that the turbulent would not then assemble, in any force, to oppose the army; but that, under the pretense of opposing the army, they might plunder or destroy their fellow citizens, and quit a country in which they could no longer remain. Some fears also existed, justly provoked as the army was, that it would not be possible to restrain all of them from some intemperate acts, which might provoke at least secret revenge, and introduce general destruction. On all these grounds, representations were sent down to the President of the changed state of the country, and those who sent them were willing to give yet stronger assurances of sincerity, and risk the peace of the country on its internal exertions.[29] The propositions were honestly meant. Perhaps their rejection was wise. Consequences shewed that it was. The army conducted itself with unexampled discipline and tenderness to an offending country, and manifested a temper equalled only by the spirit which roused them in defence of the laws and constitution. The peace of the country, and energy of the laws, which otherwise might have been the work of some time, were suddenly restored; and a precedent of the force of government, and the danger of sedition has been set before the people of this country, which, I trust, they will never forget, and, I believe, will never need to be repeated.

Notwithstanding the settled malignity in the minds of several, perhaps many, individuals, considering the country the country [sic] in general, I believe there is a compleat practical reformation produced among us.

Yet the plan of leaving part of the army for some months in this country, appears to me a prudent one.[30] Many of the turbulent spirits have fled from the settlement, thinking that their concealment would be but temporary, and thinking that they might soon return without fear of punishment. But, as part of the army remains, they will be convinced that they must submit either to the laws or to permanent exile. And countenanced by this remainder of military force, not a hostile army, but a body of citizens armed to support the laws, the people of this country will acquire the habit of aiding and obeying publick authority.

These are my sentiments. I may be mistaken, but I am sincere. This is a statement of opinions not facts; and the opinions of different men on the same facts will vary from various circumstances. You will qualify my opinions by your own observations, and the information of others.

I am Sir &c&c A. A.
23 Novr. 1794

NOTES

1. No record of any request by Lee has been found, but the tenor of the first paragraph of Addison's letter, particularly the use of the past tense, suggests strongly that Lee may have made his request orally and that Addison replied orally, then wrote the letter for the record. Lee was in Pittsburgh and its environs from about November 9 to November 26 (Leland D. Baldwin, ed., "Orders Issued by General Henry Lee During the Campaign Against the Whiskey Insurrectionists," *Western Pennsylvania Historical Magazine* 19 [1936], 103; *Gazette of the United States* [Philadelphia], December 5, 1794).

2. This is supposition, in the absence of any explanation by Lee as to why he wanted Addison's opinion, or any contemporary reference to the Addison document. Since Lee asked specifically about the impact of the government's actions on suppressing the rebellion, he was probably worried about the army leaving the area. When the troops moved into Pittsburgh in early November, Secretary of the Treasury Alexander Hamilton feared that the population would submit to the law sullenly—unwillingly—only as long as troops were present, and that as soon as the army left, the rebellion would resume (Hamilton to Rufus King, October 30, 1794, to George Washington, October 31, 1794, in Harold C. Syrett, et al., eds., *The Papers of Alexander Hamilton* [New York: Columbia University Press, 1972], 17: 348, 351–352). Hamilton and Lee also worried about the patience of the eastern militia: how long it would willingly remain away from home, how it would suffer with winter soon approaching, and whether in the best of circumstances the army could be maintained in the area without friction, or even violence, between the soldiers and the local inhabitants (Hamilton to Thomas Mifflin, October 10, 1794, to Lee, October 20, 1794, in *ibid.*, pp. 317–318, 331–336; George Washington to Lee, October 20, 1794, and to Hamilton, October 26, 1794, in John C. Fitzpatrick, ed., *The Writings of George Washington* [Washington, D.C.: Government Printing Office, 1931–1944], 34:5–9; Lee to Mifflin, October 25, 1794, to the inhabitants of the four western counties, November 8, 1794, in John B. Linn and Wm. H. Egle, eds., *Pennsylvania Archives*, 2d ser., [Harrisburg: B. F. Meyers, 1876], 4:420–421, 445–446). Apparently Lee and Hamilton decided to require the inhabitants of the area to sign oaths of loyalty to the Constitution and obedience to the laws, and at the same time to seize all suspected leaders of the rebellion immediately. Then the army could be withdrawn quickly, and a detachment left to make certain violence or resistance did not recur. See Hamilton to King, October 30, 1794, to Tench Coxe, November 8, 1794, and to George Washington, November 8, 1794, in *Papers of Hamilton* 17:358–359, 361; Lee to William Irvine, November 9, 1794, in *Pennsylvania Archives*, 2d ser., 4:447–448. The request for Addison's opinion might have also been intended to put the judge on record as agreeing that the rebellion was suppressed, both to protect Lee personally and the administration politically in the decision to withdraw the army, which was ordered on November 17, and to issue a general pardon to the inhabitants, which Lee did on November 29 (General Orders, November 17, 1794, in Baldwin, ed., "Orders Issued by . . . Lee," p. 108; Proclamation of Pardon, November

29, 1794, in *Pennsylvania Archives*, 2d ser., 4:479–480). A final motive may have been distrust of Addison himself. Hamilton had long suspected that Addison, who opposed the excise tax, might even have participated in an indirect way in the rebellion. See Conference Concerning the Insurrection in Western Pennsylvania, August 2, 1794, Hamilton to Washington, September 2, 1794, in *Papers of Hamilton* 17:13, 186–190. Once the army, administration officials, and the federal judge and marshall for Pennsylvania returned to Philadelphia, Addison would be the chief judicial officer in the Pittsburgh region, responsible for enforcing the excise law if federal officials under the new June 1794 law decided to use state courts, and necessary in gathering evidence so that the leaders of the rebellion could be prosecuted in federal court. (See William Rawle to Addison, November 24, 26, December 29, 1794, *Pennsylvania Archives*, 2d ser., 4:472–473, 474, 500–502.) In what may have been a reply to Addison's letter, Lee wrote Addison that "I am persuaded the wisdom and vigor which will be displayed by the officers of justice . . . will probably be found equal to all future exigencies." If not, Lee added, the troops left "cannot fail in the immediate suppression of every irregularity, and will, I trust, be instantly restored to" (November 26, 1794, in *ibid.*, p. 474).

3. For background on Addison, see G. S. Rowe, "Alexander Addison: The Disillusionment of a 'Republican Schoolmaster,' " *Western Pennsylvania Historical Magazine* 62 (1979), 221–250; Leland D. Baldwin, *Whiskey Rebels: The Story of a Frontier Uprising,* rev. ed. (Pittsburgh, Pa.: University of Pittsburgh Press, 1968), pp. 51–52; Hugh G. Cleland, "John B. C. Lucas, Physiocrat on the Frontier," *Western Pennsylvania Historical Magazine* 36 (1953), 95, 147–152; John Robinson Wagner, "The Public Career of Alexander Addison", M. A. thesis, University of Pittsburgh, 1951; Whitfield J. Bell, Jr., "Washington County, Pennsylvania, in the Eighteenth Century Antislavery Movement," *Western Pennsylvania Historical Magazine* 25 (1942), 135–142; Boyd Crumrine, *The Courts of Justice Bench and Bar of Washington County, Pennsylvania . . .* (Washington, Pa.: Washington Bar Association, 1902), pp. 40–43.

4. For the Federalist interpretation of the origins of the rebellion, see Richard H. Kohn, *Eagle and Sword: The Federalists and the Creation of the Military Establishment in America, 1783–1802* (New York: Free Press, 1975), pp. 201–202. In denying a conspiracy, Addison agreed with Hugh Henry Brackenridge. See his *Incidents of the Insurrection in the Western Parts of Pennsylvania In the Year 1794* (Philadelphia: John McCulloch, 1795), particularly 3: appendix, pp. 140, 141.

5. See *The Speech of Albert Gallatin . . . relative to the Western Insurrection* (Philadelphia: William W. Woodward, 1795), p. 28; William Findley, *History of the Insurrection* (Philadelphia: Samuel Harrison Smith, 1796), pp. 70–75, 223–225.

6. Information on Isaac Craig is in Baldwin, *Whiskey Rebels*, pp. 46–47.

7. Samples of Isaac Craig's handwriting are in the Craig Papers, Carnegie Library of Pittsburgh, Pittsburgh, Pa.; of Addison in the Alexander Addison Papers, Arlington Memorial Library, University of Pittsburgh, Pittsburgh, Pa., and Addison to Alexander James Dallas, July 24, 1794, RG 26, Executive Correspondence, box 12, Pennsylvania State Archives, Harrisburg, Pa.; of Presley Neville in Neville to Craig, September 12, 1794, Craig Papers; of John Neville in his correspondence with George Clymer, September 1791, vol. 19, Oliver Wolcott Papers, Connecticut Historical Society, Hartford, Conn. The letter is on paper of the kind commonly used in the nineteenth century during the Jacksonian era.

8. For Neville Craig's handwriting, see his letters to Henry Carey Baird in the 1850s

in the Henry Carey Baird Papers, Edward Carey Gardiner Collection, box 4, Historical Society of Pennsylvania, Philadelphia.

9. Neville B. Craig, *Exposure of a few of the Many Misstatements in H. M. Brackenridge's History of the Whiskey Insurrection* (Pittsburgh: John S. Davidson, 1859), p. 73. Information on Craig and the battle with Brackenridge is in *ibid.*; the last box of the Craig Papers; *Memoirs of Allegheny County, Pennsylvania: Personal and Geneological with Portraits* (Madison, Wis.: Northwestern Historical Association, 1904), pp. 357–359; Daniel Agnew, "Address to the Allegheny County Bar Association, December 1, 1888," *Pennsylvania Magazine of History and Biography* 13 (1889), 46–47.

10. In none of the research for *Eagle and Sword* did I find any other copy of the document, nor any contemporary reference to it. I also checked the following newspapers for reference: *Pittsburgh Gazette,* December 1794–May 1795; *Carlisle Weekly Gazette,* December 1794–May 1795; *Pennsylvania Gazette* (Philadelphia), December 1794–May 1795; *American Daily Advertiser* (Philadelphia), December 1794–January 1795. The *Gazette of the United States* (Philadelphia) and the *General Advertiser* (Philadelphia) were read earlier.

11. See particularly the deposition of Judge Addison, n.d., *Pennsylvania Archives,* 2d ser. 4:390–391; "Remarks on the late Insurrection," December 1794, in Alexander Addison, *Charges to Grand Juries of the Counties of the Fifth Circuit in the State of Pennsylvania* (Philadelphia: John Colerick, 1800), pp. 120–123.

12. Addison wrote "what I should say" after "that" and lined the words out.

13. Parliament taxed alcoholic beveridges as early as 1643, and distilleries as early as 1690. As direct taxes, excises were opposed from the beginning as being unfair because they added to the price of necessary staples for daily life and taxed the poor. See Townsend Ward, "The Insurrectiion of the Year 1794, in the Western Counties of Pennsylvania," *Memoirs of the Historical Society of Pennsylvania* 6 (Philadelphia: J. B. Lippincott, 1858), 6:120–124; William Kennedy, *English Taxation, 1640–1799: An Essay on Policy and Opinion [Series of the London School of Economics and Political Science,* No. 33] (London: G. Bell & Sons,1913), pp. 52, 76–77, 107, 122–123; Stephen Dowell, *A History of Taxation and Taxes in England from the Earliest Times to the Present Day,* 3d ed. (New York: Augustus M. Kelley, 1965), 2:53–54, 69–77; 4:69–77,177–180.

14. Using the 1790 census, Baldwin (*Whiskey Rebels,* pp. 21–22) estimates that the most numerous groups in western Pennsylvania at this time were English and Scot in origin, including Scots from Ireland. However the populace was polyglot, including German, Dutch, and Irish Catholic. The earliest and chief church was Presbyterian and the Scots-Irish "apparently" gave "the tone to frontier life," making it "easy for contemporary travellers to assume that the Monongahelans were overwhelmingly 'Irish' " (*ibid.*, p. 22).

15. The boundary between Pennsylvania and Virginia, west of Maryland's western border, was uncertain in the colonial era because of conflicting colonial charter claims. In the 1770s, jurisdiction over the area south of the Ohio and Allegheny Rivers and west of Laurel Ridge, settled both by Pennsylvanians and Virginians, was claimed by both colonies. A compromise was reached in 1779 and 1780, and a boundary surveyed in the 1780s. See Solon J. Buck and Elizabeth Hawthorn Buck, *The Planting of Civilization in Western Pennsylvania* (Pittsburgh, Pa.: University of Pittsburgh Press, 1939), 156–170.

16. Agitation for a separate state in the area began during the Revolutionary War and continued into the 1780s. The Pennsylvania legislature "in 1782 . . . enacted a law de-

claring any attempt to organize a new state within the boundaries of Pennsylvania to be high treason and prescribing the death penalty'' (*ibid.*, p. 171).

17. Pennsylvania taxed and regulated spirits throughout its early history. The last state excise enacted before the rebellion was in 1781, supplemented in 1783, and repealed in September 1791. See Baldwin, *Whiskey Rebels*, pp. 56–58, 78.

18. William Graham of Philadelphia was appointed Pennsylvania excise collector for Washington, Fayette, and Westmoreland counties in April 1783 (*ibid.*, p. 58).

19. This incident occurred at Cross Creek, Washington County, in 1784. While Graham had been subjected to ridicule and intimidation earlier, this time he sued and won damages from twelve leaders of the mob. He resigned soon after the incident (*ibid.*, pp. 59–60).

20. The U.S. excise law was passed March 3, 1791, and amended May 8, 1792, and June 5, 1794. See the *Papers of Hamilton* 17:2–3, n. 1.

21. Resistance to the law between 1791 and 1794 is described in Baldwin, *Whiskey Rebels* ch. 4.

22. David Bradford, a Marylander by birth, was a popular lawyer in Washington County, and one of the leaders of the insurrection. He served as deputy attorney general for the county from 1783 until 1794, and was elected to the state assembly in 1792.

23. The U.S. marshall for the District of Pennsylvania was David Lenox of Philadelphia. Lenox's serving of processes which required distillers delinquent in registering their stills to appear in federal court in Philadelphia touched off the attack on General Neville's estate, and the rebellion.

24. One of the chief complaints of western Pennsylvanians was that legal actions under the excise law took place in federal court, which in Pennsylvania was in Philadelphia. A law to allow use of state courts went through Congress in April and May of 1794, and was signed by the President on June 5. The processes served by Lenox, for appearance by delinquent distillers in Philadelphia, were issued in May while the new law was being passed. (For a dating see Ward, ''The Insurrection,'' *Memoirs of the Historical Society of Pennsylvania* 6:155–156). This led Addison to note rather pointedly that the government *chose* to use the federal courts. Republicans like William Findley argued outright that the government, by prosecuting in federal court when it could have waited two or three weeks and used the state courts, actually provoked the rebellion. See Findley, *History of the Insurrection*, pp. 70–75.

25. Addison wrote ''papers'' after ''his,'' but lined it out.

26. Neville's estate was attacked on July 16 by about forty men, and sacked and burned on July 17 by several hundred. For these events, see Baldwin, *Whiskey Rebels,* pp. 115–124; the documents in *Pennsylvania Archives*, 2d ser., 4:69–70, 73–75; and the documents in *Papers of Hamilton*, pp. 3–4, n. 2.

27. On July 26, near Greensburg, mail from Washington, Pennsylvania, and from Pittsburgh bound for Philadelphia was seized from the post rider and delivered to insurgent leaders. After reading the letters, the insurgents called for the militia of the area to assemble on August 1 at Braddock's Fields, about eight miles from Pittsburgh on the east bank of the Monongahela. See Baldwin, *Whiskey Rebels,* pp. 138–139; Circular . . . to the Militia Officers, July 28, 1794, *Pennsylvania Archives* 2d ser., 4:78–79.

28. Addison was probably referring to Republican congressmen William Findley and John Smilie, and Republican stalwart Albert Gallatin, a member of the Pennsylvania legislature. These three, all from the Pittsburgh area, were frequently named by Federalists as the real fomenters of the rebellion. See, for example, Oliver Wolcott, Jr. to his father,

September 23, 1794, George Gibbs, *Memoirs of the Administrations of Washington and John Adams* (New York: W. Van Norden, 1846) 1:159.

29. On October 9 and 10, at Carlisle, William Findley and David Redick met with the President and Alexander Hamilton, both accompanying the right wing of the militia army on the march toward Pittsburgh. Findley, the congressman from Westmoreland County, and Redick, the lawyer with whom Addison had read law and also an officeholder in Washington County, had been appointed by a popular meeting at Parkinson's Ferry on October 2 to transmit to the president promises to submit to the law and to federal authority. Addison was secretary of the meeting (Baldwin, *Whiskey Rebels,* pp. 217, 228–229).

30. A detachment of troops numbering over a thousand men were left in the Pittsburgh region, under the command of General Daniel Morgan, when the army withdrew in late November. Morgan's force was disbanded in June 1795 (Don Higginbotham, *Daniel Morgan: Revolutionary Rifleman* [Chapel Hill: University of North Carolina Press, 1961], pp. 193–198).

Hugh Henry Brackenridge,
Incidents of the Insurrection

Hugh Henry Brackenridge, a Pittsburgh attorney, emigrated to Pennsylvania from Scotland in 1753. He graduated from the College of New Jersey (Princeton) in 1771, and served as a schoolteacher in Maryland for five years. He simultaneously studied divinity and in 1776 emigrated to Philadelphia where he edited the *U.S. Magazine*. Following that brief sojourn in journalism, Brackenridge served as a chaplain in the army. He migrated to Pittsburgh at the close of the war to practice law. He aided in establishing the *Pittsburgh Gazette* in 1786 and contributed literary and political material to it throughout his lifetime.

Brackenridge held elective office only once: he served as an assemblyman from Westmoreland County during 1786–1787. As an assemblyman he sponsored legislation separating Pittsburgh and the surrounding area from Westmoreland County and creating the new county of Alleghany. He also supported the call for a state convention to ratify the proposed federal Constitution and published a number of essays in the *Gazette* in support of ratification. In this Brackenridge was at odds with many of his constituents and he failed to win a seat in the state convention. Undaunted by that defeat, Brackenridge continued to assail anti-Federalism throughout the winter of 1787–1788 in the columns of the *Gazette*. Brackenridge remained an active Federalist during the ensuing first federal elections as well, despite some personal pique over not being on the Federalist ticket.

While Brackenridge's Federalism alienated his rural constituents, he also antagonized the influential Federalist, General John Neville. Brackenridge claimed the source of Neville's animosity was a civil suit he prosecuted. In any case, by 1790 Brackenridge found himself politically powerless and professionally insecure. His fortune was on the mend, however, when the events of 1794 intervened. During the rebellion, Brackenridge served as a mediator between the rebels and the town of Pittsburgh, which was considered threatened because it housed Neville, the collector of the excise for the district, and his allies. In doing so, Brackenridge further antagonized Neville and "the connection." This led, he claimed, to aspersions being rumored about him by Neville and his son Presley, first among the troops sent west to quell the rebellion, then among the countryside, and ultimately across the nation. It was with an eye to correcting these false rumors and allegations that Brackenridge wrote detailing his every action that related to the rebellion, with frequent asides to counter various rumors or innuendos current at the time, and to offer possible reasons for those rumors.

Despite this narrow focus, Brackenridge also offers an interpretation of the causes of the rebellion. Conceding that there was a long-standing tradition of resistance to excise taxes among the Scots-Irish in the west, he nonetheless insisted that the principal cause of the rebellion was the excise tax and the unjust burden it levied on the area. Brackenridge's view, which was shared by William Findley and other contemporaries, has been accepted by a substantial share of the historians of the rebellion. Brackenridge was less successful in refurbishing his own reputation, and his son reports that as late as the 1850s the people of Pittsburgh still referred to "that insurgent" Brackenridge.

Brackenridge composed his history in 1795 while in Pittsburgh and sent it piecemeal to the printer in Philadelphia. It was initially scheduled to be three volumes and is so paginated. Once it was completed, however, the printer decided to bind the three volumes as one and to release it under the title, *Incidents of the Insurrection* (Philadelphia, 1795). The portion printed below is from section 1, p. 3, and section 3, pp. 9–30, 39.

INCIDENTS OF THE INSURRECTION IN THE WESTERN PARTS OF PENNSYLVANIA IN THE YEAR 1794

What I write is with a view to explain my own conduct, which has not been understood.[1] It is possible I may not be able to remove the misconception of everyone. I am aware how difficult it is to change opinion, even with the best cause on my side. But, I may support those who have undertaken my defense in conversation and it may satisfy others who are disposed to find men innocent rather than criminal.

****

Such was the state of the public mind with regard to excise laws when that of the United States was enacted.[2] This was of March 3rd, 1791.

The bill had been brought before the House of Representatives in Congress on the January preceding, the legislature of Pennsylvania then in session also.[3] The Pennsylvania House of Representatives took the matter up and entered into resolutions expressive of their sense with regard to excise laws and directing those resolutions to be communicated to the senators representing the state of Pennsylvania in the Senate of the United States. To these resolutions, carried by a majority of 36, there was a dissent of six members; not on the principle of justifying an excise system, but on that of the impropriety of the state legislature interfering in the deliberations of the federal government.[4] They take notice also of the inconsistency of that house objecting to an excise law under the United States when "an act of their own, of the same nature, existed unrepealed, and in operation in the state; an act also which involved powers far more obnoxious and oppressive to the people than those in contemplation in the act of Congress."[5]

The majority, in support of these resolutions, entered on the journals the reasons for their votes on the question when the yeas and nays were called. A member, who had not been present the first moving of the question, entered on the journals the reasons of his dissent from the resolutions. This was Thomas Ryerson, of Washington.[6]

This gentleman, having been a member of the house with James Marshall the preceding year, had differed from him in a vote with regard to the continuation of a state tax. The state debt being assumed by the federal government, a tax was not necessary as to that object. Marshall thought that the people, being in the habit of paying, would not be dissatisfied at the continuance of a light direct tax and there were great public objects to be accomplished: opening roads, clearing rivers, &c. I thought Marshall right at the time, and Ryerson, who differed from him, wrong. But Ryerson had the popular side, the keeping clear of paying money, and he run Marshall down, so that at the next election [October, 1791] he was left out.

When the vote of Ryerson was announced in the case of the resolutions, Marshall, in his turn, came forward against Ryerson. He became a leader in the opposition to the excise law.[7] It may easily be supposed that Ryerson was left out at the next election.

All the members, on their return from Philadelphia, in order to enhance the merit of their services, may easily be supposed to have been strong in testimony borne against the excise law of Congress, which they had so strenuously, though unsuccessfully, opposed. The resolutions and the reasons were published in the *Pittsburgh Gazette* of March 1791, and read and commented on at all public meetings and places.

David Bradford, who had not before this time interfered in political affairs, came forward in an open and direct manner to arraign the law. Whether for the sake of popularity; or from a personal pique against Thomas Scott, the sitting member of Congress who had voted for the law; or against Alexander Addison, who at this time came forward in the *Pittsburgh Gazette* with a strong publication in favor of it;[8] or whether it was that he conceived it would drain the country of circulating cash and injure the profession of the law; or on general principle, I declare myself at a loss to say. But it would seem to me that he had not reach of mind, nor information sufficient, to entertain objections on elementary principles of its being a tax on domestic manufacture and dangerous as introducing that principle, extendible to any length.

William Findley, of Westmoreland, who had been several years in the legislature of Pennsylvania and had meditated no blow at the excise law of Pennsylvania, was now of the House of Representatives in Congress, and saw great evils in that of the United States. He fell back amongst the people with all his weight to reprobate it.[9]

[John] Smilie, of Fayette, also then a member of the House of Representatives in Congress, and who also had been of the legislature of Pennsylvania several years, having voted with Findley in the opposition, upon returning to his county, added his influence to fix, if anything was necessary, the rivets of prejudice more strongly against the law.[10]

But if these had all be quiescent, the prejudice was of itself irresistible. Had they attempted to reconcile the people to the law, they would have been instantly unpopular and have descended to the level whence they rose. It was not anything celestial in the form or talents of these men that made them popular, it was their standing with a party and consulting the prejudices of the people. The moment they opposed the feelings of the multitude, they were damned with them to a lower bed than those whom they had never favored. But it was not enough for them even to be silent. They were charged publicly in the *Gazette* with their unpardonable inattention, while members of the legislature of Pennsylvania, in having suffered an excise law to exist in the government. They were under the necessity of acknowledging it to have been a great oversight, to atone for which they would have the state excise taken away, and would redouble their diligence in having that of the United States repealed also. The state excise law was repealed at the next session of the legislature the September following; nothing now remained but to have that of the United States repealed also. Findley and Smiley must do, or at least seem to be doing, something in order to keep their seats at the next election. Perhaps the men may have acted on the same principle with the people, viz. from an absolute dislike of it and prejudice against it. I only state grounds of conduct which would be sufficient with me to account for their opposition independent of the abstract principle of any inconsistency in the law with equality of tax or principles of liberty.

Alexander Addison, who had come forward at an early period in defending, or at least in apologizing for the law, though possessing an independent situation, yet was shortly obliged to take in his sails and slacken course.[11] He would soon have ceased to have been regarded in all he could say to a jury in his charges and his person itself would have been insecure in his riding the circuit had he persisted.

Such had been the state of things and situation of the country when General [John] Neville, shortly after the passing of the act, had accepted the office of inspector for the survey comprehending the four Pennsylvania counties on the west of the mountain and that of Bedford on the east.

I had never considered General Neville as possessing an extensive popularity, yet, at the same time, he had a respectable share of it, and what was in his favor, he stood well in his own neighborhood. But he had been a member of the legislature of Pennsylvania when the resolutions against the excise law were moved and carried. He had absented himself from the House when the vote was taken and his conduct was afterwards attributed to his having previously looked forward to an appointment under the law. The circumstance of a man whom the people have sent forward in a legislative capacity looking out for a profitable office that he may retire has at all times an appearance of selfishness and intro-duces the suspicion of having himself more in view than the public. If that man is already wealthy, and has no need of offices, as was the case with General Neville, it increases the charge of covetousness and accumulates the odium of his conduct. Had General Neville stood forward in the House, and on the local ground of the unequal operation of the tax to the western country, supported the resolutions of the house (and I am clear, they had a right to instruct their senators as immediately appointed by them); if he had, I say, acted this part and, after the law had passed, had pointed out to the government some firm and respectable character in the western country whom he might induce to accept the office, and have returned home, free from all suspicion of interested motives, to recommend an acquiescence to the law, and to support the officer as far as he could indi-vidually; he would have acted the part of a patriot. As the case was, he contributed to fix the odium of the office more deeply in the minds of the people by the circumstances under which he took it.

I had been employed as counsel in defending the rioters on the indictments at the prosecution of [William] Graham, the state collector of excise. It is to be presumed that I had been of the same opinion with my clients—that the excise laws were odious and that an honest fellow ought not to be severely treated who had done nothing more than to shave the under hairs from the head of an excise man who wore a wig at any rate. I had appeared for the seventy distillers that were sued in Allegheny County and in defending them was lead unavoidably to avail myself of arguments drawn from the odious nature of the excise laws as a ground of strict construction against their operation. I was thought by the people to be staunch against all excises. I did not like much to lose my character in this respect, nor indeed could I well afford it. I had been at the head of the practice at the bar in the year 1786, when, in order to accomplish a particular purpose, the obtaining a new county comprehending Pittsburgh, I procured my-self to be elected to the legislature of the state. The members of the surrounding counties, out of which the new county must be taken, were of course opposed to a dismemberment, and I was under the necessity of making friends elsewhere. There were two parties at the time in the house, known under the name Con-stitutional and Anti–Constitutional. The western members were Constitutional-ists, I was therefore obliged to join the Anti-Constitutionalists in order to get their interest to accomplish my object. Of course, when the western members returned, I was represented as a traitor who had betrayed my country because I had gone with a wrong party. They were 9 to 1 against me. Findley was the head of them, and I had thought to have defended myself by writing,[12] but only made the matter worse for the people thought it impossible that plain, sensible men could be wrong and a profane lawyer right.

Another circumstance had taken place during the session which accumulated odium upon me; that was the calling a convention to new model the federal government. I supported that measure and when the convention had sat and published a Constitution, I supported the adoption of it. All my colleagues from the westward came home Antifederalists and held me up in a worse point of view, if possible, than before.[13] My character was totally gone with the populace. My practice was lost and James Ross and David Bradford and others, whom I left at the bar just beginning, got it all. Pride and good policy would not permit me to leave the country until I had conquered the prejudice. I knew that to be practicable by lying by until the popular fury should waste itself. It required time, but I had patience. But it was necessary for me to be silent and add nothing more to the popular odium. It was the first experience I had ever had in life of unpopularity and I found it a thing more painful to sustain and more difficult to remove than I had thought it to be. Had I possessed an independent fortune, I would have cared less about it, but I had just laid the foundation of making something by the practice I had established, and this was now taken from me. It is astonishing what an effect political character has upon professional success. It was not to be expected under these circumstances, let my sentiments have been what they might, that I would have come forward as the champion of government in the case of the excise law. It would have been excuseable had I taken some advantage of the popular gale, having been so long becalmed or detained by headwinds where I lay. But the fact was, though an advocate for the federal government, I had not been an admirer of it. I speak of the legislative department. The funding system, in all its branches, was contrary to my wishes and all ideas of justice.[14] I am conscious I was influenced by no motives but abstract principles of what I thought right or wrong. At the same time I am not calling in question the integrity of the framers, but what I give them leave to call in question with me: the judgment. The excise law I considered as a branch of the funding system and I felt a hatred to the offspring on account of its stock. At the same time I saw the operation to be unequal in this country, the people having put themselves generally in the way of distilling and spirits from domestic manufacturers being chiefly in use. It is true that the excise paid by the country would be that only on spirits consumed in it. But even in the case of exports, the excise must be advanced in the first instance by the distiller and this would prevent effectually all the poorer part from carrying on the business.[15] I was opposed to the law on these grounds and would have preferred a direct tax with a view to reach unsettled lands which all around us have been purchased by speculating men who kept them up in large bodies and obstructed the population of the country. Nevertheless, I was shackled by my connections. The party to which I belonged in the legislature and who had finally enabled us to succeed in obtaining a county were rather on the side of the funding system and the excise law. Thomas Scott of Washington was a friend of mine and he had voted for the law.[16] Alexander Addison had supported it in the public paper and he was a friend of mine. I had been upon such terms with the Neville connection that it was disagreeable to me to come forth and strongly in the opposition to the law when the head of that house was the officer for carrying the law into execution. Moreover, Findley, Smiley, and others of my political enemies had come forward to reprobate the law. I did not like to be ostensibly in the same party with them. Besides, in my *Gazette* writings against Findley and others, I had treated with such ridicule, the arts of seeking popular favor that I was afraid of being suspected of that myself.[17] Had it not been for these circumstances, I am persuaded I should have come forward against the law more than I have done and have given my adversaries much greater presumption of having contributed to the insurrection than exists as things now are. If I had not been shackled by the terms on which I was with the Neville connnection particularly, it is not improbable that I might have exercised at least attempts at wit at the expense of the officer or the office and excise duties might have been sung here as Wood's half pence in Ireland. And I know well that if any other had been the officer, there is no man that would have enjoyed it more than General Neville. But if I had written ever so much in the way of wit or invective, it would be absurd to charge me with the acts of others, for the distinction is infinite between constitutional and unconstitutional opposition. A man has a right to arraign the policy of a law as well after it is enacted, in order to procure a repeal, as before, in order to prevent the enacting of it.[18] I shall now return to the history of the opposition.

A meeting was held at Redstone, Old Fort, now called Brownsville, on the 27th of July, 1791, at which meeting it was understood that Findley, Smiley, and Marshall, with a great number of the inhabitants of the western counties, were present. Albert Gallatin was clerk of the meeting. He was, at that time, a member of the legislature and had voted with the majority in support of the resolution to instruct the senators on the excise bill in Congress.[19] Edward Cook was chairman, who had been a decided Federalist, so that it was not considered to be a question of federalism or antifederalism. Nor had it been so considered in the legislature of the state, numbers of the firmest Federalists voting with the majority in the case of the resolutions with regard to the excise bill. It was at this meeting resolved[20] "that it be recommended to the electors of each election district in the several counties of Westmoreland, Washington, Fayette and Allegheny, to meet on the third Tuesday of August next at the place of holding their annual elections and there to choose not more than three representatives for their district to form a county committee. That the representatives thus chosen do meet at the seat of justice of their county, respectively, on the fourth Tuesday in August next, and having fairly collected the sense of the people within their respective counties, shall respectively choose out of their own body three members to form a general committee.

"That the members thus chosen by the several county committees shall meet on the third Tuesday of September next at the house of Mr. [Adamson] Tannehill, in the town of Pittsburgh, and there draw up and publish in the *Pittsburgh Gazette* a set of resolutions expressing the sense of their constituents on the subject of the excise law. That the said general committee, if in their opinion it shall be necessary, shall draw up an address to the legislature of the United States on this subject, wherein they will express the sense of their constituents with decency and firmness.

"That they shall draw up and communicate a circular letter and general address to the neighboring counties in Pennsylvania, Virginia, and Kentucky, calling upon them for their exertions in a cause which is common."

Agreeably to the above resolution, district elections had taken place through the greatest part of the four counties and the members from the districts having met at the seat of justice, chose deputies to meet in a general committee on the first Tuesday of September at Pittsburgh.

At the meeting of the district members in the town of Washington on the 23rd of August, delegates were chosen to the general meeting and certain resolutions were adopted of a violent nature with regard to the law in question.

James Marshall, whose first spring in this business might in some degree have been his contest with Ryerson, but who doubtless had the same general impressions with the others, had been at Pittsburgh occasionally, having at that time a contract with the public for the purchase of horses for the wagons of the army; had conversed with me on the subject of the excise law; and finding my sentiments in unison with his, not only with regard to the excise law, but the funding system in general, expressed a wish that I would come forward and get myself elected a member from Allegheny County. I declined it on the ground of having suffered in practice, not only from the obloguy against me, but the impression the people had that I made political subjects more the object of my attention than law. This was true, but the chief reasons why I did not come forward were those I have before assigned. Marshall excused me, but thought I could have no objections to assist in drawing up the addresses proposed to the public or to the representatives in Congress. I had no objections to that.

James Marshall was a man for whom I had all along entertained respect. When I came to this country in the year 1781 a strong party existed in favor of the establishment of a new state comprehending the Pennsylvania and Virginia counties.[21] Marshall was county lieutenant in Washington and had exerted himself greatly in opposition to this measure. I was with him in all endeavors to compose the country and establish the Pennsylvania jurisdiction. This produced an intimacy. After his lieutenancy he was sheriff of the county and discharged this office with general approbation from the court, the bar, and the country. During my political debates with Findley and others, he had leaned in my favor to a certain extent, I had believed from personal engagements. When a member of the convention for the purpose of adopting the Federal Constitution, he was the most moderate of all the Antifederalists and refused to sign the *Protest,* as reasons were alledged in it which did not weigh with him.[22] I had flattered myself with thinking that my opinion and representations in favor of the Constitution had contributed to make him moderate; for he is naturally a democrat, perhaps in the extreme. At the lowest ebb of my popularity, he was willing to serve me in my practice and did contribute considerably to restore it. In the difference between him and Ryerson I could not take part because I was friendly to both.

I state these things in order to explain the standing on which I was at this time with Marshall.

The committee met at Pittsburgh on the 7th of September. Agreeably to my engagement to Marshall I had prepared a sketch of resolutions and a draught of an address to Congress; this last drawn with great care and to the best of my ability. On the day Marshall came forward with a rough draft of an address to the people. Bradford also had drawn something. These were put into my hand with a request to new model them and to give them any polish that they might seem to want. I did so, and my address to Congress was copied by Marshall, and that to the people copied by Bradford. My sketch of resolutions was copied by a member of Westmoreland.

I was present as a spectator some time during the debates in the committee until the papers, some of which I had written, had been committed to three persons: my brother of the bar, who was then of the committee, David Bradford, and Edward Cook, chairman. I heard no more of them until the day after, when, being in the printing office, I saw the proceedings with the printer to be published. And I made this observation to him, ''The first draughts of some of these writings were by me. They are totally changed, and rendered inconsistent, and absurd, and I disclaim all responsibility.'' They had been new modelled in the committee. I understood my brother of the bar had alledged there were treasonable expressions in the first draughts. I never heard of a sentence he has quoted; all I can say is that he mistook a figure for a threat and had not literary taste sufficient to distinguish.

A report of the Secretary of the Treasury on the excise law was made to the House of Representatives on the 6th of March, 1791. It begun to be published in the *Pittsburgh Gazette* of April 7th, 1792, and was continued through several papers. Strictures on it had been published in the *National Gazette* under the signature of Sydney, said to be written by William Findley.[23] These strictures were copied into the *Pittsburgh Gazette*, I have understood by request. They were continued through several papers at considerable length, from the paper of May 19th to that of November 3d, 1792.

A great variety of publications had appeared in the meantime in the western paper on the subject of the excise; some of which were attributed to me, but in which I had no hand. A publication of considerable length signed John Neville had appeared in a pamphlet.[24] The object was to reconcile the people to the law. It was answered in a variety of publications in the *Gazette*. I was not the author of any. The address was of no use. Professions of disinterestedness were held out which were thought to be absurd as it must have struck everyone that in accepting the office he could have no other object in view but the making money.

A second general meeting took place at Pittsburgh on the 21st day of August 1792. I do not find any previous advertisements in the gazettes calling that meeting, nor do I know how it was brought about. An extract from the resolutions entered into at that meeting, I subjoin in a note.[25]

I had been elected a delegate from Allegheny County, but declined serving. I recollect to have been asked by some of the members whether the going so far could be construed treason. I thought not. I was told by the member that the same question had been put to my brother of the bar and that he was of opinion that it did not amount to treason. It struck me to be going to the utmost boundary of right reserved by the people. On the principle of political virtue nothing but extreme necessity could justify it. It is the last step short of using actual force. It is a thesis I would like to see well discussed. Gallatin, in his speech in the legislature of Pennsylvania on the question of the western election, seems to have given it up and calls it his "political sin."[26] He would seem, on reflection, to have considered it not, as I presume, as a misdemeanor cognizable by the law, but as censurable on the ground of abstract political virtue. I would certainly think it is so, the case stated, viz., as the last step before using force.

A Democratic society was instituted in the town of Washington in the month of April, 1794, on the same principles and in correspondence, as I have understood, with societies of the same denomination in New York, Philadelphia, and elsewhere. I have traced no resolutions or proceedings of this society of Washington with regard to excise law.[27]

Prior to this a society of a nature much more democratic had been instituted in the neighborhood of Mingo Creek. The place of convening was usually the meeting house.[28]

Various principles combined to produce this society. Some of the leaders in it had been disappointed in their wishes to be justices of the peace, or to be upon the bench as associate justices; others were harassed with suits from justices and courts and wished a less expensive tribunal; others favored it as an engine of election for county offices, or for the state legislature; others from a desire natural to men of being conspicuous. This society was the cradle of the insurrection. They did not, as a society, project the first outrages, but they naturally sprung from that licentiousness of idea with regard to law and liberty which the articles of their institution held out or were calculated to produce.

A society of a *singular* nature was instituted in a part of the county of Allegheny in April following. We have the first account of it in the *Gazette* of April 26th, 1794.[29]

The articles of this society are to the same effect with that of Mingo Creek and equally calculated to abstract the public mind from the established order of the laws.

The account given me by Mr. McDonald, the secretary, or rather the apology made for instituting the society, was that the people of the settlement were outrageous to do something on account of the excise law, the costs of the suits before justices, court expense, and the salaries of officers; and were determined to do something; and had talked of breaking up General Neville and burning Pittsburgh; and that the instituting a society was thought of by the more moderate as a means of employing the people's minds and keep them deliberating instead of acting. Be this as it may, it does not seem to have had the effect, but rather to have accelerated the commencement of actual violence. It appears that at the June court at Washington, 1794, there was a conversation, and by some of the members of that society of a nature with that mentioned by McDonald, viz., the seizing Neville and the breaking up the office in Pittsburgh.

It was on the verge of Mingo Creek settlement that the marshall was opposed in serving the first process. He had served process without molestation in the counties of Bedford, Westmoreland, Washington and Fayette; and in Fayette county a meeting of distillers had been called, at which Gallatin assisted, and it had been determined to employ counsel at the federal court to defend the suits. It was in serving the remaining process in the county of Allegheny, on the verge of the Mingo creek settlement, that the opposition broke out into actual hostility. The marshall had served several writs in a single neighborhood in the course of one morning. Those on whom he had served the first had collected and pursued him while he was serving the last. The people left the harvest fields and took up arms. There was no pre-concert, no determined object. It had nothing in it but the essence of a mob. I attribute little to the circumstance of General Neville being in company or to that of a writ being served in a harvest field amongst a group of reapers; nor do I attribute much even to the circumstance of a number of men being assembled at a board of appeals in case of fines for a neglect of militia duty held that day by the inspector of brigade at Benjamin Parkinson's. I resolve it rather into the established temper of the country than into accidental causes. Be this as it may, the inflammation spread rapidly. The quitting harvest fields, a most urgent business with the farmer, was a strong proof to me of the violence of the people. The whole settlement was in commotion suddenly. The first party that attacked Neville's house were but a squad from the bulk that were behind, in agitation consulting what measures to pursue. Holcroft, in his retreat, was met at Couche's fort by numbers who had come forward disposed to violent purpose. These returning roused others and in the course of one night the body was assembled to the amount at least of 500 men that met at Couche's fort. A committee was here chosen to direct the operations and it was under orders, occasionally given, that the people marched. The flags passed and repassed between them and those that attempted to defend the house of the inspector.

From the preceding statement it will appear that the idea of "an individual projecting the insurrection" is without foundation. It originated on the broad basis of popular prejudice. However, it may be that leading men, at home or abroad, contributed by speeches or by writings to foster and support that prejudice. I am persuaded that no digest was ever made in the minds of anyone to rouse the people to an actual and general outrage.

Having given the preceding history of incidents which led to it, I address myself to rebut those presumptions that I have heard alleged against myself as projecting the disturbance or having a privacy with the counsels of those who did. As to the grounds of my intimacy with Marshall, or my supported privacy with his councils, I have stated every particular that is within the recollection of my mind. As to Bradford, I was upon terms of apparent intimacy and of that I give the following account.

It is well known to gentlemen of the bar that lawyers who reside in a county usually bring the suits and its rests with them in most cases to recommend to clients the assistants out of those who ride the circuit, whom they may employ on the trial of the cause. Bradford, though not a great lawyer, was a popular one and I had found it useful, at a time when I was struggling to restore my practice, to stand well with him. I had found my account in it still on and the very advantage which I had derived, independent of any principle of philanthropy, established in my mind a good will for the man. But I was thought to have an intimacy with him which I had not. It was in appearance considerable, but not much in fact, for he was not a man of much sentiment, and my accordance with him went no further tha[n] the interest which I had in sharing business.

I have heard it predicated loudly by those who wished to involve me in any prejudice that may exist against Findley, Smilie, Gallatin, &c., that I had fallen in with them and formed a conjunction on the west of the mountain. After an established difference with Findley, I had come so far in the course of nine years as to exchange a common saluation, but the first time I gave him my hand was at Brownsville the morning I was going forward with Gallatin to support the propositions of the commissioners. I gave him my hand and said it was time to forget differences and join in our endeavors to avert a civil war. With Smiley I never had any difference, except what was political and abstract, but I have not exchanged with him seven words these seven years. With Gallatin, I do not recollect that I have ever exchanged a word in my life, until in the course of our transactions in composing the disturbance. With none of these have I ever corresponded; to none of these have I ever sent a message, nor they to me. I was never of a committee or other meeting where any of them were present or with which they had anything to do. If I have not the credit of individual patronage, why should I be subject to the odium?

It has been said that disappointment had soured my temper with the federal government and that I was disposed, if not to overthrow, at least to embarass it. In proof of this it is alledged that in my correspondence with some gentlemen of Philadelphia some years ago I expressed chagrin with the federal party in the state and said they would find the effect of having affronted me. It is true I was chagrined and did write to this effect. Let me explain it. It has been seen that while a member of the legislature of Pennsylvania in the year 1787, I had found it necessary to join myself to a party. This was distinguished at the time by the name of Anticonstitutional, or those opposed to the frame of government which Pennsylvania had adopted. Having stood firmly in the house with those on all questions, I had become obnoxious to the opposite. It was the Anticonstitutionalists that brought forward the bill for a convention to revise the federal government; the model framed by this convention was supported by the party in the house to which I was attached. On my return from the legislature, I became the advocate for it in the western country; I fought a hard battle in its favor until it was adopted.[30] The election for the first representatives was to be general through the state and not by districts. In order to frame a ticket two district conventions were held at Lancaster and Harrisburgh. That at Lancaster was the Federal, as it was called, or the interest to which I had been attracted. Findley, who had been my adversary, was to be taken up, as it was understood, by the Harrisburgh, or Antifederal ticket. It struck me to have my name brought forward in the Federal ticket in opposition to him. I procured a delegation from the four counties of two gentlemen who attended at the Lancaster convention and presented my name. It was rejected. I felt the indignity and considered myself as absolved from the party and expressed myself to this effect. But that had nothing to do with my attachment to individuals or to the government itself that had been established. My resentment reflected merely the party in the state and nothing else. It had been no object with me to be a representative. I had cared nothing about it. But merely on a principle of opposition to my adversaries, I had suffered my name to be carried forward; and that being the case, I was affronted to have it thrown aside. I felt it with sensibility until I came to understand how it took place; viz., that it was not on the ground of personal disrespect to me, but on that Thomas Scott, whom they took in my place being less exceptionable at the time with their adversaries, and of course his name would serve the ticket more.[31]

I have now finished the detail which I had in view. That my information may not have been correct in all cases; that my memory may have led me into error; that my imagination may have colored facts, is possible; but that I have deviated from the strictness of truth knowingly is what I will not admit. That I have been under the painful necessity of giving touches which may affect the feelings of some persons is evident. But it has been with all the delicacy in my power, consistent with doing justice to myself. If I have done them injustice, they have the same means with me in their power, an appeal to the public. This is the great and respectable tribunal at which I stand.

NOTES

1. Brackenridge claimed that John and Presley Neville portrayed him to General Lee and others "as the damnedest rascal that ever was on God's almighty earth" (*Incidents*, sec. 2, p. 48). Brackenridge's letter to Tench Coxe, in which he stated: "Should an attempt be made to suppress the people, I am afraid the question will not be whether you will march to Pittsburgh but whether they will march to Philadelphia" (*Pennsylvania Archives*, 2 ser., 4:140–44) was also cited as evidence of his treason. Brackenridge took measures to secure depositions from men in the west who could rebut the erroneous interpretation of his letter which were printed as an appendix to the volume. See particularly the depositions by Abraham Tannehill, *ibid.*, 4:103 and John Lucas, *ibid.*, 4:107–08. Despite this effort, according to his son, Henry Marie Brackenridge, as late as the 1850s Brackenridge was still referred to as "the insurgent Brackenridge" (Henry Marie Brackenridge, *History of the Western Insurrection* [Pittsburgh, 1859], p. vii.

2. In the intervening sections Brackenridge outlined the history of the colony and

state excise in the western country from the 1750s to 1791. He argued that the collectors appointed were consistently treated with contempt and the tax was not collected throughout the period.

3. Secretary of the Treasury Alexander Hamilton introduced his Report on the Public Credit January 9, 1790. In it he proposed an excise on domestically produced spirits. On the legislative history of the excise act of 1791, see William Barber, "Among the Most Techy Articles of Civil Police," *William and Mary Quarterly*, 2d ser., January 1968, 25:58–84.

4. The resolutions carried by a vote of forty to sixteen. William Findley, who voted with the majority, had some initial reservations on these grounds. See chapter 5.

5. January 22, 1791, *Journal of the First Session of the House of Representatives,* (Philadelphia, 1791), pp. 108–11.

6. *Ibid.*

7. Marshall, a Washington County attorney, had represented that county in the state convention that ratified the Constitution and served as a county lieutenant and sheriff. He attended the September 7, 1791, meeting in Pittsburgh and was a member of the committee of twelve that met with commissioners of the state and federal government on August 21, 1794.

8. The files of the *Pittsburgh Gazette* are incomplete for the period 1791–1794, and no copy of this publication has been found. Brackenridge makes repeated reference to essays from the *Gazette*. In cases where they have been located, that information will be noted. If the particular issue is no longer extant, there will be no note.

9. On Findley's role in the opposition to the excise, see the introduction to his *History of the Insurrection,* in chapter 5.

10. Smilie served in the House from 1793 to 1795 and again from 1799 to 1813. A constitutionalist in state politics, Smilie had opposed ratification of the U.S. Constitution, served in the state House and Senate in the 1790s and was a Jeffersonian presidential elector in 1796.

11. In "Revisionary Notes" that concluded the volume, Brackenridge added, "I have represented him [Addison] as being under necessity 'of taking in his sails, and slacking course.' By that I do not mean any derelection of duty, but necessary prudence in not continuing to be an evangelist of the law, for it must be acknowledged that he did not fail to reprehend, in his charge to the grand juries, the masked attacks upon excise officers and to recommend strict cognizance of the offenses. . . . I mention these things the more minutely because his reputation has been attacked by insinuations as not having acted with sufficient firmness or as winking at the outrages in their commencement." On Addison's role see Kohn, "Judge Alexander Addison," in chapter 3.

12. William Graham served as the collector of the state excise for the counties of Westmoreland, Fayette, and Washington in 1783 and 1784. While attending county court at Greensburg, Westmoreland County, Graham was attacked. Graham pressed charges against his assailants, but to no avail. Following additional assaults, he resigned.

13. Brackenridge defended his role in creating Allegheny County and his support for the Constitution in the columns of the *Pittsburgh Gazette*. On the former, see for example, "An Answer to Criticisms by William Findley," March 24, 1787. For his defense of the Constitution, see, for example, "A 'sermon' in favor of the Federal Constitution," March 22, 1788. A complete list of Brackenridge's writings is printed as appendix 2 in Claude M. Newlin, *The Life and Writings of Hugh Henry Brackenridge* (Princeton, 1932).

14. In 1791 Congress funded the existing debt of the United States, calling in all

outstanding forms of indebtedness and issuing new four percent interest bearing bonds to replace them. Brackenridge opposed funding the existing debt at full face value because much of it had changed hands during the preceding years at a discount as high as 90 percent. Brackenridge also opposed the federal government's assumption of the revolutionary war debts of the states. His opposition to the funding system, "in all its branches," meant that he also opposed the excise tax of 1791, a tax necessitated by and therefore a part of the funding system.

15. On this unequal impact of the excise, see Dodee Fennell, "By Calculation Oppressed," unpublished manuscript in the possession of the editor.

16. Thomas Scott, a Federalist lawyer from Washington County, served in the First and Third United States Congresses. He alone among the western representatives supported Hamilton's economic program.

17. Brackenridge had repeatedly satirized Findley, whom he referred to as the "Westmoreland Weaver," during the debate over ratification. See for example his "On the Popularity of [William Findley]," *Pittsburgh Gazette*, December 1, 1787, and *Modern Chivalry* (Philadelphia and Pittsburgh, 1792–1797).

18. Brackenridge's view was not shared by Secretary of the Treasury Hamilton who argued that men like Brackenridge were chargeable with the excesses of others. Washington, in his proclamation of September 15, 1792, also blurred the distinction between nonviolent proceedings intended to secure a repeal of the law and violent action intended, in the short run, to nullify it. For a contrasting view, see Findley's *History*, in chapter 5.

19. *Pennsylvania House Journal*, p. 49.

20. No other copy of these resolutions is extant.

21. On the dispute over the Pennsylvania and Virginia boundary, and the move to create a separate state, see Solon Buck, *The Planting of Civilization in Western Pennsylvania* (Pittsburgh, 1929). "The Address and Reasons of Dissent of the Minority of the Convention of the State of Pennsylvania to their Constituents," *Pennsylvania Packet*, December 18, 1787.

22. Marshall's moderation was also reflected in a letter to John Nicholson, state comptroller general, who initiated a petition campaign to repeal Pennsylvania's act of ratification. Marshall doubted "that a petition would be very generally signed," adding, "I feel strongly inclined to wait . . . for it may be I shall be obliged to live under it [the Constitution]" (Merrill Jensen, ed. *The Documentary History of the Ratification of the Constitution* [Madison, Wis.: 1976–], 2:713.

23. No evidence has been located which substantiates this.

24. No copy of this pamphlet has been located.

25. Brackenridge's note reads:

That whereas men may be found amongst us so far lost to every sense of virtue and feelings for the distresses of the country as to accept the office for the collector of the duty, resolved therefore, that in future we will consider such persons as unworthy of our friendship, have no intercourse or dealings with them, withdraw from them every assistance, and withhold all the comforts of life, which depend upon those duties that as men and fellow citizens we owe to each other, and upon all occasions, treat them with that contempt they deserve; and that it be, and it is hereby earnestly recommended to the people at large, to follow the same line of conduct towards them.

26. *The Speech of Albert Gallatin . . . Touching on the Validity of the Elections held in the Four Counties of the State, on the 14th of October, 1794* (Philadelphia, 1795).

27. The society passed resolutions critical of the excise and several of its members, including its President James Marshall, were active in the rebellion. See Eugene P. Link, *The Democratic Republican Societies, 1790–1800* (New York, 1942), p. 146.

28. The United Freeman at Mingo Creek associated in February, 1794. On February 19, the society approved resolutions opposing excisemen who seized whiskey and all of its known members were active in the rebellion. See *ibid.*, p. 147.

29. The *Gazette* report of a meeting of delegates from different districts in Allegheny County on April 19 was signed, Thomas Morton, Chairman.

30. Brackenridge's efforts on behalf of the federal Constitution are detailed in Newlin, *Life and Writings*, ch. 10. The broader context in which Brackenridge acted is illustrated in Jensen, *Documentary History* 2: *passim*.

31. Brackenridge attended various meetings in each of the four western counties and was instrumental in securing the appointment of James O'Hara and John Wilkes, Jr., as the "representatives of the whole western country." Despite whatever disappointment he felt for not being placed on the Federalist ticket, Brackenridge endorsed the slate and campaigned for its election. See "Allegheny, Fayette, Washington, and Westmoreland County Meetings," and "Hugh Henry Brackenridge's Report of the Proceedings," both 25 October, 1789, in Jensen, *Documentary History* 1:318, 327.

William Findley, *History of the Insurrection*

William Findley shared with many of his generation a concern that an accurate record of the events of that era be preserved. Toward that end he wrote a lengthy autobiographical letter and a history of the state of Pennsylvania. It was not merely an abstract commitment to historical truth that prompted Findley to write the *History of the Insurrection*. Secretary of the Treasury Hamilton and Hugh Henry Brackenridge, both long-time political opponents, had offered their views on the rebellion. Findley wrote, in part, to correct their factual errors, and to rebut their analyses of the origins of the rebellion.

In contrast to Hamilton and Brackenridge, Findley argued that the principal cause of the Whiskey Rebellion was the economic isolation of the western country which made the tax burden of the excise tax heavier on those near-subsistence rural dwellers than on their counterparts in the east. That, coupled with a long-standing tradition of opposition to all excise taxes, predisposed westerners to resist the federal law. Findley goes further, however, for he argues that culpability for the Whiskey Rebellion lay specifically with Alexander Hamilton whose inconsistent enforcement of the law and unwillingness to protect those who complied with it in 1791 and 1792, encouraged more overt resistance and created an opportunity for Hamilton's self-aggrandizement at the head of the federal troops that marched west.

Findley never retreated from that position. He did, however, acknowledge errors of fact in his text. In order to remedy those defects, he prepared a corrected manuscript. It was lost en route to the printer, however, and Findley, not having retained a copy, abandoned the enterprise. The full title of the volume is *History of the Insurrection in the Four Western Counties of Pennsylvania in the Year MDCCXCIV With a Recital of the Circumstances Specially Connected Therewith and an Historical Review of the Previous Situation of the Country by William Findley, Member of the House of Representatives of the United States*. (Philadelphia, 1796). The selections are from pp. 37–46; 58–76; 313.

CHAPTER III

Federal excise, opposition to its execution by meetings, resolves, etcetera[1]

When the federal government was organized, and before provision had been made for the public debt, the assembly of Pennsylvania repealed the law for levying a direct tax and left the excise unrepealed. This measure was much influenced by one of the members of Congress [Thomas FitzSimons] (who resided in the city) and had newly returned from Congress at New York; the same who always introduced the measures originated by the secretary of the treasury in the form of resolves in the House of Representatives; but it was opposed by a numerous minority, of which the western members composed a part. They wished to continue the direct tax a year longer that the earliest opportunity might be taken of repealing the excise law. So much embarrassed were the revenues of that state by the premature repeal of the direct tax that in the next session the legislature had to borrow sixty thousand pounds from the Bank of North America on mortgage and to negotiate with the late properietaries to get them to receive certificates instead of cash for a debt due them by the commonwealth. How far disappointing the public creditors of the state, by prematurely embarrassing its revenues and continuing the state excise when the direct tax was repealed was intended to promote the plan for assuming the state debt and levying a general excise, which transpired soon after, the reader who has been attentive to those measures in their progress will be able to judge for himself.[2]

It is well known that the plan reported by the secretary of the treasury to the second session of the first Congress was rejected at that time and again brought forward in the last session of that Congress and enacted into a law, Congress then sitting in Philadelphia.[3]

The legislature of the state being then also in session, the members of the house of representatives became exceedingly alarmed at the introduction of an excise and adopted resolutions expressive of their sense of the excise bill then before Congress. The resolves were designed to have been sent to the Senate of the United States, not as instructions by which they were to be bound, but as a declaration of the sense and wishes of the state of Pennsylvania respecting an excise system.

The substance of these resolutions were: First, A declaration of a right in the state legislature to give an opinion on every thing of a public nature which has a tendency to destroy the rights of the people: Second, That the proceedings of Congress, tending to the collection of a revenue by means of an excise, ought to attract the attention of the house: Third, That no public emergency then existed to warrant the adoption of any species of taxation that would violate the rights which were the basis of the government and thereby exhibit the singular spectacle of a nation opposing the oppression of others, to enslave itself.[4]

In the discussion of these resolutions there were none who argued in favour of the excise. The objections were confined to the right of the house to interfere in federal measures. I was a member at the time, and voted in favour of the resolutions; but had at first some difficulty with respect to the right of interference. Since that time we find, however, that other state legislatures have frequently interfered by giving their opinion on important federal measures without being censured for it. The Yeas and Nays were taken on the resolutions and the reasons given at large on the journals. By the journals of that session of the house of representatives of the General Assembly it appears that there were forty votes in favour of the resolutions, and sixteen against them. Some, at least, of the minority were as much opposed to the excise as those who voted in the majority, but thought the interference improper. The name of John Neville, now inspector of the western survey, stands with the majority.[5] Considering the difficulty of the question of interference, this was a very unanimous declaration of the representatives of Pennsylvania and could not be ascribed to the influence of a faction. The truth is the resolutions were moved and seconded, and zealously supported by Col. Francis Gurney and Mr. Richard Wells, of the city of Philadelphia, well known to be respectable citizens and zealous federalists. They were also supported by consultations with other inhabitants of the city at the Coffee-house where the principles of excises were discussed freely, and at these consultations, and in the debates in the House of Representatives, the testimony given by the old Congress against excises was much relied on. The western members did not assist at the consultations at the Coffee-house.

A great proportion of the people of Pennsylvania had expressed their sense of the excise law by the alarm they discovered on receiving information of the secretary's report in favour of an excise system and the joy they expressed at hearing that it was rejected. This circumstance gave the members of assembly a good opportunity to know the sentiments of the people on the subject, and this disposition was not confined to any particular place. Only one member from the city of Philadelphia and two from the county voted against the resolutions, and but one member from the western counties voted in their favour.[6]

The first ill treatment given to an exciseman under the federal law was in Chester county, but the rioters were convicted and punished severely by the state courts. On that occasion the foreman of the jury told the Attorney General that he was as much or more opposed to the excise law than the rioters, but would not suffer violations of the laws to go unpunished.[7] I expect sensible jurors every where would act from the same laudable principle. There were several other attacks made on excise officers in other parts of the east side of the mountains which it is not necessary to be particular in stating.

The people in the western counties anticipated their experiencing peculiar hardships from the excise. Without money or the means of procuring it, and consuming their whiskey only in their families or using it as an article of barter, which, though it in some respects answered the place of money, yet would not be received in pay for the excise tax, they thought it hard to pay as much tax on what sold with them but at from two shillings to two shillings and six pence as they did where it brought double that price. These and such like arguments were not new.[8] I found them in use against the state excise when I went to reside in that country. They arose from their situation, and the simplest person feeling their force knew how to use them.

Some talked of laying aside their still altogether till they would have time to observe the effects of the law on other places and have time to reflect on the subject; and this method was advised in preference to a more violent mode of opposition by some who were apprehensive of outrages being committed. But though several peaceable men laid aside their stills or sold them, yet there never was any association or resolutions among the inhabitants to that purpose. The contrary has been asserted by pretty high authority.[9]

In the month of June, 1791, the first year on which the stills were to have been entered, there were no offices of inspection opened in the western counties: And although the people were in great consternation, no public or general consultation was held on the subject till the latter end of July following when a meeting was advertised to be held at Red-stone old fort [Brownsville]. Individuals attended from different places, but not by delegation, and, being in harvest, few attended from a distance. There were four or five from Westmoreland, few from Allegany, or the distant parts of Washington or Fayette. The hardships naturally resulting from the execution of the excise law to that country were explained, but at the same time the constitutional authority of Congress to enact it was asserted. It was resolved to petition Congress for relief, and no petition being prepared, a committee was appointed to meet at Pittsburgh to draught one. The committee was also authorized to correspond with the citizens in other places who might be disposed to petition Congress on the subject, and it was recommended to the different counties to appoint committees to superintend the signing the petitions and forwarding them to Congress.

How this meeting could have been ranked by the Secretary of the Treasury in his report to the President preparatory to calling out the militia among the causes of the insurrection, and given as one of the instances of unlawful combination, I know not.[10] Surely such a meeting may be held and such resolves passed in Great Britain, even after the sedition bills, which have thrown that nation into such a flame, are enacted into laws. I never knew that a meeting to petition government respectfully was esteemed criminal in any country that had the least pretentions to freedom.

The truth is, as far as I was acquainted with the design of that meeting, it was intended to promote submission, and not opposition, to the law. There was no other alternative; for to have argued that the law was just and salutary would have had no effect; nor did I know of any person then in the country that approved of or advocated it as a good law. Some who wrote in favour of submission to the excise law in the *Pittsburgh Gazette* were present at the Red-stone meeting.[11]

Several of those who kept the largest distilleries that I was acquainted with in these counties designed at that time to enter their stills if there was an op-

portunity. Some of these however afterwards changed their mind. Many of the
uninformed people, being told by the warm advocates of the federal government
that after it was ratified we would have no more excises,[12] considered the excise
law therefore as unconstitutional. At the Red-stone meeting this mistake was
openly combated. It is not easy to convince people that a law, in their opinions
unjust and oppressive in its operation, is at the same time constitutional.

In August a committee met at Washington, agreeably to the recommendation
of the Red-stone meeting, and in September a committee, composed of persons
from the western counties, met at Pittsburgh. I presume none of them were
delegated, except perhaps from Washington county, for only in it had there been
a county committee. From Westmoreland there was but one person, and he was
not delegated.[13]

A petition was proposed by the general committee at Pittsburgh to be signed
by the people, and several resolves were published in the gazette, some of which
were intemperately expressed and respected subjects but little connected with
the excise law, such as the salaries of office, the funding system, etc.[14]

About eleven months after, in August 1792, a number of persons from Washington, Fayette, and Allegany counties formed the second and last committee
of that kind that was held at Pittsburgh. They prepared and published another
petition to Congress praying for the repeal of the excise law to be signed by the
people.[15] The Committee also published its sentiments on the principles of taxation, and the supposed impropriety and injustice of an excise system. Though
it did not censure any other measures of government, it resolved to take all legal
methods of obstructing the operation of the excise law, and to have no fellowship
with such as accepted offices under it, and to withdraw from them every assistance, to withhold the comforts of life, etc. They also recommended to the
people to follow their example. A similar resolution had been published by the
committee of Washington about a year before.[16]

I never knew that this example was followed by the people in any instance
or that the resolution was obeyed by even all the members of the committee.

On the ground of discretion these resolutions were censurable, and were in
fact disapproved by many through the state who also heartily disliked the excise
law. That they were not, however, contrary to law is acknowledged by the
secretary himself who informs us of his procuring testimony in order to prosecute
the persons who composed the committee; but he adds that the attorney general
did not think it actionable.[17] There is no doubt but it is morally wrong in many
cases to refuse our charity or assistance to any of our fellow men when their
necessities require it; but these duties being of imperfect obligation, we are only
responsible to our own conscience and the opinion of the world for the proper
discharge of them. There are, no doubt, persons in society whose manners are
so disagreeable or their character so objectionable as to justify us in resolving
to have no fellowship with them; and where the excise law is almost universally
believed to be unjust and oppressive, men of this description will be found pretty
readily among the excise officers. Indeed this observation need not be restricted

to places so situated; it corresponds with the sentiments of people generally where excises have been long established and is the language of their laws.

These resolutions, however, were censurable on the ground of policy. They disgusted those members of Congress that would otherwise have been disposed to have eased, if not to have fully relieved them from their grounds of complaint, and offended the citizens at large who had sympathized with them;[18] in short, they undoubtedly occasioned less respect to be paid to their petitions.

A desultory meeting was held, in consequence of an advertisement, in Allegany county; it formed rules of association and published some intemperate resolutions, but never had a second meeting.[19] Col. Morton, the chairman, near whose residence the meeting was held, behaved always in an orderly manner and discovered great firmness and discretion through the whole of the insurrection. A meeeting was advertised to have been held at Greensburgh in the same winter, James Guthry, chairman; but the supposed chairman contradicted the advertisement in the next week's gazette, denying that there was any such meeting or that he was chairman, and we heard no more of it. It may be remarked that Guthry has uniformly supported the character of a good citizen. In short, there was a disposition prevailing with a few people to have the country organized into committees, but not exclusively to oppose the excise. The wages of the assemblymen had been raised the year before, and people living at such a distance from market, having the necessaries of life cheap and not being sensible of the increased expense of living in Philadelphia, were offended. From this circumstance a greater number than usual wished to bring themselves forward as candidates, not to lower, but to receive, the high wages; to take a lead in committees seemed a probable means of success. This circumstance was suspected to have promoted the progress of the disturbance in some places, but the conduct of these characters came into disrepute soon enough to prevent their success.[20]

CHAPTER V

Riots committed previous to the insurrection

The first actual outrage was committed in September 1791, on a Robert Johnson, collector of excise for Washington and Allegany counties, by a party of armed men disguised. The attack was made on him near Pigeon creek. After cutting his hair, they tarred and feathered him, and in this situation compelled him to walk some distance.

The next act of violence was committed on a man of the name of Wilson, who was in some measure disordered in his intellects, and affected to be, perhaps thought he was, an excise-man, and was making enquiry for distillers. He was pursued by a party, taken out of his bed, and carried several miles to a smith's shop; there they stripped off his cloaths and burnt them, and burning him in several places with a hot iron, they tarred and feathered, and in that situation dismissed, him.[21]

Not long after this one Roseberry suffered the punishment of tarring and feathering for advocating the excise law. An armed banditti seized and carried off two persons who were witnesses in the case of Wilson, who had been abused by the rioters.[22] A formidable attempt was made to seize the inspector himself in Washington town, where he was expected, by a numerous party disguised. He had been apprised of their coming and did not attend at the office. In August 1792, Capt. [William] Faulkner, who had let his house to the inspector to hold his office in, was attacked on the road by a person with a drawn knife, and threatened that his house should be burned for permitting an office of inspection to be held in it. He escaped on giving a promise to prevent the further use of his house for an office, and accordingly gave public notice in the newspapers that the office should be no longer kept in his house.

In April 1793, an armed party attacked the house of [Benjamin] Wells, whose residence is in Fayette county, but did not find him at home. They broke open the house and threatened the family. On the 22nd of November following, the house of Wells was attacked again in the night. They then obliged him to surrender his commission and books, and required him to publish a resignation of his office within two weeks in the newspapers on pain of having his house burned.

James Kiddoe and William Coughran, who had entered their stills, were first threatened, and afterwards attacked. Some pieces of the grist-mill of the former were carried away, and the still of the latter was destroyed, his saw-mill rendered useless, and his grist-mill materially injured; and he was ordered to publish what he had suffered in the *Pittsburgh Gazette*.

An armed party in disguise attacked and broke into the house of John Lynn, where the office was kept, and after prevailing on him to come down stairs, they tied and threatened to hang him; then took him to the woods, cut off his hair, tarred and feathered him, and swore him never to disclose their names, or permit an excise office to be held in his house; and binding him to a tree, left him in that situation till morning, when he extricated himself. These outrages all happened south of the Monongahela.

In June 1794, Wells, the collector for Westmoreland and Fayette counties, opened his office at the house of a certain Philip Regan in Westmoreland county. The house was at different times attacked by armed men in the night, who frequently fired on it; but they were always repulsed by P. Regan and Wells the younger.

I have taken this enumeration from the secretary's report.[23] However, I have passed one instance mentioned by him, viz. that Wells the collector was injuriously treated at Greensburg, in Westmoreland, in 1792. I passed it because I was convinced it was without foundation.[24] On the most minute enquiry I have not found the smallest trace of any injury or insult that he received there; nay, he got assurances that none in the town would injure him. He was told indeed in friendly conversation that they could not undertake for other parts of the county, and that since no person in the county would accept of the office, he might conclude that his holding it there would not be acceptable. Though the man's person was little known in that county, yet few were strangers to his personal character previous to his obtaining the office.

The account of his being ill treated at Greensburgh is connected by the secretary with a similar assertion respecting the treatment he received at Union Town, in Fayette county. This, however, also appears to have but little foundation. On the first day appointed for entering the stills a number of distillers attended; but the collector did not appear. On the second day, for he was to have attended one day in the week, a greater number of distillers appeared; but the collector was not to be found, though called and diligent enquiry made for him. He was known to be a timid man, and very probably was afraid of their numbers, and this might have been the reason why a greater number attended the second day; but they were neither armed with weapons nor threats. When he undertook the office he ought to have discovered more boldness and less apprehension. This conduct invited to further insults. I am persuaded that at this time no plan for attacking or mal-treating excise-men had been concerted or matured by the distillers.[25]

When either public or private trusts are undertaken by men who dislike the business themselves, they cannot be expected to discharge it with energy. To obtain the compensation will be their principal aim, and all their efforts will be directed to that object. It will be the same with such as possess neither principle nor sense of honour, and such may be expected to obtain offices where the field for selection is very much narrowed. How far this observation will apply to the case of the excise officers in the western counties, will be seen in its proper place.

In two instances the barns of persons who had given information against offenders, &c. in Allegany county were burnt, probably by the offenders themselves, though this could not be proved.[26] Some other injuries were committed, and threats were published in the newspapers under the signature of Tom the Tinker. These threats, contained in letters signed by Tom the Tinker, were directed to certain persons with express orders to have them published; and the editor of the *Pittsburgh Gazette* did not think it prudent to refuse to admit them. I cannot give a better account of the famous signature of Tom Tinker, which figures so highly about this time, than by adopting the words of Mr. Brackenridge on that subject.

"A term had come into popular use before this time, to designate the opposition to the excise law; it was that of Tom the Tinker. It was not given, as the appellation of whig originally was, as a term of reproach for adversaries; but affirmed by the people who were active in some of the masked riots, which took place at an early period. A certain John Holcroft was thought to have made the first application of it. It was at the time of the masked attack on a certain William Coughran, who rendered himself obnoxious by the entry of his stills; and the menders, of course, must be tinkers, and the name, collectively, became Tom the Tinker. Advertisements were put up on the trees, and in the high ways, or in other conspicuous places, under the signature of Tom the Tinker, threatening individuals, or admonishing them in measures with regard to the excise law.''[27]

It afterwards appeared that they did not originate with Holcroft, though the inventor of them has never been discovered; these letters were only made use of in the settlements adjacent to the Monongahela till after the insurrection broke out. Then, however, they were sent to distant places.

In the latter end of 1793 and the beginning of 1794 there appeared to be a very general wish among the distillers, and other people of reflection, that the stills should be entered, and a general submission to the law enforced.[28] They were convinced that the desultory, outrageous, and incendiary opposition that was given to the execution of the law was likely to introduce a very bad state of society. That it was putting it in the power of bad men, emboldened by the habit of committing daring outrages, to disturb the peace of society, and to render the enjoyment of life and property insecure. They knew that though the present outrages were only directed against the execution of the excise law, if these escaped with impunity, the execution of every other law might share the same fate in its turn. The demand for whiskey for the supply of the army put it in the power of the distillers to procure cash for the payment of the excise tax, and the contractor confining his purchases to spirits on which the excise had been paid, gave a powerful inducement to a compliance with the law.[29]

With a view to promote this compliance a number of the most influential distillers agreed to promote submission to the excise laws on condition that a total change was made in the officers, and such men put into office as the people could confide in; they also expressed their willingness to recommend such characters and render themselves responsible for their fidelity. This agreement was entered into at the court of Fayette county in the winter or spring previous to the insurrection.[30] I had the first information of it from James Ross, Esq. Senator of the United States, who had been present and contributed to this agreement before he came to the Senate in April 1794. I asked him how far the change of the officers was intended to go, and if they were confident they could procure good men to accept of the offices. He told me the change was intended to go to all the officers of the survey, and that they were confident of being able to procure such as would faithfully discharge the duties of the respective offices and enjoy the confidence of the people, and he asked me if I could recommend such for Westmoreland county. I told him that having been long from home, and having no opportunity of consulting, I could not recommend: That if I did recommend a good man without knowing whether he would serve or not, and he declined it, it would render it more difficult to get another to accept of it. I had experienced this inconveniency under the state excise.

This disposition coming to the knowledge of those who were obstinate and undiscerning, and who had already committed excesses, they became more outrageous, proceeded to fresh acts of violence, and expressed as great a degree of resentment against those who complied with the law as they did against the officers who acted under it. The exertions of those who opposed the law being the result of an infatuated state of mind and a mistaken zeal were vigorous, and being conducted in a clandestine manner, there could be no defence against their effects; this encreased the disposition of discreet men to submit, but it deterred them from actually entering their stills. They were surprised that no coercive exertions were made by the federal judiciary in support of the law and those who complied with the duties it required.[31] About that time I received letters from different distillers near Loyalhanna in Westmoreland county requesting my opinion both as to their best mode of proceeding, and whether government was likely to make any exertion to put the law in execution, and protect those who were willing to submit; for though there had been no riots in that part of the country, neither had there been any office of inspection, nor entries of stills; but they had heard of the treatment those had met with who entered them in other counties, and did not know but they might be treated in the same manner. I informed them that it was their duty to enter their stills whether they used them or not, that there was no ground to expect that the law would be either repealed or altered in that respect during the session of Congress, but referred to themselves to judge of the safety of their persons or property.[32] I had suspected no danger of that kind in that part of the country when I left home. With respect to the opportunity of entering, that laying with the inspector, I could tell nothing about it. Some of those in the mean time, compounding privately for the excise in Pittsburgh, sold their liquor to the contractors. They would have much rather entered their stills; but even selling their liquor to the contractors raised suspicions against them, and occasioned threats from a distance and resentment from some of their neighbors, and rendered it necessary for them to temporize during the troubles that followed more than they otherwise would have done. The new alterations in the excise law were not enacted till some time in the month of June, and could not be known at that distance till after that month was expired.

From the relation already given it is evident that an opposition to, or non-compliance with, the execution of the excise law had existed in the western counties of Pennsylvania for the space of three years; or, to use the expressions of the secretary of the treasury,

"The opposition to those laws in the four western counties of Pennsylvania was as early as they were known to have passed. It has continued, with different degrees of violence in the different counties, and at different periods. But Washington has uniformly distinguished its resistance by a more excessive spirit than has appeared in the other counties, and seems to have been chiefly instrumental in kindling, and keeping alive the flame."[33]

There might be some differences of opinion between the secretary and others about the instances that are entitled to the term opposition. Perhaps circulation of opinion or declaration of sentiments, and every lawful means of promoting remonstrances against it, or petitions for its repeal, or even resolving to cease from distilling, if that had been done, might be better expressed by the term disapprobation. But not to contend about this, it will be admitted that the attack on Robert Johnson on the 6th of September, 1791, and all the subsequent acts of violence, were acts of opposition to that law, and were so many defiances to the power of the judicial authority of the United States. Various and flagrant instances of opposition I have already recited till I have brought the narrative to the avenue of that crisis when the opposition burst forth with an explosion that, as has been said by respectable authority, electrified the whole United States. It remains to be enquired what means the responsible head of the executive department exerted to coerce this opposition and to prevent its more general spread.

CHAPTER VI

The protection offered to officers and complying citizens by the head of the revenue department was calculated rather to excite than to suppress opposition

The first instance that we find of coercion having been attempted was the sending Joseph Fox, deputy marshal, to serve processes issued by the district court against the persons concerned in the riot of [Robert] Johnson [collector for Washington and Allegheny counties].[34] He went to the inspector [of the excise, General John Neville] and on his advice returned home again without going to the proper place or attempting to serve the writs. But with the inspector's advice also, he sent the processes under cover as private letters by a poor simple man who had been usually employed in driving cattle, etc. If the inspector could have contrived a surer method to degrade the government in the esteem of the rioters and invite insults, it is beyond my comprehension; and unhappily the poor man [John Connor], who was ignorant of what he was doing, was the victim of this injudicious plan.[35]

What better could the inspector expect. If the people were well disposed where the process was to be served, why discourage the deputy marshal from going forward? If they were not well disposed, why send a poor creature who, not knowing what he delivered, could not give testimony of his having served the processes? Would not this contemptible method of serving processes irritate even a well disposed man on whom it was served? The authority of a commission from government, and the respectability attached thereby to the person that bears it, generally procures a degree of reverence to an officer of justice. The sheriff or constable will be respected when the officious bum will probably be well flogged, but in this instance the poor man was taken for a bum and treated accordingly without knowing the nature of the service he was employed about. He was seized, whipped, tarred and feathered, and it is said that his money was taken from him, and finally, being blindfolded, he was tied in the woods and remained in that situation for five hours.[36]

No farther exertion was made on the part of the government till the fall of the year 1792, that the supervisor of the revenue [George Clymer] was sent "to ascertain the real state of the survey, to obtain evidence of the persons who were concerned in Faulkner's case and of those who composed the meeting at Pittsburgh, to uphold the confidence and encourage the preseverance of the officers acting under the law, and to induce, if possible, the inhabitants of that part of the survey which appeared least disinclined to come voluntarily into the measure by arguments addressed to their sense of duty and exhibiting the eventual dangers and mischiefs of resistance."[37]

I wish for the sake of the personal respect I have long entertained for the supervisor of the revenue and his family that he had not introduced journey to Pittsburgh, and put me to the disagreeable necessity of animadverting on it.[38] Were I indeed to relate it in the manner I have heard it described, the reader would be induced to think it a romance rather than a real narrative. It is sufficient for my purpose to state that he went to Pittsburgh in the most clandestine manner possible, confined himself within a very narrow circle of the citizens while he remained there, refused to go to Washington town, though he was warmly solicited to go there and assured of safety, and though it was in that county that the offence was committed, to prepare for the prosecution of which was the principal object of his mission, and where only evidence was to be procured. Staying but a few days at Pittsburgh, he returned to Philadelphia with the rapidity of a post rider, accompanied by a military guard through the most peaceable part of the country where there were many respectable citizens with whom he was well acquainted and others who would have been glad to have seen him and would have thought it a pleasure to do him any reasonable service.

Not contented with discovering this total want of confidence in the most discreet people of that country, when he returned to Philadelphia he made an unprovoked attack in the news-papers on the magistrates, clergy, and all the other inhabitants of the whole western counties, I say unprovoked, for though a ludicrous account of his journey had been published in the *Pittsburgh Gazette* and republished in Philadelphia, yet if it was a crime, it could not be ascribed to the people whose character he traduced, for few of them knew he had been up till they heard of his being gone again.[39] Though I reside within two miles of the great road by which he returned, the first information I had of his having been up was from the very publication in the [Pittsburgh] *Gazette*. If I had known he had been there I would undoubtedly have waited on him and invited him to my house. There were others who would have done so as well as me.

There had been no insult offered or injury done to any excise officer, nor actual opposition given to the execution of the law in all the country through which he passed and repassed, and at that time the distillers there generally would have been easily induced to have complied with the law; but the supervisor's conduct went far to suppress the growing disposition towards compliance, which even the Secretary [of the Treasury, Alexander Hamilton] himself acknowledges to have existed at that time. He indeed procured evidence against two men [Alexander Beer and William Kerr] for being concerned in the riot at Faulkner's, but the evidence was false. The two men were not only innocent but meritorious, and the proofs of their innocence were so decisive as not to leave the least doubt remaining; therefore, though a bill had been found at the district court, in consequence of the perjury the prosecution was discontinued.[40]

The witness was a recruit and at that time a hostler of Capt. Faulkner's. I know nothing of his character but I have sufficient reason to presume that Captain Faulkner's own testimony would condemn no person before a court of justice where his character was known. I never knew who it was that suborned the witness to swear against Mess. Kerr and Beer, but I am persuaded the supervisor's moral principles were too good to permit him to be knowingly concerned in it. All the information the Secretary is pleased to communicate on this is that there was a mistake in the persons; fortunately the mistake operated against persons whose character and situation protected them from falling victims to the most gross and flagrant depravity. It might have been otherwise with persons equally innocent.

We are further informed that testimony was procured by him of the persons who composed the Pittsburgh Committee and in a letter of the Secretary to the Governor [Thomas Mifflin] he says that Mr. Albert Gallatin was one of them. This is also a mistake for Gallatin and myself were both attending the General Assembly of the state in Philadelphia at the time of the Pittsburgh Committee.[41]

These proceedings encouraged those who were disposed to oppose the execution of the excise law to exult in the weakness of the administration of the revenue and confirmed their belief that a law which could not be executed would be repealed. When the head officer of the district was ashamed to appear in defence of it, people who knew there was no danger did not ascribe his behavior to fear. Even those who were convinced of the necessity of submission and would otherwise have contributed to promote it thought it prudent to be silent.

From this time the number and boldness of those who violently opposed the law and maltreated the officers who executed it and the citizens who complied with it visibly increased. It was not till after this that persons were put in jeopardy for entering their stills and the Secretary acknowledges that the laws appeared during 1793 to be gaining ground, that several principal distillers who formerly held out had complied, and that others discovered a disposition to comply, which was only restrained by the fear of violence. I will add that as far as I was acquainted with the distillers, the compliance would have been general if adequate protection had been afforded by government.

It was not however an expensive protection that was desired or necessary. The presence and authority of a court of justice would have answered every necessary purpose and less would not do.[42] The necessity of a federal court going into that country, of or competent powers being vested in the state courts, had been suggested to the President and urged on the Secretary of the Treasury, who at that time was not only the responsible head of the revenue department, but who also at that time originated the revenue laws as well as directed the arrangments for the execution of them.

On a full conviction of the propriety of this measure Congress in March 1793 enacted a law to enable the federal judiciary to hold special sessions nearer the place where crimes were committed than those to which the sessions of the circuit court had been fixed by law.[43] Those who anxiously wished to see the dignity and authority of the laws supported expected that a special session would have been held in the western counties with all convenient speed. If this had been done, I am certain there would have been no Insurrection.

But far from applying this cheap, rational and efficacious remedy, the disorders were permitted to go on and increase till July 1794. Previous to this, however, on the fifth of June, authority was vested in the state courts to try causes arising under the revenue laws.[44] Though this important improvement in the laws was too long delayed, yet if it had been fairly exercized, even at this late period, extraordinary exertions would have been unnecessary, but these ordinary and salutary methods of preventing the evil appear never to have been seriously designed.

Previous to the necessary powers being vested in the state courts processes had privately issued out of the district court at Philadelphia, but the execution of them was delayed till July following, when the marshal [David Lenox] was sent to the western counties to serve the processes in the midst of the hurry of harvest, when men's minds are agitated with unusual care and their bodies with vigorous exertions, and when to the heat of the season and the competition of labor is generally added the stimulus of ardent spirits. At this unfortunate period the marshal arrived and served the processes which required the distillers to appear at the district court in Philadelphia. I do not mean that people drink more ardent spirits in harvest in this country than in other places where there is no other substitute. It is drunk on these occasions in as great quantities on the east side of the mountains as it is on the west.

He served all the processes that were directed to the distillers of Fayette County, thirty four in number, without interruption and had been equally successful in serving all those in Washington County till the very last writ when he unfortunately went into Pittsburgh.

Before I proceed further it is proper to remark that during the first two years the number who committed infractions on the laws were comparatively small and confined to but a few places; that in the last years as the disposition among the distillers to comply with the law became more evident, the opposition to it became more violent and was carried on in other and more alarming methods; that during this period the treasury department either wholly neglected it or tampered with it in such a manner as was only calculated to encourage the opposition and discourage every exertion of well disposed citizens to support the law. It is an undoubted fact that the manner in which the execution of the law was conducted, while it invited opposition, gave alarming apprehensions to men of discernment for they could not otherwise account for it than by supposing that the disorders were designedly fostered until they would produce a more serious issue. Many of them knew that he who stood at the helm of the revenue department had no aversion to being employed as a pilot in a storm. When the whole method of conducting the coercion of the laws, both as to time and manner, is compared with the crisis produced by it, and the subsequent proceedings relative to that crisis are taken into consideration and judiciously examined, the candid reader will be the better qualified to judge of the reasonableness of these apprehensions.

It is true the secretary assigns some reasons in his report for this negligence, but they are not sound, they are indeed scarcely plausible. Did the laws give him any more power to dispense with the application of their coercive powers than it did to the people in their non-compliance. The Constitution has indeed vested the human and salutary power of pardoning in the President, but has not vested the power of granting impunity in the commission of crimes nor of dispensing with the execution of the laws in the Secretary. That impunity, which evidently contributes to promote opposition to the laws and increase the number and the crimes of offenders, is undeserving of the name of lenity. It is a refinement in cruelty.

CHAPTER XXII

An inquiry, whether the insurrection was the result of a preconcerted plan, and whether the expedition was necessary to restore order in the western counties . . .

I have suggested oftener than once that the head of the revenue department conducted the execution of the law in the western district in a manner that was calculated to promote the event that happened. To support a suggestion of this nature positive proof cannot be obtained. To me, however, it appears better established than could reasonably have been expected. From the means I had used to promote a due execution of the law and the observations I had made on the manner in which it was conducted, I had suspected his design and for some time looked forward to the event with dread. But in the spring of 1794, when competent powers were vested at the state courts, my prospects brightened and I blamed myself for my suspicions. But the mine was ready to be sprung when I had flattered myself that the danger was over. I will not, however, recapitulate the grounds upon which my opinion was founded, but leave the reader to examine and compare the facts for himself and judge of the result. The facts are truly stated.

NOTES

1. In the preceding chapters Findley discussed the initial settlement of the western country, the boundary dispute with Virginia, and the state excise law. In both chapters he stressed the general willingness of westerners to settle their grievances peaceably.

2. Pennsylvania had paid much of its Revolutionary War debt. Its momentary inability to continue payments was another argument in favor of Hamilton's proposal for the federal government to assume the debts of the states, a proposal that evenly divided the Pennsylvania delegation in Congress. On the importance of funding and assumption, see E. James Ferguson, *The Power of the Purse: A History of American Public Finance, 1776–1790* (Chapel Hill, N.C., 1961). For more specifics on Pennsylvania's reaction to assumption, see Jacob E. Cooke, *Tench Coxe and the Early Republic* (Chapel Hill, N.C., 1978)

3. See William Barber, "Among the Most Techy Articles of Civil Policy," *William and Mary Quarterly*, 2d ser., 25 (1968), 58–84.

4. January 22, 1791, *Journal of the First Session of the House of Representatives* (Philadelphia, 1791), pp. 108–11.

5. *Ibid.*, p. 111.

6. Findley is in error here as he, Albert Gallatin, John Neville, and a number of other western representatives voted for the resolutions. See the roll call in the *Journal*, pp. 110–11.

7. Governor Thomas Mifflin to George Washington, October 5, 1792, in *Pennsylvania Archives*, 2d ser., 4:33–34.

8. Findley had stressed this basis for opposition to the law as early as 1792. See his letter to Governor Thomas Mifflin, November 21, 1792, in *ibid.*, 2d ser., 4:48–51.

9. See Hamilton's report to Washington (in chapter 2), in which he asserts private associations were formed, not to discontinue distilling, but to "forbear compliance with the law."

10. Findley elsewhere in the *History* (pp. 263–65) defended his role in the meeting when he explained,

In June 1791 the operation of the excise was to commence, but in the western counties, and I presume in many other districts in the union, officers were not provided for the entering of stills and the law on experiment proved to be in so great a measure impracticable that a revision of it was immediately found to be necessary. An advertisement was published inviting citizens of the western counties to meet at Redstone Old Fort [Brownsville], to consider and give advise how they should proceed with respect to the excise law. On hearing of the intended meeting, reflecting on the chagrin that prevailed in the minds of the people on account of the unexpected introduction of a system which they so much abhorred, and knowing that the violent opposition that had been given to the execution of the state excise law in some parts of the country, I was considerably alarmed less that if only such people attended the meeting that were so violently opposed to the excise law, measures unfavorable to the peace of the country might be promoted. Therefore, though no correspondence had taken place between those who promoted the meeting and the people in the county in which I reside, I determined to attend it and to take some discreet men with me. I never yet knew who first promoted the meeting, but the design was lawful and proper, it was to conduct measures for petitioning Congress in order to quiet the minds of people . . . After the meeting was opened and the hardships that would result from the excise law explained in some addresses to the chair, I observed that though the principles of the excise law and the local oppressive effects it would have on the western counties were developed, yet the constitutional power of Congress to levy it was not sufficiently explained. This induced me to address the chair in a discourse of some length in which I first asserted and explained the constitutional authority of Congress to levy excises and said that they themselves had acknowledged that right by adopting the government, electing representatives to it, and having the state officers sworn to uphold it. I next proceeded to show the bad effects of violent opposition to it and endeavored to convince them that the only choice they had was either to pay the tax or otherwise refrain from stilling, and suggested that to refrain from stilling, altogether was much more tolerable evil than any mode of actual opposition, and that in the mean time it was their duty to lay their grievances before Congress by petition, but that as petitoning itself was an acknowledgement of the authority of government in the case respecting which they addressed it, petitioning was therefore inconsistent with opposition. I concluded by pointing out the evils in the excise law and hardships peculiar to their local situation to which their petition should apply and too, particular care not to invite them to expect an immediate repeal, but encouraged them to look for relief to be obtained by a revision of it as I knew it could never be executed till it was revised, and informed them that in its present state it was impracticable.

11. No list of the men attending the meeting is extant. Perhaps the reference is to Alexander Addison who had published essays urging compliance with the law in the *Gazette*.

12. There is no such explicit statement extant, but Federalists did, in response to anti-Federalist charges that an excise would be the inevitable result of adoption of the Constitution, insist that an import tax would in all likelihood be sufficient to the needs of the government. See for example, James Wilson, Speech in the State House Yard, 6 October, *Pennsylvania Herald*, October 9, reprinted in the *Pittsburgh Gazette*, October 19, 1787.

13. According to the minutes of the Meeting, two men, Nehemiah Stokely and John Young, attended from Westmoreland County. Young served as secretary of the meeting.

14. Findley is referring to the resolutions adopted by the Washington County meeting of August 23. The resolutions of the Pittsburgh meeting were restricted to the excise act. See *Pennsylvania Archives*, 2d ser., 4:20–22.

15. The meeting was held at Pittsburgh on August 21 and 22, 1792. The resolutions, signed by Albert Gallatin, are printed in *ibid.*, 2d ser., 4:20–31.

16. The resolutions of the Washington County meeting of August 23, 1791, printed in an issue of the *Pittsburgh Gazette* no longer extant, were enclosed in a letter from John Neville to George Clymer, September 8, 1791. The resolutions, which were unanimously approved, are quoted in note 6, Alexander Hamilton to George Washington, August 5, 1794, Harold Syrett, et al., eds., *The Papers of Alexander Hamilton*, New York, 1972, 17:28–29.

17. Findley's view of the legality was shared by Brackenridge but not Washington. See chapter 4.

18. Findley was a member of Congress at the time and presumably was aware of Congressional reaction to the petitions. Congress did, nonetheless, revise the excise in May, 1792.

19. *Pittsburgh Gazette*, April 26, 1794.

20. Hamilton also saw opposition to the excise as an electioneering ploy in his report to Washington. See chapter 2.

21. This assault occurred in October, 1791.

22. Prosecutions for the assault on Wilson were discontinued after Wilson left the area. Those involved, however, in preventing witnesses from appearing before the court were prosecuted, convicted and fined. See Alexander Addison to Governor Mifflin, November 4, 1792, in *Pennsylvania Archives*, 2 ser., 4:36–37.

23. Hamilton's report is, as the editors of the Hamilton papers note, "A standard—and often the only—source for those who have written about the opposition in western Pennsylvania to the excise laws in the period before August 1794." Findley confirmed the validity of this statement when he declared, "I have had resource to it [the report] as an authority respecting the riots committed against revenue officers, not having heard of several of these riots through any other channel (*History*, p. 291).

24. Niether Hamilton nor the editors of the Hamilton papers offer any evidence to substantiate this report.

25. This is in direct contrast to Hamilton's charge of a preconcerted plan as early as 1792.

26. This information is also drawn from Hamilton's report to Washington.

27. Brackenridge, *Incidents of the Insurrection*, (Philadelphia, 1795), pp. 78–79. An example of "Tom Tinker's" warning is printed in *Pennsylvania Archives*, 2d ser., 4:71–72.

28. Even Hamilton concedes the law was making headway in the spring.

29. This point is discussed at length in Dodee Fennell, "By Calculation Oppressed" (unpublished manuscript in possession of the editor).

30. According to Alexander Addison, during March "some of the most respectable gentlemen of that country, and most strenuously opposed to the excise law, proposed that a meeting of the inhabitants of the county should be called, in which it should be agreed that they would all enter their stills, provided Benjamin Wells was removed from office, and some honest and respectable person appointed instead." To Governor Mifflin, May 12, 1794, in *Pennsylvania Archives*, 2 ser., 4:63. Leland Baldwin suggests that the Fayette meeting marked a real turning point in the opposition for once the large distillers agreed to comply with the law, that laid a more onerous burden on the smaller producer, the latter increasingly resorted to violence (*Whiskey Rebels* rev. ed. [Pittsburgh, Pa.: University of Pittsburgh Press, 1968], p. 40).

31. In contrast, Hamilton in a September 2 report to the president, placed the burden of responsibility on state officials for their "neglect to bring to justice offenders . . . who were at the same time breaking the peace of Pennsylvania," *Hamilton Papers*, 17, pp. 180–90.

32. These letters have not been found.

33. See chapter 2.

34. Johnson was attacked on September 16, 1791.

35. Fox believed that had he attempted to deliver the processes, "he should not have returned alive," a judgment shared by General Neville and Hamilton. In his report, however, Hamilton did agree with Findley that the alternative adopted, that of sending the processes with John Connor, was "injudicious and fruitless."

36. In the details, although not the interpretation of this incident, Findley follows Hamilton's report.

37. The quoted material is from Hamilton's instructions to Clymer as summarized by Hamilton in a letter to Commissioner of the Revenue Tench Coxe, September 1, 1792, *Hamilton Papers*, 12:306–10.

38. Clymer traveled to Pittsburgh in late September, 1792. His experiences are summarized in his letters to Hamilton, September 28 and October 4 and 10, in *ibid.*, 12:495–97; 517–22; and 540–42.

39. The *Pittsburgh Gazette* printing has not been located. The account was reprinted in the *Philadelphia National Gazette*, November 28, December 1, 5, 1792.

40. See Hamilton's report to Washington, in chapter 2.

41. Findley is in error here, for Gallatin attended the August, 1792, Pittsburgh meeting and served as secretary.

42. This is contradicted in part by a petition of Westmoreland County inhabitants who asked General William Jack to form a "small corps of militia volunteers" to maintain peace and protect those "well disposed citizens" who were willing to submit to the law. Findley signed the petition (*Pennsylvania Archives*, 2d ser., 4:65–67). Alexander Addison, however, insisted that if "the excise were in proper hands it might now be made." To Governor Mifflin, March 31, 1794 (*ibid.*, 2d ser., 4:50–61). Addison wrote from Washington, Pa., the center of the most vigorous opposition.

43. Findley is in error here. Congress considered such a measure, but did not adopt it. See, Alexander Hamilton to George Washington, chapter 2.

44. "An Act Making Further Provision for Securing and Collecting the Duties on Foreign and Domestic Distilled Spirits, Stills, Wines and Teas," Richard Peters, ed., *The Public Statutes at Large of the United States of America, 1789–1873* (Boston: Little, Brown, 1850–1873), 1:378–81.

A New Look at the Whiskey Rebellion

> Thus, without shedding a drop of blood, did the prudent vigour of the executive terminate an insurrection, which, at one time, threatened to shake the government of the United States to its foundation. That so perverse a spirit should have been excited in the bosom of prosperity, without the pressure of a single grievance, is among those political phenomena which occur not infrequently in the course of human affairs, and which the states-man can never safely disregard. When real ills are felt, there is something positive and perceptible to which the judgment may be directed, the actual extent of which may be ascertained, and the cause of which may be discerned. But when the mind, inflamed by suppositious dangers, gives a full loose to the imagination, and fastens upon some object with which to disturb itself, the belief that the danger exists seems to become a matter of faith, with which reason combats in vain.[1]

With these words, John Marshall encapsulated a version of the Whiskey Rebellion that in time achieved as much credence as the opinions he wrote as chief justice of the United States. It is a masterful statement by a skillfull and experienced advocate. In a few lines he vindicated the decision of the Washington administration to send 15,000 troops into western Pennsylvania to silence objections to the whiskey tax and isolated its opponents from the company of rational men. The mass meetings and occasional violence that had accompanied attempts to collect the excise and, in one instance, to serve processes were elevated to the status of an insurrection that threatened the republic. How a few misguided rebels on the frontier who had only imaginary grievances could pose such a danger is a question that Marshall did not address. It was enough to assert that the germ of rebellion was contained and that it dissolved when confronted by the might of the new nation manifested in military power.

The fact is, however, that what Marshall wrote was not—in popular terminology—the truth, the whole truth, and nothing but the truth. To be sure, Marshall was not writing a definitive history of the events of 1791–1794. He was celebrating George Washington's virtues in a hagiographic biography of the Father of his Country. In that context, the insurrection was merely an episode in the apotheosis of the great American hero. The few pages that Marshall did devote to the Whiskey Rebellion are nonetheless important because they helped establish an interpretation that was startlingly incomplete, yet one that has remained largely unchallenged to the present.

That interpretation, stripped to its essentials, is that the Whiskey Rebellion was a brief uprising carried on by a few backwoods farmers in western Pennsylvania.[2] These farmer-distillers disliked paying taxes to the government, especially taxes on their moonshine. Although the excise may have imposed some burden on them, their protest was out of all proportion to their injury. The settlers' discontent made them vulnerable to self-seeking politicians organized in ''self-created'' Democratic Societies that encouraged resistance and violence, and thus threatened the stability of the nation.[3] The administration responded by amending the statute to remove some of its objectionable features and, in the summer of 1794, by sending negotiators to persuade the distillers to end their opposition. But they stubbornly refused any gestures of reconciliation. Because the insurgents were concentrated in four counties (Allegheny, Fayette, Washington, and Westmoreland) it was possible to plan a military solution, and the administration reluctantly but firmly did just that. Faced by 15,000 nationalized militia representing the might of the federal government, the insurrection dissolved. Two of its leaders stood trial for treason and were convicted, but they were magnanimously pardoned by the president. The timely use of military power brought harmony as well as peace, and the republic was saved.

Versions of this story are found in every American history textbook while the variations in scholarly journals are generally directed toward specifying the role of the Democratic Societies or Secretary of the Treasury Alexander Hamilton, and to illuminating the decision to use force to crush the rebellion.[4] But there are two other aspects of the rebellion that have somehow escaped notice: the actual extent of the opposition to the tax, and the effect of the suppression of the ''rebels'' on the subsequent operation of the law. It seems now astonishing that the Federalists—for this was a partisan issue—could manage the news (and therefore history) as successfully as they did. Thousands of people knew at the time that resistance to the excise was neither as isolated nor contained as it was alleged to have been, nor did it end with the appearance of the troops in 1794. They also knew that although there were occasional acts of violence, there was no real threat to the established government. Fortunately for historians, some of those people left widely scattered documents that show that the whiskey tax was unpopular from the beginning, that noncompliance spread far beyond Pennsylvania's borders, and that it continued for years after the ''insurrection'' was suppressed.

''An Act repealing, after the last day of June next, the duties heretofore laid upon Distilled Spirits imported from abroad, and laying others in their stead; and also upon Spirits distilled within the United States'' was enacted on March 3, 1791.[5] Three months earlier, the legislature of North Carolina had instructed its senators that they should ''strenuously oppose every excise and direct taxation law.''[6] One of that state's members of the House of Representatives reported to his constituents that, indeed, there had been ''a most strenuous opposition, and much time spent in debate'' in the House. The opposition was sectional, however, and was outnumbered thirty-five to twenty-one, with all but five of the negative votes coming from states south of the Mason-Dixon line.[7]

Those in the minority opposed the law for various reasons. Some objected to the purpose for which the tax was intended—to pay interest on the states' debts assumed by Congress in 1790. Others disliked a provision that permitted warrantless inspections of the premises that housed stills. Some protested that a tax on products of domestic distillation made foreign spirits relatively less expensive and to that degree handicapped the competitive position of home production. Farmers without capital charged that because they and not consumers had to remit the duties, distilling required specie that they did not have and that was, in many regions, difficult to obtain.[8]

The most enduring complaints came from those who lived west of the Appalachian Mountains who thought the excise discriminatory because it fell on their only exportable product. As long as Spain withheld free navigation of the Mississippi River, western farmers could not sell their grain, hogs, hemp, or tobacco in eastern markets because the cost of transporting those products across the mountains was greater than their intrinsic worth. The only economical way to sell grain was to distill it. Whiskey had the greatest value for the least weight and volume, and in vast areas of the frontier, it was the only cash crop. Even teetotalers were, in Albert Gallatin's words, ''distillers through necessity, not choice, that [they] may comprehend the greatest value on the smallest size and weight.''[9]

The disaffection was widespread enough and the pressure on Congress such that in November 1791 the House of Representatives directed Secretary of the Treasury Alexander Hamilton to report on difficulties encountered in executing the statute and to recommend amendments that might make it more palatable.[10] Hamilton, in turn, instructed Commissioner of the Revenue Tench Coxe to gather the necessary information, and the following March recommended several amendments that were incorporated into the second internal revenue act of May 1792.[11] Even as Congress approved Hamilton's recommendations, the House coupled its cooperation with a request for further information. That proved as difficult to obtain from some areas as compliance with the amended statute.

Over the following months, Hamilton received scattered reports about widespread resistance to the law. By late summer, he knew that there was, as Coxe euphemistically described it, ''an uneasiness about the revenue law . . . in part of Kentucky.''[12] He knew that there was opposition in some parts of Virginia and in North Carolina, and that there were no returns at all on the country stills in South Carolina.[13] He also knew that in Pennsylvania, opponents of the tax tarred and feathered a collector and later a messenger who tried to serve process on the putative culprits.[14] Yet from the very beginning Hamilton decided to minimize the extent of noncompliance outside Pennsylvania, even as he pressed for sanctions and eventually the use of military force there. That decision is reflected in Coxe's 1794 report to the House, which blurred the evidence of resistance by noting duties *arising* and revenue *accruing*—not, as formerly, duties paid and revenue received.[15]

The extent of noncompliance before the "official" Whiskey Rebellion can only be surmised pending further research in the court records and related documents of the federal and state governments. Those that have been examined thus far suggest that the determination to intervene in Pennsylvania was not based upon isolated resistance in that state alone, although the administration may have genuinely feared that insurgency might be contagious.[16] Nor were the actions against Pennsylvania the only aspects of the rebellion over which the nationalist glaze of Hamilton, Washington, and others has obscured the operation of the excise laws during the Federalist era. For notwithstanding the president's claims to the contrary in his addresses to Congress in the fall of 1794, it is clear that massive—if largely passive—resistance to the whiskey tax continued throughout the decade.[17] In some instances, at least, distillers obeyed the law only after Jefferson's election brought the promise of repeal.

But not all the evidence lies in long overlooked court records. One widely known source that indicates that the conventional wisdom about the Whiskey Rebellion is incomplete is *American State Papers, Finance*. There lie the annual reports that the House required of the Internal Revenue Department, documenting some of the difficulties of collection and the extent of opposition. For example, months after the "insurrection" had been put down and the troops had reportedly aroused citizens to their duty, the March 1795 report admitted "certain irregularities and delays in the returns" which made it "impracticable . . . to state, with precise accuracy, the productiveness of the revenue, and the expense of collection; nor the number nor names of the officers employed in the collection."[18]

Information about the duties from stills and domestic spirits in some areas remained elusive throughout the decade. When Coxe reported in March 1796 on the year ending June 30, 1795, he admitted that the law could not be executed in the recently established Ohio District, consisting of Kentucky and the settled portion of the Northwest Territory.[19] Twenty months later, those returns were still "partial and imperfect"—and returns from New Jersey "deficient."[20] In that report Coxe returned to the practice of listing duties payable, and to revenue accruing, a practice followed by his successor William Miller in reports for the years ending June 30, 1797, and June 30, 1798.[21] What proportion of those payable duties was ever paid evidently was not reported to the House, and because of the Treasury fire in 1833 may never be known with certainty.

What is certain is drawn chiefly from the order books of the federal court in Kentucky. Like Pennsylvania, the Bluegrass State produced abundant harvests of grain for distillation, both for local consumption and for export. Also like Pennsylvania, resistance to the internal revenue laws began soon after their passage. Ironically, the earliest evidence that John Marshall's version of the Whiskey Rebellion was incomplete lies in a long-lost correspondence that his own father wrote to revenue officials.[22] Colonel Thomas Marshall was the chief revenue officer in Kentucky, and like his son was an ardent Federalist determined to see that Hamilton's policies were carried out. From the time of his appointment he had trouble finding men to serve as collectors, but he had tried to organize his district and to get his fellow Kentuckians to register their stills. They did not choose to do so, however, and by March 1792 he was complaining to his superior about "the many violent enemies the law had."[23]

Marshall's problems were compounded by confusing, complicated, and sometimes unworkable statutes. Distillers were expected to register their stills and to keep complete records—but they did neither. The law distinguished between distilleries in cities, towns, and villages on one hand (which were taxable according to the quantity and proof of the distilled product), and country stills on the other (which were taxable according to the capacity of the still). Rating the tax of the former was impossible because of the absence of records. Computing the tax of the latter was equally inexpedient: Colonel Marshall quickly complained about "the impracticability of measuring the stills on account of their being all at work."[24] Other statutory distinctions between distilleries and private stills were inapplicable in Kentucky, where almost every farmer was a distiller. And the provision that the penalties of the law were not to apply to persons who owned only one still not exceeding fifty gallons encouraged many to ignore the law altogether.[25]

In October, Commissioner of Revenue Tench Coxe tried to be helpful by reporting that in Maryland, "aid to the Government has been derived from information being given by the trade. No persons are so much concerned to prevent infractions of the laws as the fair complying distiller."[26] But in Kentucky, as the court records show, no member of the general public was willing to act as an informer even for half the penalties and forfeitures. And the collectors had enough problems without filing informations against distillers.

Soon Marshall and the collectors stood alone. In December 1792, the United States attorney for the district resigned his office, and for four years there was no one to prosecute violators of the law.[27] The revenue officers could only threaten and cajole, and neither method was effective.[28] In the spring of 1793, Collector Brooks was assaulted in Nelson County.[29] Later, in the summer, Collector Hubble bought some whiskey for the army only to have it "rescued" from him.[30] The following winter Hubble spent the night with a distiller, and while they slept the house was attacked and Hubble's money, saddlebags, and records for Mason and Bourbon Counties were stolen.[31] Some time later, the collector of Fayette County was pulled from his horse, tarred, and rolled in leaves.[32]

What was equally remarkable was the role of the federal court. During all this period, grand juries were convened who proffered no presentments. No informations were filed with them and, of course, no indictments were handed down in the absence of a federal attorney. Marshall and his superior in Virginia, Edward Carrington, were forced to resort to civil procedures. In December 1793, Carrington brought two suits in Case, apparently to recover the value of the stolen whiskey.[33] The suits were continued at the March 1794 term and dismissed in July. To add insult to injury, Carrington was ordered to pay the defendants' costs.[34]

Meanwhile, Alexander Hamilton thought of an ingenious way to secure compliance. Because the Treasury Department was already in the business of purchasing supplies for the army, it occurred to Hamilton that distillers might be persuaded to pay their taxes in whiskey.[35] When he was in western Pennsylvania with the troops during the Whiskey Rebellion, he wrote of Coxe: "It has been much insisted upon, that this part of the Country could not without oppression pay the duty in cash. The supply of the Western Army enable us to accomodate [sic] in this particular, an option may therefore be either to pay in cash or in Whiskey."[36]

But most Kentuckians would not be humored into compliance. Apparently, the only distillers who took advantage of Hamilton's offer were those who sold whiskey to the army. Interestingly enough, these sales were arranged by middlemen like Thomas Marshall and Thomas Carneal—who, because they were also revenue officers, were able to require payment as a condition of purchase.[37] The whiskey credited to duties in this way went to the army. But no money was forwarded from Kentucky, and evasion of the excise continued.[38]

Eventually an earlier concession was repeated. In 1793, Secretary of State Thomas Jefferson had agreed to forgive arrearages for the first year upon the promise of distillers that they would pay the tax in the future.[39] An extension of the grace period had been refused later that year, but by 1795 the administration was willing to try again.[40] When James Innes returned from his placating mission to Kentucky to inform residents there about the reopened negotiations for navigation of the Mississippi, he evidently convinced the central government that there was no possibility of securing compliance unless arrearages accruing before 1794 were forgiven.[41] The Treasury Department apparently believed that a bargain had been struck, but both Hamilton and his successor, Oliver Wolcott, underestimated the determination of Kentuckians. Five years later Wolcott complained bitterly: "Influential Gentlemen of the State of Kentucky gave assurance in 1795, that by forebearing to demand the duties and penalties which had accrued prior to July 1794, a general compliance with the Law, would be thenceforward assured. A compromise was authorized on the principles suggested, but without securing the desired effect."[42]

By 1796 the Treasury Department was becoming desperate. Military action was inadvisable if not impossible, and the carrots of payment in whiskey and forgiveness of arrearages and penalties had been rejected. The stick of legal action was all that remained. But Wolcott had become suspicious about the absence of activity in the federal court, and he wrote Coxe to instruct Colonel Marshall to consider bringing suit. Equal application of the law was clearly not what Wolcott had in mind, as an early draft of his letter reveals:

The first demand ought to be made of those delinquents, whose examples in opposition to the Law has been most influential. If they shall manifest a disposition to submit to the Law . . . the Supervisor ought to settle with them. . . . If however, opposition is made to a compromise on these Principles, suits ought to be commenced against this class of Men generally. With respect to persons of inferior consideration and influence, suits may be suspended until further instructions shall be received. ~~In making the experiment care should be taken to render it so general as that the issue may completely demonstrate, the efficacy of judicial concern~~ [crossed out in original]. If for any reason it shall appear adviseable to the Supervisor to institute some of the suits in the State Courts no objections will be made at the Treasury.[43]

This strategy was, for the time being, as unsuccessful as its predecessors.[44] Marshall could find no attorneys to assist him, and except for the suits in case brought earlier by Carrington in the federal court, its records indicate that term after term passed with no hint that federal statutes were being avoided or evaded. Grand juries were regularly empaneled, but until March 1795 they did nothing but approve the first census.[45] Their only presentment during this period was against Andrew Holmes, charged with retailing wine at his tavern in violation of an act that laid duties on foreign wines and foreign distilled spirits.[46] That presentment was quashed at the next term for "uncertainty and informality," and no grand juries were empaneled at any of the succeeding six terms.[47] The marshal was evidently violating the rule adopted in June 1791 that required a grand jury at each term. But there is no indication in the records that he was censured by Judge Harry Innes, although he did not hestitate to reprimand the marshal (and the clerk) for inattention to their duties on other occasions.

There was still no United States attorney for the Kentucky District to take the initiative in prosecuting suits. Even Colonel Marshall's son-in-law, William McClung, had declined the office. The colonel suspected some kind of conspiracy and he expressed his frustration repeatedly in letters, including one to his son John, upon his appointment as United States attorney general:

Now I hope we may be informed why we have no Attorney in this State for the United States. I have complained of this in every letter I have written on the subject of revenue. I cannot possibly have the revenue collected, as no one will comply with the laws without compulsion, and the government has not put it into my power to compel compliance. This I have tried, but without success; . . . there might be political reasons assigned for the neglect. But if that be the case, why am I repeatedly written to by the Commissioner of Revenue, as if it was expected that I could go on with the business in the same manner as if there were no impediment.[48]

Matters seemed about to change in December 1796, when William Clarke accepted appointment as attorney for the district, and the four-year vacancy in that office finally ended. On the day after he presented his commission of office to the court, the grand jury brought presentments against James Smith and Peter Utman for having forcibly obstructed a revenue collector.[49] Responding to the new situation, Judge Innes promulgated new rules "to regulate penal laws when fines and imprisonment are instituted, or fines only."[50] The rules provided for issuance of subpoenas, conditions for default judgments, acceptable pleadings, and other details which were to be completed "in the same manner as in Common Law." The only unexpected requirement was that the attorney for the district was to file an information on every presentment, stating the charge and the informer's name and residence.[51]

The movement toward criminal litigation continued at the March term, when two related charges were brought. One was a presentment against Peter Smelzer for keeping an unregistered still (on an information filed by a collector); the second was an indictment against Joseph Steele for assault and battery against another revenue agent. Of equal significance was Clarke's response to the instructions given by Commissioner Coxe to Colonel Marshall the preceding June: he filed informations against men whose opposition to the law he believed had been influential. And the attorney chose to make examples of two who were unquestionably prominent: Thomas Jones, justice of the peace for Bourbon County and an elector of the state senate, and United States Senator John Brown, Judge Innes's closest friend.[52]

Colonel Marshall, confident that at last the forces of law and order had triumphed over neglect of duty, resigned his inspectorship. He wrote to President Adams:

It may possibly be asked why, after holding the office during the most critical of troublesome times, I should now resign it, when I am no longer insulted, and abused. . . . In truth, this very change . . . furnishes a reason. . . . For having once engaged in the business of revenue I presently found myself of sufficient importance with the enemies of the government here to be made an object of their particular malevolence—and while this was the case, I was determined not to be driven from my post.[53]

But Marshall's confidence was premature. No grand juries were empaneled at the next two terms of the court (in June and November 1797) nor did the new attorney file any more informations. Marshall and Carrington, it seemed, could depend only on each other. In November, Carrington filed four suits in Debt, and Marshall filed one. Both men sued in their own names "and for the benefit of the United States" against four different defendants.[54] Despite Coxe's instructions, however, none of these defendants appears to have been particularly prominent. One was the man whom Carrington had sued in case in 1793; another was sued by both Carrington and Marshall, so that there were only four defendants although there were five suits.[55]

This second use of civil actions proved little more productive than the first. Carrington discontinued the cases against three of the defendants and paid the costs. The fourth defendant, sued by both Carrington and Marshall, confessed judgment for $165.72 in 1798 but was able in 1802 to get a *supersedeas* staying proceedings on collection.[56]

A similar examination of the disposition of the earlier cases indicates that the first four criminal charges (those against Smith, Utman, Smelzer, and Steele) were also proving futile. The charge against Utman was abated by his death. The charge against Smith was continued at every term until July 1798, when he was able to prove to the satisfaction of the court that process had been served on the wrong James Smith. He then recovered his costs from Clarke. A new information was filed and new process issued against James Smith, merchant. This case, like many others, remained open throughout the remainder of the period under examination.[57] The charges against Smelzer and Steele, brought in March 1797, were continued the following June. In November Steele's charge was quashed for informality. Smelzer's case was continued until March 1798, when it was discontinued on the motion of Clarke, with the defendant paying costs.[58]

Still the attorney persevered. He filed an information against Dudley Mitcham for using an unregistered still and got a presentment from the grand jury in March 1798.[59] But no grand jury was empaneled in July, and Clarke could only file informations against two more distillers, John Shawhan and James Caldwell.[60] It was uphill work. Finally, in November 1798, Judge Innes announced a new rule:

No person shall on whom any process shall be served returnable to this Court, or has a Suit depending herein, or who may be summoned as a witness in any suit or question depending in the Court, *or who is a distiller of Spirits within this district*, shall be summoned as a Grand Juror, and the Marshall before he summons a Grand Juror is directed to make the necessary inquiry agreeably to this Regulation.[61]

The new rule had an immediate impact: the November grand jury issued presentments against five persons for operating unregistered stills.[62] For the first time in the seven years since passage of the internal revenue act, grand jurors brought charges based on their own knowledge of violations of the law. And once begun, the trend continued: in March 1799, thirteen distillers were presented; in July, another; in November, five more; in March 1800, an additional six. The charges were substantially the same in every case.[63] Meanwhile, Clarke continued to file informations. He brought five in November 1798, two in March 1799, and one each in March and November 1800.[64]

However, these presentments and informations were not followed by convictions. When the cases came to trial, it became evident that petit jurors refused to convict their neighbors of criminal charges when their only crime was violating the revenue acts. As Judge Innes had pointed out in his address to the first federal grand jury:

Trials by Jury have from time immemorial been considered as the basis of Liberty. . . . They are the great bulwark which intervenes between the Magistrate and the Citizen. . . .

In Criminal Cases . . . no Offender can be arraigned at the Bar, until his Offence hath been inquired into by the Grand Inquest . . . and found to be true by the voice of twelve of them at least, his trial then comes on before a Petit Jury where a unanimous voice is necessary to find him guilty.[65]

Petit jurors in Kentucky apparently saw themselves as such a "great bulwark" between the government and its citizens, and Judge Innes assisted them by rigidly maintaining procedural safeguards. Together, the judge and the jurymen prevented enforcement of the unpopular revenue laws through criminal charges.

Thus, of the fifty criminal charges brought from December 1796 through November 1800 (the period of Clarke's tenure), not one of the accused paid the full fines, penalties, or forfeitures provided by the laws. It made no difference whether the charge was distilling without a license or obstructing revenue agents: criminal charges simply were not acceptable. Seven cases went to petit juries, and in every instance they found for the defendants. Judge Innes then ordered the accusers to pay the costs of the suits. Failure to appear and plead resulted in eight default judgments, but two of these were later set aside. Two other defendants acknowledged their failure to enter and pay duties; they were assessed only those duties and costs of the suits, minus the district attorney's fees. The remaining thirty-three cases were abated by the death of the defendants, or quashed, dismissed or discontinued.

Among the defendants were two men who were evidently being harassed by Clarke and the grand jurors, but Innes and the petit jurors refused to cooperate. Nothing in the records explains why William Trimble and Ambrose Bush inspired such attention, but the number and variety of charges against them indicated that they were marked men. Trimble first appeared in the Order Books in November 1798, when he was presented by a grand jury on two counts of using stills which had not been entered and on which duties had not been paid. Bush was also presented twice at that term on the same charges, and their cases seem to be related because the two defendants acted as surety for each other in the actions brought against them.[66] The following March another grand jury again presented Trimble on the same charges, specifying different dates.[67] While the grand jury was deliberating, Supervisor of Revenue James Morrison filed civil suits for debt against Bush and Trimble, and, in addition, Clarke filed informations against them.[68]

The first of all the charges against Trimble to come to trial was a debt case, in July 1799. He pleaded, that he "doth not owe the debt in the declaration demanded," and a petit jury agreed.[69] The finding was important because this was the first civil suit brought under the revenue acts that had reached a jury. The result was not, however, surprising: five members of the jury had similar causes pending before the court.[70]

The marshal's choice of petit jurors, and the court's acceptance of them, seem clearly to have been in violation of the spirit of the rule regarding grand jurors announced in November 1798, which had resulted in the first grand jury charges

not based on informations. The officials of the court were evidently unsympathetic with Clarke's methods. What is perhaps more surprising is that Clarke
apparently did not challenge the selection process. But it might not have made
any difference if he had. Although all nine civil and criminal charges against
Trimble and Bush eventually went to petit juries, in every instance the jurors
found for the defendants or acquitted them.

The July 1799 term was a personal disaster for Clarke. He was subjected to
a scathing lecture on legal history in the Jones case and he lost the civil suit
against Trimble. To add to Clarke's embarrassment, Morrison brought an action
of debt against *him* for failure to pay internal revenue duties. (A juror was
withdrawn at his trial to avert a verdict, probably because agreement was reached.)[71]
Finally, completing Clarke's humiliation, Commissioner of Revenue Miller
strongly criticized the handling of the Trimble case in a letter to Morrison:

The interests of the United States have been committed by this defeat, in a way that is
mortifying. . . . It is an important concern to avoid the introduction of suits, unless in
cases of urgency. . . . In such cases and none others, in my opinion, ought there [be]
resort to proceedings which must become expensive, tedious, and . . . uncertain in their
decision.[72]

Given the failure of criminal prosecutions, the Revenue Office wanted Clarke
and Morrison to use the statutory provision for distraint (seizure) and sale, a
method earlier rejected even by the determined Colonel Marshall.[73] Clarke un-
wisely complied with Miller's request, and the result was the wounding of the
marshal and his deputy when they tried to serve a writ of *fieri facias*.[74] Obviously
distraint and sale were unlikely to gain the cooperative support of the marshal,
and given the attitude of Kentuckians toward the revenue acts, such procedures
also were unlikely to be any more productive than criminal charges.

Criminal charges had failed; distraint and sale had misfired. But there remained
a third way to achieve compliance with the revenue acts: to bring civil suits for
debt (for the amount of duties accrued) against noncomplying distillers. In November 1798, Supervisor James Morrison decided to experiment with this new
procedure and chose his defendants carefully. He brought six suits against Stith
and Thomas Daniel of Jefferson County. The Daniel brothers were major distillers—and Stith Daniel had been appointed a revenue collector by Colonel
Marshall.[75] When their cases were continued in March 1799, Morrison continued
the experiment by filing seven more debt cases. In July, the government won
its first victory of any kind in the eight years since passage of the internal revenue
acts: a petit jury assessed the Daniel brothers 259.12\frac{1}{2}$, 928.38\frac{3}{4}$, and $312.25.[76]
It was an instructive lesson for the defendants, who thereafter acknowledged
their debts.[77] It was also instructive for Morrison, who vigorously pursued the
new policy. He filed twenty-three more debt suits in July, sixty-three in November, forty-eight in March 1800, twelve in June, and twelve in November.
Even more notable was that the government won fourteen more judgments in

July 1799, nineteen in November, eight-one in March 1800, twenty in June, and seven in November.

But the victory proved to be a limited one. During these same months, twenty-six judgments went for the defendants, and twenty-seven judgments that had earlier gone for the government were set aside. The judge and the attorney for the district were on a collision course: Innes was absolutely rigid about legal technicalities and Clarke was notoriously casual about form. Some defendants were able to get judgments arrested because suits had been brought in the name of the United States, instead of in the name of Supervisor Morrison "for the use of the United States."[78] Other defendants pleaded successfully that no demand for payment could be proved, whereupon their cases were dismissed. A third group pleaded that revenue agents (who were often the only witnesses) were inadmissible as witnesses because of their interest in the judgment. (During this period, no one could testify in a proceeding if he had a pecuniary interest in its result). Since the collectors received 6 percent of their collections and 50 percent of all penalties and forfeitures, Innes refused their evidence and judgments went for the defendants.

The pleading which brought the most serious disagreement between Innes and Clarke was that offered by Trimble and upheld by Innes in a July 1799 debt case. Trimble claimed that no duty could be collected on stills that had not been entered. Innes agreed that a distiller could be charged the penalty for not having entered his still, but not the duties which might have accrued during the period of nonentry. Clarke had apparently failed to specify the penalty in his declaration, and sued only for the duties. He was so vehement in his opposition to the judge's ruling that Innes suspected that complaints about him were being made to the Treasury Department. He wrote to Thomas T. Davis, a member of the House of Representatives, to find out what Clarke might be reporting. After two inquiries from Davis, Secretary of the Treasury Oliver Wolcott acknowledged that there had been some correspondence concerning Innes's ruling in the Trimble case.[79]

Wolcott assured Davis that Clarke's "representations" had "ever been temperate and respectful," and that "the decision of the Judge must be conclusive, in case it shall not be controuled by a Superior Judicial Tribunal."[80] What apparently frustrated Secretary Wolcott (and perhaps Clarke, as well) was that most of the Kentucky distillers had never lived up to the 1795 agreement (that arrearages would be forgiven and compliance assured). While the Treasury Department duly noted the amount of excise in its reports, the figures were always identified as "accrued" and never as "paid." By the spring of 1800, the administration had lost the earlier optimism occasioned by Clarke's appointment. He had failed to secure the cooperation of the people, and he was clearly no match for the distillers, their lawyers, or the federal judge.

Clarke's failure to win support in the community and Innes's lack of respect for him eventually took their toll of the attorney. When the March 1800 grand jury made six presentments, Clarke immediately moved to quash them, presumably because he would not or could not effectively prosecute the cases.[81] Even the number of new actions in debt brought by Morrison dwindled in the June term: he, too, had become convinced of Clarke's incompetence.[82] By then it was apparent to all that Clarke's effectiveness had ended. Finally, the Marshalls in Kentucky used their connections in the Adams administration to remove Clarke from a situation that must have become for them, as it certainly was for him, "exceedingly difficult and embarrassing."[83] Fortunately for them, Governor William Henry Harrison was eager to get the new court for the Indiana Territory established, and the position of chief judge offered a convenient berth. President Adams was in no hurry to make the appointment, but the combined pressure from Governor Harrison, Secretary of State John Marshall, and Secretary of the Treasury Wolcott brought him around.[84] Clarke was given a recess appointment in October 1800 which was confirmed by the Senate in December, and in January he took the oath of his new office.[85]

Meanwhile, there was a strange interregnum in Kentucky while the Marshalls were arranging to have a political ally (and future brother-in-law) appointed to succeed Clarke.[86] Finally, in November 1801, Joseph Hamilton Daveiss became attorney for the district. From the day he presented his commission to the court it was obvious that a new regime had begun. Daveiss was energetic and competent, and those qualities proved to be more important than his Federalism, his membership (by marriage) in the Marshall family, and his alliance with Humphrey Marshall. Innes and Morrison could work effectively even with a political enemy if he was capable, and the Kentucky distillers soon learned that their ten-year escape from internal revenue taxes had ended. Ironically, their compliance was achieved only after Jefferson had been elected, and the taxes were being repealed.

Daveiss began his first day in court by getting two indictments from the grand jury, amending earlier cases brought by Clarke, and with Morrison docketing 121 civil cases in debt against distillers. One of the indictments charged a distiller with obstructing the service of a process for distraint and sale, a procedure that had not grown more popular with time. The other eventually resulted in the only petit jury conviction on a grand jury indictment against a distiller during the entire period under examination. Daveiss had chosen his case carefully, and the verdict was undoubtedly influenced by evidence that the defendant had used two pistols to prevent service of a warrant charging that he had hidden spirits to evade payment of the excise.[87]

Daveiss even secured a jury conviction on an information filed against a distiller.[88] But criminal prosecutions were relatively unprofitable, and the results of other informations were similar to those during Clarke's tenure: three were dismissed, one discontinued, three defendants acknowledged their debts and paid costs, one judgment went for the defendant, and two judgments went for the government. Forfeitures and fines resulting from these were later remitted by Secretary of the Treasury Albert Gallatin who was, of course, unsympathetic with the revenue laws.[89]

The massive docketing of debt cases during Daveiss's first term indicated his awareness that compliance with the internal revenue acts could most successfully be achieved through civil action. He was careful not to risk failure through sloppiness in procedure: all of the 161 suits filed in November 1801, and the 51 filed in May 1802, were brought in the name of the revenue officer (usually Morrison) "for the use of the United States." (As noted earlier, Daveiss amended earlier declarations to comply with this technicality.) After his first term, Daveiss seldom used criminal charges to enforce the revenue acts. The Jeffersonians repealed the internal revenue taxes in April 1802, but a few cases continued to trickle in until the five-year statute of limitations took effect. Altogether, Daveiss filed 315 debt cases during the six years he was attorney.[90] The message must have been clear to Kentucky distillers: few of Daveiss's cases ever went to juries, because most defendants acknowledged their debts and paid the duties. Although Kentuckians complained until the excise was repealed, they did belatedly comply with the law—after Jefferson became president.[91]

The parallels between Kentucky and Pennsylvania are striking. The differences are also important. In Pennsylvania, the federal court was in the East, and the noncomplying distillers were in the West. Indeed, one of their major grievances was that any who were charged with violating the law in the federal court had to travel all the way to Philadelphia to appear and plead.[92] In Kentucky, the federal court was right in the middle of all the distillers. Even more important, federal judge Harry Innes obviously sided with *them* whenever criminal charges (as contrasted with civil charges) were brought. But Innes was not alone. Obviously, the Jeffersonian political establishment in Kentucky would not cooperate in even token compliance until after the federal government provided access to the Mississippi River and protection from the Indians. The decision to tolerate evasion of the internal revenue acts probably prevented the degree of violence experienced in Pennsylvania, and perhaps kept Kentucky in the union.[93]

It is equally clear that the administration decided to ignore the massive resistance in Kentucky, despite grumblings among individual cabinet members after a mass meeting in Lexington in May 1794 had produced remonstrances against the federal government.[94] The administration knew how exceedingly difficult it would be to raise another army (or continue this one in service), send it so far west, and equip and supply it—among a frankly hostile population.[95] Further, they could not depend upon the Kentucky militia as they eventually were able to depend upon that of Pennsylvania, because they needed Kentucky troops to serve under General Anthony Wayne in the Indian war that culminated in the Battle of Fallen Timbers in August 1794. Surely they must have understood that if the militia of other states were sent into Kentucky while its own was absent, there would have been a full-scale rebellion—or secession. No evidence has yet been found that any member of the administration acknowledged for the record that he agreed to enforce the law in one state but ignore it in another. Yet all must have realized that using troops in Pennsylvania constituted exactly that. And one of the consequences of choosing to ignore what was going on in Kentucky was to set in operation a coverup of those events that lasted almost 200 years.

With the stage set for intervention in Pennsylvania, Hamilton wrote a narrative of events that was so convincing that even participants relied upon it when they wrote their own memoirs.[96] Yet every member of the cabinet, every member of Congress from Kentucky and some other states, and thousands of noncomplying distillers and their families throughout the nation knew that if there was an insurrection it was not confined to Pennsylvania. All also knew that whatever term was used to describe the events in the West that there was no threat to the established government. Among the prominent, only Thomas Jefferson objected—and he expressed his objections privately.[97] Edmund Randolph went along with the administration, but with such obvious reluctance that he became a target for Hamilton's allies. A year later they forced him out of the cabinet and severed his lifelong attachment to Washington.[98]

John Marshall made his contribution to the official history of the insurrection a decade after the event. He knew from his own father that what he wrote was not the complete truth, and many of his readers knew, also. But Hamilton's death in the year of publication of Marshall's *Life of George Washington* contributed to the dramatic potential of the alleged Whiskey Rebellion. With heroic figures like Washington, Henry "Light Horse Harry" Lee, and the martyred Hamilton on one side, and irrational, anarchic frontier distillers on the other, the Whiskey Rebellion manifested a dualism common in Western culture. It was also in 1804 that Napoleon crowned himself emperor of France. Even Francophiles must have been impressed by the providence that had protected the fruit of the American Revolution and—in words that Francis Scott Key would write a few years later—preserved us a nation. Perhaps the chief justice was right, after all; perhaps there had been an insurrection; perhaps the use of force in Pennsylvania was a necessary act. The United States was still a republican nation, and France was not.

It is disconcerting to discover that thousands of people whose experience was otherwise accepted a version of events that they knew was not an accurate one. It is even more surprising to discover a volume of data that, however scattered, reveals evidence so different from the official accounts. Yet for almost two centuries, the Federalist account of the Whiskey Rebellion prevailed and became incorporated into the common understanding of the early Republic. That account has four components: that there was a genuine insurrection, that it was limited to four western counties, that a massive show of military power ended it, and that thereafter opposition to the excise on stills and distilled liquors ceased. But a reexamination of familiar sources and the rediscovery of unfamiliar ones— especially court records—casts doubt on those traditions. It is quite possible that the Federalists won a greater victory in the history books than they did in Pennsylvania.

NOTES

1. John Marshall, *The Life of George Washington, Commander in Chief of the American Forces During the War Which Established the Independence of His Country, and*

First President of the United States: Compiled Under the Inspection of The Honourable Bushrod Washington, from Original Papers Bequeathed to Him by His Deceased Relative, (New York: Walton, 1930 [orig. publ. Philadelphia, 1804]), 2:411. Blood was shed, however. Two civilians were killed (a boy and a man who may have been deranged or intoxicated), apparently because of the nervousness of the untrained militia (Thomas E. Templin, "Henry 'Light Horse Harry' Lee: A Biography," Ph.D. diss., University of Kentucky, 1975, p. 399).

2. E.g., Richard B. Morris, ed. *Encyclopedia of American History*, rev. ed. (New York: Harper and Row, 1965), pp. 123, 126.

3. Washington used the phrase "self-created societies," referring to the Democratic Societies, in the report on the Whiskey Rebellion contained in his Sixth Annual Address in November 1794 (James D. Richardson, ed., *A Compilation of the Messages and Papers of the Presidents* [New York: Bureau of National Literature, 1913], 1:155).

4. Richard H. Kohn, "The Washington Administration's Decision to Crush the Whiskey Rebellion," *Journal of American History* 59 (1972): 567–584, which includes a convenient bibliography on p. 567, n. 2.

5. Richard Peters, ed., *The Public Statutes at Large of the United States of America, 1789–1873* (Boston: Little, Brown, 1850–1873), 1:199 (hereafter cited as 1 *Stat.*).

6. Noble E. Cunningham, Jr., *Circular Letters of Congressmen to Their Constituents, 1789–1829* (Chapel Hill: University of North Carolina Press, 1978), 1:6, n. 4.

7. John Steele to William Blount, Jan. 27, 1791, in *ibid*. 1:4.

8. A comprehensive list of complaints, together with the responses of Secretary of the Treasury Alexander Hamilton are in "Report on the Difficulties in the Execution of the Act Laying Duties on Distilled Spirits" [Mar. 5, 1792], in *The Papers of Alexander Hamilton*, eds. Harold C. Syrett, et al., (New York: Columbia University Press, 1961–1979), 11:77–106.

9. Henry Adams, ed., *The Writings of Albert Gallatin* (New York: Antiquarian Press, 1960 [orig. publ. Philadelphia, 1879]), 1:3.

10. Hamilton, "Report on the Difficulties," in *Hamilton Papers*, 11:77, n.; Walter Lowrie and Walter S. Franklin, eds., *American State Papers, Finance: Documents, Legislative and Executive of the Congress of the United States*, (Washington, D.C.: Gales and Seaton, 1834), 1:250–251.

11. 1 *Stat.* 267.

12. Tench Coxe to Hamilton, May 20, 1792, *Hamilton Papers* 11:405–408. The letters referred to in p. 408, n. 12, are in Whiskey Rebellion Papers, RG 58, Records of the Internal Revenue Service, National Archives.

13. Daniel Huger to Hamilton, June 22, 1792, in *Hamilton Papers* 11:541; Washington to Hamilton, Aug. 31, 1792, in *ibid*. 12:304; *American State Papers, Finance* 1:250.

14. Hamilton to Coxe, Sept. 1, 1792, in *Hamilton Papers* 12:305.

15. *American State Papers, Finance* 1:280–281.

16. "Conference Concerning the Insurrection in Western Pennsylvania," Aug. 2, 1794, in *Hamilton Papers* 17:9–14. See especially Hamilton's opinion on p. 12.

17. Richardson, *Messages and Papers of the Presidents* 1:154–164.

18. *American State Papers, Finance* 1:355.

19. *Ibid*. 1:391.

20. *Ibid*. 1:562.

21. *Ibid*. 1:593, 618.

22. These letters were discovered in 1954 among papers that had been removed from

the Internal Revenue files at some unknown time in the past. The collection is correctly labeled "Whiskey Rebellion Papers," and there are many references to affairs in Kentucky as well as in Pennsylvania (Whiskey Rebellion Papers, National Archives).

23. Thomas Marshall to Edward Carrington, Mar. 8, 1792, in *ibid*. At the time that the revenue laws went into effect, Kentucky was the western district of Virginia; Marshall therefore reported to the Virginia supervisor. In 1794 Marshall's district was reorganized and renamed the District of Ohio (1 *Stat*. 270).

24. *Ibid*.

25. 1 *Stat*. secs. 15, 21, 36, 43; *ibid*., 267, sec. 1. Section 15 of the latter statute, passed in May 1792, lowered duties but contained a bribe (or threat) to those on the frontier: any deficiency in the returns from the excise was to be made up from money raised for the protection of the frontiers.

26. Coxe to Marshall, Oct. 31, 1792, in Letters Sent by the Commissioner of the Revenue and the Revenue Office, 1792–1807, M-414, roll 1, Records of the Internal Revenue Service, 58, National Archives. (Hereafter cited as Letters Sent, Revenue Office, M-414.)

27. The difficulties encountered in trying to fill this office are described in Mary K. Bonsteel Tachau, *Federal Courts in the Early Republic: Kentucky 1789–1816* (Princeton, N.J.: Princeton University Press, 1978), pp. 65–76.

28. Both are reflected in advertisements in the *Kentucky Gazette* (Lexington). See, for examples, the following issues: June 18, 1791; Mar. 24, Apr. 21, Apr. 28, and Nov. 24, 1792; Jan. 12, July 27, Aug. 31, and Nov. 23, 1793; Feb. 22, 1794.

29. Coxe to Carrington, Mar. 27, 1793, in Letters Sent, Revenue Office, M-414, roll 1.

30. George Nicholas to Marshall, Aug. 25, 1793, in Whiskey Rebellion Papers, National Archives. Nicholas was Edmund Randolph's brother-in-law, and wrote him frequently about Kentucky affairs.

31. Marshall to Carrington, Mar. 20, 1794, in *ibid*.; *Kentucky Gazette*, Feb. 22, 1794. President Washington received extracts of Marshall's letter, describing these events in Kentucky (Proceedings of the President, July 14, 1794, George Washington Papers, Manuscript Division, Library of Congress, reel 13).

32. Coxe to William Clarke, May 11, 1797, in Tench Coxe Section, Coxe Papers, Manuscript Collection, Historical Society of Pennsylvania, Philadelphia.

33. Case was a form of action used to recover damages which were the indirect consequence of the defendant's act. See *Carrington* v. *Saunders;* and *Carrington* v. *Trotter,* United States Court for the District of Kentucky, Order Book A, Dec. 17, 1793, p. 44. (Hereafter cited as DC OB).

34. *Ibid*., Mar. 18, 1794, p. 54; July 22, 1794, p. 61. Nicholas had strongly recommended to Marshall that the suits be dropped (Nicholas to Marshall, Aug. 25, 1793, Whiskey Rebellion Papers, National Archives).

35. The Treasury Department had taken over this function from the War Department after St. Clair's defeat had been attributed in part to the inefficiency of earlier supply arrangements. Legislation authorizing the transfer was passed in February 1792 (1 Stat. 279). See John C. Miller, *The Federalist Era 1789–1801* (New York, 1960), p. 147; Leonard D. White, *The Federalists: A Study in Administrative History* (New York, 1948), p. 121.

36. Hamilton to Coxe, Nov. 17, 1794, in Whiskey Rebellion Papers, National Ar-

chives. A copy of this letter, addressed to Henry Miller (acting quartermaster general of the militia army), is in *Hamilton Papers* 17:376.

37. Marshall to Coxe, Mar. 20, 1794, in *ibid*. For their dual roles and purchase advertisements, see *Kentucky Gazette,* Nov. 24, 1792; Mar. 29, 1794; Jan. 17, 1795.

38. *American State Papers, Finance* 1:390, 391, 562, 593, 618; Coxe to John Brown, Mar. 30, 1797, Coxe Papers; Coxe to Marshall, Jan. 2, 1796, in Letters of Tench Coxe, Commissioner of the Revenue, Relating to the Procurement of Military, Naval, and Indian Supplies, 1794–1796, in M-74, Records of the Bureau of Indian Affairs, 75, National Archives; Treasury Department [Oliver Wolcott] to Thomas Carneal, Oct. 21, 1797, in Oliver Wolcott Papers, Manuscript Collection, Connecticut Historical Society, Hartford, 33:44.

39. Thomas Jefferson to George Nicholas, July 15, 1793, Domestic Letters of the Department of State, 1784–1906, in M-40, roll 5, General Records of the Department of State, 59, National Archives. (Hereafter cited as Domestic Letters, Dept. of State, M-40.) It was Jefferson's refusal to extend the grace period that prompted Nicholas to decline, for a second time, the appointment as United States attorney for the Kentucky District (Nicholas to Marshall, Aug. 25, 1793, in Whiskey Rebellion Papers, National Archives).

40. Hamilton to Coxe, Nov. 17, 1794; Jan. 27, 1795, in Whiskey Rebellion Papers, National Archives.

41. In the summer of 1794, Edmund Randolph persuaded President Washington to send James Innes (brother of the judge of the Kentucky federal court) to Kentucky to inform its citizens about the administration's new initiatives in trying to gain free access to the Mississippi River from the court of Spain, to find out why Kentuckians were resisting the whiskey tax, and how they felt about the government. The mission is described in Tachau, *Federal Courts in the Early Republic*, pp. 49–51. Randolph kept Washington informed about events in Kentucky by passing along correspondence. See, for example, Randolph to Washington, Feb. 27, 1794, in Miscellaneous Letters of the Department of State, 1789–1906, M-179, roll 11, General Records of the Department of State, RG 59, National Archives. (Hereafter cited as Misc. Letters, Dept. of State, M-179.)

42. Wolcott to Thomas T. Davis, Feb. 25, 1800, in Innes Papers, Library of Congress, vol. 21, pt. i, pp. 1–89.

43. Wolcott to Coxe, June 27, 1796, in Wolcott Papers, pp. 31, 49 (the final draft omitted the words crossed out); Wolcott to Coxe, June 27, 1796, in Whiskey Rebellion Papers, National Archives. Coxe transmitted the final draft verbatim to Marshall (Coxe to Marshall, June 30, 1796, in Letters Sent, Revenue Office, M-414, roll 2).

44. The strategies apparently did not work in Pennsylvania, either, according to a letter written by Coxe's successor to Marshall's successor (William Miller, Jr. to James Morrison, June 2, 1798, in Whiskey Rebellion Papers, National Archives). Furthermore, Oliver Wolcott doubted that even the military action there had been successful in securing compliance. In 1799 he wrote President Adams that "though the insurrection has been suppressed the spirit which occasioned it still exists, and the friends of government and its officers have lost much of the influence which they once possessed" (Wolcott to Adams, Nov. 18, 1799, in Wolcott Papers, 40:68).

45. DC OB A, Jan. 12, 1792, p. 18. The failure of grand juries to act is further evidence of the nonpartisan nature of the resistance to the whiskey tax. Under Kentucky statute, grand jurors were summoned by the marshal, and this practice was followed in

the federal court (Harry Innes to John Breckinridge, Dec. 27, 1801, Breckinridge Family Papers, Manuscript Division, Library of Congress, 21:3559). The federal marshal during this period was Samuel McDowell, Jr., a cousin of the Marshalls and a strong Federalist.

46. 1 *Stat.* 376; DC OB A, Mar. 17, 1795, p. 82.

47. DC OB A, June 17, 1795, p. 97. "Informality" meant lack of legal form.

48. Thomas Marshall to John Marshall, Nov. 6, 1795, quoted in W[illiam] M[cClung] Paxton, *The Marshall Family* (Cincinnati, 1885), p. 22. Colonel Marshall apparently did not realize that his son had declined the appointment, just as he had earlier refused to serve as United States attorney for the District of Virginia (Washington to Hamilton, Oct. 29, 1795, in *Hamilton Papers* 19:357).

49. DC OB A, Dec. 21, 1796, p. 142.

50. *Ibid.*, Dec. 23, 1796, pp. 143–45.

51. *Ibid.* Historically, presentments resulted from the knowledge of grand jurors, but the result of this rule was that subsequent presentments carried the names of informers who were revenue agents, not grand jurors.

52. DC OB A, Mar. 22, 1797, p. 151; William Clarke to Tench Coxe, May 11, 1797, in Coxe Papers; W. T. Smith, *A Complete Index to the Names of Persons, Places and Subjects Mentioned in Littell's Laws of Kentucky* (Lexington, Ky., 1931), p. 97.

53. Marshall to Adams, Apr. 28, 1797, in Misc. Letters, Dept. of State, M-179, roll 15.

54. Marshall's and Carrington's cautiousness in observing the proprieties (suing in their own names and for the benefit of the United States) is in marked contrast to the carelessness of Clarke, noted below.

55. *Carrington v. Saunders, Carrington v. Ravenscraft,* and *Carrington v. Helm,* DC OB A, Nov. 20, 1797, p. 169; *Carrington v. Horine* and *Marshall v. Horine, ibid.,* Nov. 21, 1797, p. 174.

56. The action may have been used because of Marshall's death in 1802. No further proceedings were recorded that might have revived the debt case in the name of his heirs or in the name of the United States (*Marshall v. Horine,* DC OB A, July 9, 1798, pp. 196, 197; *Horine v. Marshall,* DC OB C, Nov. 20, 1802, p. 368; Dec. 1, 1802, p. 418).

57. DC OB A, Mar. 21, 1797, p. 147; June 20, 1797, p. 162; Nov. 20, 1797, p. 170; July 12, 1798, p. 211; DC OB B, Nov. 19, 1798, p. 4.

58. DC OB A, Mar. 21, 1797, pp. 146, 147; June 20, 1797, p. 162; June 21, 1797, p. 165; Nov. 20, 1797, pp. 168, 170; Nov. 21, 1797, p. 171; Mar. 12, 1798, p. 180.

59. *Ibid.*, Mar. 12, 1798, p. 178.

60. *Ibid.*, July 12, 1798, p. 211.

61. DC OB B, Nov. 26, 1798, 27, italics added. The rule was evidently put into effect before it was recorded in the Order Book.

62. *U.S. v. Trimble, U.S. v. Bush, U.S. v. Hardwick, U.S. v. Lewis,* and *U.S. v. McKenney,* DC OB B, Nov. 19, 1798, p. 1. Because of the limitations on joinder, two presentments were made for two of these men (Trimble and Bush) for failure to enter on two different dates. The total number of presentments was, therefore, seven.

63. *U.S. v. Trimble, U.S. v. Hockaday, U.S. v. Singleton, U.S. v. Bayer, U.S. v. Galbraith, U.S. v. Dodson, U.S. v. Ellis, U.S. v. Stewart, U.S. v. Bogio, U.S. v. Gouge, U.S. v. Wills, U.S. v. Peeples, U.S. v. Logan,* DC OB B, Mar. 12, 1799, pp. 44–48. *U.S. v. Farrow, ibid.,* July 8, 1799, p. 87; *U.S. v. Jackman, U.S. v. Teter, U.S. v. Adams, U.S. v. Shackleford, U.S. v. Price, ibid.,* Nov. 18, 1799, pp. 130, 131; *U.S.*

v. *Randolph, U.S.* v. *Allen, U.S.* v. *Dawson, U.S.* v. *Spaulding, U.S.* v. *Keith, U.S.* v. *Barbee, ibid.*, Mar. 11, 1800, pp. 238, 239.

64. *U.S.* v. *Beauchamp, U.S.* v. *Payton* (two charges), *U.S.* v. *Lee* (two charges), DC OB B, Nov. 11, 1798, p. 16; *U.S.* v. *Trimble, U.S.* v. *Bush, ibid.*, Mar. 11, 1799, pp. 34, 36; *U.S.* v. *Heath, ibid.*, Mar. 10, 1800, p. 229; *U.S.* v. *Robinson, ibid.*, Nov. 18, 1800, p. 479. The list of names indicates that the Scots-Irish did not dominate the distilling industry, as is commonly supposed.

65. Draft address, undated but prepared for the grand jury that convened Jan. 12, 1792 (Harry Innes Papers, Manuscript Division, Library of Congress 18: 2–123).

66. DC OB B, Nov. 19, 1798, p. 2.

67. *Ibid.*, Mar. 12, 1799, p. 47.

68. *Ibid.*, Mar. 11, 1799, pp. 34, 35.

69. *Ibid.*, July 8, 1799, p. 85. As discussed below, the declaration apparently specified the duties that had accrued before the stills were entered, and not the penalty for failure to enter. The duty was 54¢ per gallon per year; the penalty was $250 and forfeiture of the still. The judge's opinion is in [Harry Innes] ''Cases in the Court of the United States for the District of Kentucky, from its first Organization to the year 1806 Inclusive,'' United States Court for the Western District of Kentucky, Louisville, p. 103.

70. Dudley Mitcham, DC OB A, Mar. 12, 1799, p. 178; Robert Peeples, DC OB B, Mar. 12, 1799, p. 47; William Ellis, *ibid.*, p. 46; John Galbraith, *ibid.*, p. 45; and Ambrose Bush, whose cases were cited above.

71. *Morrison* v. *Clarke*, DC OB B, July 13, 1799, p. 113.

72. Miller to Morrison, Oct. 23, 1799, Letters Sent, Revenue Office, M-414, roll 2.

73. Distraint and sale was first specified as a method of enforcement in the act of Mar. 3, 1791, 1 *Stat.* 199, sec. 23; and later in 1 *Stat.* 597, sec. 15; 2 *Stat.* 22, sec. 28; and 3 *Stat.* 366, sec. 2.

74. A writ of *fieri facias* was a court order commanding the sheriff to collect the amount of the judgment from the personal property of the defendant. The incident occurred Apr. 13, 1800. *U.S.* v. *Caldwell, U.S.* v. *Matthew Hemphill, U.S.* v. *John Hemphill,* and *U.S.* v. *Andrew Hemphill*, DC OB B, Nov. 17, 1800, p. 468. Caldwell confessed and was sentenced to one hour in jail, a fine of $40, and costs; the Hemphills found it convenient to move out of the district and their cases never came to trial (DC OB C, Nov. 18, 1802, p. 323).

75. *U.S.* v. *Stith and Thomas Daniel*, DC OB B, Nov. 21, 1798, p. 10; *Kentucky Gazette*, Nov. 24, 1792; Nov. 15, 1794.

76. Fractions of cents were not uncommon in the judgments of the court but they were usually expressed in mills. *U.S.* v. *Daniel* (three cases), DC OB B, July 12, 1799, pp. 104, 105.

77. DC OB B, Nov. 21, 1799, p. 185.

78. While it is not now possible to prove that this oversight was Clarke's and not Morrison's, it was Clarke's responsibility to see that the government's suits were prepared properly. His successor found it necessary to amend the identification of the plaintiff in at least 21 of the government's cases during his first term in office. See DC OB C, Nov. 16, 1801, pp. 52–54.

79. Davis to Innes, Feb. 28, 1800, in Innes Papers, Library of Congress, vol. 27, pt. i, pp. 8–12; Wolcott to Davis, Feb. 25, 1800, in *ibid.*, vol. 21, pt. i, pp. 1–89.

80. Wolcott was apparently hoping that one of Clarke's cases would be carried to the United States Supreme Court. Innes was not opposed to this because he thought it would

give him an opportunity to expose Clarke's incompetence. Wolcott to Davis, Feb. 25, 1800, in Wolcott Papers 37:146; Innes to Brown, Mar. 18, 1798, in Innes Papers, Library of Congress 28:9–210.

81. DC OB B, Mar. 11, 1800, pp. 238, 241.

82. Innes to Brown, Mar. 5, 1800, in Innes Papers, Library of Congress 28:9–217.

83. Wolcott to Clarke, Aug. 5, 1800, in Wolcott Papers 38:38.

84. John Marshall to Adams, Aug. 26, 1800, Miscellaneous Permanent Commissions, Appointment Office Files, B (1789–1802), Department of State, quoted in Clarence E. Carter, "William Clarke, First Chief Justice of Indiana Territory," *Indiana Magazine of History* 34 (1938), 1–13; Carter, ed., *The Territorial Papers of the United States,* vol. 7, *The Territory of Indiana 1800–1810* (Washington, D.C.: 1939), p. 20.

85. Carter, *Territory of Indiana,* pp. 7, 16–19.

86. Humphrey Marshall to Joseph Hamilton Daveiss, Nov. 24, 1800, in Joseph Hamilton Daveiss and Samuel Daveiss Papers, Manuscript Dept., Filson Club, Louisville, Ky.

87. The defendant was released on $300 bail provided by Thomas Marshall, Jr., and the judgment was later arrested because of errors in the warrant. Innes's opinion stressed not only the heinous nature of the crime but also the danger of general warrants and quoted the Fourth Amendment as well as English decisions. The proceedings may be traced in *U.S.* v. *Mannen,* United States Court for the Sixth Circuit, DC OB C, Nov. 17, 1801, p. 106; *ibid.,* May 17, 1802, p. 191; United States Court for the District of Kentucky, DC OB C, Nov. 17, 1802, p. 345; *ibid.,* Nov. 28, 1802, p. 349; *ibid.,* Nov. 29, 1802, p. 413; *ibid.,* Dec. 2, 1802, pp. 434, 437; DC OB D, Dec. 3, 1802, p. 15; *ibid.,* Dec. 6, 1802, p. 31.

88. *U.S.* v. *Pleu,* DC OB C, Nov. 30, 1801, p. 179; May 17, 1802, p. 193; Nov. 24, 1802, p. 387; DC OB D, Mar. 17, 1803, p. 107; *ibid.,* July 5, 1803, p. 195; *ibid.,* Nov. 7, 1803, p. 304.

89. Authority to remit forfeitures and penalties was granted in the first internal revenue act, 1 *Stat.* 199, sec. 43.

90. He also filed 79 other charges, making a total of 394 prosecutions.

91. G. Thompson to Breckinridge, Feb. 6, 1802, in Breckinridge Family Papers, 21:3641; Joseph Crockett to Breckinridge, Feb. 9, 1802, *ibid.,* 21:3647.

92. State courts were given concurrent jurisdiction over internal revenue cases arising more than 50 miles from a federal district court in 1 *Stat.* 378, sec. 9 (1794).

93. Randolph wrote in 1794, "The people of Kentucky . . . are restrained from hostile action by a packthread" (Randolph to Jefferson, Aug. 28, 1794, Domestic Records, Dept. of State, M-40, roll 7). As late as 1797, a Spanish agent reported to his governor at Natchez that any one of three conditions would precipitate the secession of Kentucky. The third was an attempt by the (federal) government to collect the taxes by force (Unidentified agent to Senor Don [*sic*] Manuel Gayoso de Lemos, Dec. 5, 1797 [translated from the Spanish by the Military Intelligence Division of the War Department in 1934]. Letters received by the Secretary of War, Unregistered Series 1789–1860, M-222, roll 1, Records of the Office of the Secretary of War, 107, National Archives).

94. Randolph to Bradford, Hamilton, and Knox, July 11, 1794, in *Hamilton Papers* 16:588; Hamilton to Washington, July 13, 1794, in *ibid.,* p. 600; Henry Knox to Washington, July 14, 1794, in George Washington Papers, Manuscript Division, Library of Congress, reel 105; William Bradford to Washington, July 1794, in *ibid.,* reel 106.

95. Under the Militia Act of 1792, which provided the legal basis for calling up the

militia, troops could be continued in service only thirty days after the beginning of the next session of Congress (1 *Stat.* 264, sec. 2). The administration was concerned that the army might have to be dismissed while it was still needed in Pennsylvania, and Washington asked Congress to extend the term of service (Richardson, *Messages and Papers of the Presidents* 1:157). Congress immediately complied, but specified that the service was to be in the western counties of Pennsylvania (1 *Stat.* 403).

96. Hamilton to Washington, [Aug. 5,] 1794, in *Hamilton Papers* 17:24–58.

97. Jefferson to James Madison, Dec. 28, 1794, in Paul Leicester Ford, ed., *The Writings of Thomas Jefferson* (New York: G. P. Putnam, 1895) 6:516.

98. Irving Brant, "Edmund Randolph, Not Guilty!" *William and Mary Quarterly,* 2d ser., 7 (1950), 179–198; Mary K. Bonsteel Tachau, "Edmund Randolph and the Price of Dissent" (presented at the third annual meeting of The Society for Historians of the Early American Republic, Loudonville, N.Y., July 24, 1981).

The Whiskey Rebellion and the Question of Representation

The ratification of the Constitution in 1788 was seen by its supporters as a climactic moment in the nation's history and one that promised to bring to fruition the hopes and expectations of the Revolution. George Washington acclaimed the achievement as "a new phenomenon in the political and moral world, and an astonishing victory gained by enlightened reason over brute force."[1]

Throughout the country there were joyous processions to celebrate each individual state's ratification. In Boston the day after Massachusetts ratified, 4,000 to 5,000 tradesmen marched in a parade along with a ship called the *Federal Constitution* supported by runners and pulled through the snow by thirteen white horses. The New York procession included among other things a horse-drawn frigate, designated the *Hamilton,* as well as a carriage representing the Chair of State, which was "seven feet high and four wide" and "covered with light blue satin." A joint celebration in Philadelphia of the Fourth of July and the adoption of the Constitution, however, brought forth the most impressive and massive display of joy and thanksgiving. More than half the city's population turned out to witness the procession of 5,000 people, including floats and marching units of the dozens of artisans' groups and professions.[2]

By the time Washington's second term of office began in 1793, however, much of the optimism and euphoria had worn off. Questions of foreign and domestic policy deeply split the country and raised the specter that the union might not survive. Of all those disputes, the most violent and potentially destructive was the armed insurrection by western Pennsylvania farmers in 1794.

The short-lived Whiskey Rebellion, which ultimately required the mobilization of a militia force to put it down, was a decisive landmark in the history of the early republic. It offered the first major challenge to the authority of the national government and served as a catalyst for reopening the debate concerning the nature of representation that had been waged throughout the entire Revolutionary

Era. "No political conception," Gordon Wood writes, "was more important to Americans . . . than representation." And it was this issue, according to Wood, that "had been . . . a central, if not the most fundamental issue between England and America," in leading to the Revolution.[3]

Nonetheless, although there was a brief period of harmony in the early years of Washington's administration, the ratification of the Constitution did not end the debate over the nature of representation. In fact, while there can be no doubt that the installation of the new frame of government was one of those pivotal events or crystallizing moments in American history, it is misleading to see it as a kind of a finale which ended the debates of the Revolutionary Era, as Wood seems to imply.

Proponents no doubt fervently hoped that the adoption of the Constitution would usher in a new era of peace, order, and prosperity, thus meeting their publicly expressed expectations. And from the vantage point of almost two hundred years later, it is clear that for the most part the Constitution has lived up to these expectations. But many Americans who had opposed ratification in 1788, perhaps close to half the population, did not regard the new Constitution so sanguinely, nor did they view ratification as bringing to an end the great debates of the Revolutionary Era over the nature of representative government.

And it was the Whiskey Rebellion, coming only six years later, and the Democratic-Republican Societies, to which the insurrection was inextricably tied, that most dramatically and urgently raised anew the questions of how the will of the people was to be determined; how opposition to the majority might be expressed; the proper role of an opposition in a republic; and how the rights of a minority were to be protected.

These questions revived many arguments, doubts, and fears that the anti-Federalists had raised about representation in their earlier campaign against ratification. In the 1787–1788 debate on the proposed Constitution, anti-Federalists had recommended that representatives of the people be more frequently elected (preferably annually), be rotated in office, and have close and direct relationships with their constituents. "The legislature of a free country," a Pennsylvania anti-Federalist had written, "should be so formed as to have a competent knowledge of its constituents, and enjoy their confidence." And for this to occur, "the representation ought to be fair, equal, and sufficiently numerous, to possess the same interests, feelings, opinions, and views, which the people themselves would possess, were they all assembled." Furthermore, representative bodies should be "so numerous as to prevent bribery and undue influence, and so responsible to the people, by frequent and fair elections, as to prevent their neglecting or sacrificing the views and interests of their constituents, to their own pursuits." Unfortunately, he concluded, the new Congress proposed by the Constitution failed and failed miserably to meet this test, for "the sense and views of 3 or 4 millions of people diffused over so extensive a territory comprising such various climates, products, habits, interests, and opinions, cannot be collected in so small a body."[4]

But more important and posing a much more dangerous question had been the assertion by "Philadelphiensis," a Pennsylvania essayist, that the *nature* of the conflict over ratification was *fundamental* and the differences, which threatened to destroy the union, were irreconcilable. Violent parties and factions were ever present in Great Britain, he had argued, but they had formed "not from a dislike to the fundamentals of their constitution, but on account of mal-administration: All parties glory in the constitution, and disagree only, when it is infringed, or violated." This was not the case in the United States, he had warned, where the opposition was "against the fundamentals of the constitution itself." And he had concluded with the dire prediction that no "Constitution that is not popular can possibly be established in America; or if for a short time it were established, we would have nothing but anarchy and civil war."[5]

To many western Pennsylvanians in the early years after the establishment of the new government under the Constitution, these words must have seemed prophetic. For in 1791, as part of Secretary of the Treasury Hamilton's financial program, Congress levied an excise tax on distilled liquor that so outraged western Pennsylvanians that it was virtually unenforceable. Furthermore, it seemed to confirm the warnings of the anti-Federalists that the new government was not representative of the interests of the people.

Western opposition to the tax stemmed from several sources. There was a latent and general hostility to excise laws which were regarded as a particularly odious method to raise revenue. In England they had been enforced harshly and arbitrarily, so much so that their very enforcement seemed to endanger individual liberty. This example was not lost on the Americans, and during the debate over the Constitution one of the major concerns of the anti-Federalists had been the danger of unlimited taxing power granted to the federal government.[6] More specifically, however, westerners were convinced that the tax worked a peculiar economic hardship upon their section of the country. With the lack of roads, bulky agricultural products were unmarketable, thus necessitating the production of whiskey, which was not only more transportable but also used as barter in the absence of a circulating medium.[7] It was maintained by the westerners that a land tax would be more equitable since eastern land with more improvements would carry the greatest tax burden. Furthermore, a land task would force speculators to sell their western landholdings at reasonable prices, which in turn would spur development. The last objection, not necessarily the least significant, was to the provision in the law that called for trying Pennsylvania tax offenders in the federal courts in Philadelphia. For a westerner to appear in court meant a 300-mile journey and absence from farm and home for a number of weeks.[8]

After the passage of the federal excise law in 1791, it quickly became apparent that the tax would be fiercely resisted. Almost immediately tax collectors were tarred and feathered and terrorized with threats of greater physical abuse. In addition, citizens who were sympathetic or at least were in favor of complying with the law were treated to coats of tar and feathers and had their barns and houses pulled down. At a public meeting in western Pennsylvania in August

1792, at which Albert Gallatin was among those in attendance, it was resolved that the excise, besides being "oppressive upon the poor," was also "most dangerous to the civil rights of freemen" and a threat to liberty primarily because of the excessive powers that tax officials had to have to collect the duty. The disgruntled participants further resolved that it was their obligation "to persist in our remonstrances to Congress, and in every other legal measure that may *obstruct the operation of the Law*, until we are able to obtain its total repeal." To implement this opposition, committees of correspondence in the four western Pennsylvania counties were established.[9]

The apparent institutionalization of violence as a mode of opposing the tax convinced Hamilton that a strong federal response was needed. He, therefore, recommended to the president that "vigorous and decisive measures" be taken by the federal government to convince the "well disposed part of the community" that the executive was not "wanting in decision and vigor." The language of the westerners' resolutions, which vowed to "obstruct the operation of the Law," Hamilton found particularly offensive and threatening. "This is attempted to be qualified by a pretense of doing it by 'every legal measure,' " he wrote John Jay, but this was "a contradiction in terms." Hamilton was convinced that "a high misdemeanor" had been committed.[10] His recommendations for the use of force, however, were overruled and the Washington administration instead issued a proclamation denouncing resistance to the whiskey tax.[11]

The period of relative calm that followed the president's proclamation was broken in 1794 by an armed attack upon the house of General John Neville, the federal excise inspector for western Pennsylvania. Forcing the federal troops guarding the house to surrender, insurgents ransacked and burned the property to the ground. Within several weeks more ambitious plans were laid by the rebels including the interception of the federal mails and an attack upon Pittsburgh to seize the garrison's military equipment and ammunition. The threat of violence by the rebels against Pittsburgh and the apparent escalation of lawlessness convinced a number of more moderate westerners that the situation required some action to prevent large-scale disruption and bloodshed. At a climactic meeting at Braddock's Field in August, 1794, a moderate delegation from nearby Pittsburgh met with the radicals and agreed to support the cause of resistance to the excise and to banish certain local supporters of the tax.[12] Thus Pittsburgh was spared and immediate violence prevented, but there was no indication that the rebels would be checked in their opposition to the excise. Their resistance and refusal to obey federal law continued to present a menacing challenge to the Washington administration and the authority of the new Constitution.

The use of violence by the whiskey rebels, as members of an aggrieved minority protecting their interests, was part of a long and established practice in eighteenth-century America, according to Pauline Maier, who describes in *From Resistance to Revolution* colonial uprisings in which "insurgents defended the urgent interests of their communities when lawful authorities failed to act." In the mid-eighteenth century, for example, she points to large-scale rural insurrections in New Jersey, as well as the Carolinas, where the objective was "to punish outlaws, secure land titles, or prevent the abuses of public officials only after efforts to work through established procedures failed, and the colonists became convinced that justice and security had to be imposed by the people directly." This intervention by the people to protect their interests, however, Maier categorizes as "*extra-institutional*" rather than "*anti-institutional*," since it provided society an instrument for action in the absence of law or as a result of the inability of government to cope with a particular problem.[13] The Whiskey Rebellion was part of this tradition.

The political mood of the country in the 1790s, with the exaggerated suspicions and fears political opponents had of one another[14] as well as the custom stemming from colonial days of resorting to violence as a political instrument, seriously lessened the chance for a peaceful settlement of the Whiskey Rebellion. When the news arrived in Philadelphia in the summer of 1794 of the armed attack upon General Neville's house, most members of the administration would have agreed with a correspondent from Pittsburgh who described the incident as the start of a "civil war." The immediate response the administration made was to request Pennsylvania's Governor Thomas Mifflin to call up the state militia.[15] Both Mifflin and his chief adviser, Pennsylvania Secretary of State Alexander Dallas, had been hostile to the administration and were reluctant to call state troops to suppress the dissidents. Dallas, responding in the name of the governor, argued that "the military power of the government ought not to be employed until its judiciary authority, after a fair experiment, has proved incompetent to enforce obedience or to punish infractions of the law."[16] Washington then decided against the immediate use of troops and settled upon a plan that included issuing a proclamation ordering the rebels to disperse, setting up a federal commission to begin talks with the insurgents and sending a preliminary alert to the militia forces in four other states.[17]

The commissioners' mission was not successful. After a number of meetings with the insurgents, the delegates concluded that although the extremists among the rebels were in the minority, they had a coercive power over the majority and that "the Authority of the Laws will not be *universally and perfectly* restored, without military Coercion."[18] In the meantime, the Washington administration had quietly gone ahead to mobilize a force of 15,000 men to suppress the insurrection. This action had been spurred by rumors of secession threats and of appeals for British support. In addition, the columns of a Philadelphia newspaper critical of the Washington administration, the *General Advertiser,* seemed to signal growing sympathy for the rebels: "Shall Pennsylvania be converted into a human slaughter house because the dignity of the United States will not admit of conciliatory measures? Shall torrents of blood be spilled to support an odious excise system?"[19] All of these factors appeared to indicate to the Washington administration that the situation was getting out of control and the only safe course of action for the federal government would be to use force to re-establish law and order in western Pennsylvania.

Troops from Virginia, Maryland, New Jersey, and Pennsylvania under the command of Virginia's Governor Henry Lee were dispatched into the western Pennsylvania counties to suppress the insurrection. Joining the expeditionary force were the president and Hamilton, although the former soon returned to Philadelphia. Hamilton, however, stayed with the army: "Twas very important there should be no mistake in the management of the affair—and I *might* contribute to prevent one." His enthusiasm for the coercive action was scarcely contained. The show of strength and will by the federal government, he believed, would ultimately mean "that the insurrection will do us a great deal of good and add to the solidity of every thing in this country."[20]

Hamilton was not to be disappointed. With the advance of the army into the West, the spirit of insurrection wilted, with many of the more outspoken leaders fleeing into the western interior. Westerners repented, gathering at meetings to promise "obedience to the existing laws" and pledge support for "the civil authority and all officers in the lawful exercise of their respective duties." In the aftermath most of the dissidents who were eventually brought to trial were acquitted because of lack of evidence. The two who were found guilty were finally pardoned.[21]

Closely tied to the Whiskey Rebellion in the minds of Washington, Hamilton, and most of their supporters were the Democratic-Republican Societies. These societies, according to historian Eugene P. Link, were the intellectual and institutional heirs of the American Revolultion whose popularly based, direct-action organizations, such as the Sons of Liberty and Committees of Correspondence, had acted as enforcers of the whig orthodoxy and patriot committees of vigilance.[22]

Largely formed in 1793 and 1794 to serve as institutional intermediaries between the government and the people, the Democratic-Republican Societies played an important role in articulating grievances.[23] Specifically, the members were drawn together by three general complaints. They were: (1) that the new government under the Constitution was unresponsive to its citizenry, (2) that the deferential style of representation, as outlined by Madison in *Federalist* 10, was inadequate to reflect the diversity of backgrounds, interests, and desires of the American people and (3) that some means, theretofore not provided for in the Constitution, was needed to collect, channel, and formulate public grievances so they would receive a full and sympathetic hearing. As one proponent of the societies argued, "The security of the people against any unwarrantable stretch of power" in a republic should not be "confined to the check which a constitution affords" nor to the "periodical return of elections; but rests also on a jealous examination of all the proceedings of administration."[24]

While Washington and Hamilton undoubtedly exaggerated the extent of the connection between the Democratic-Republican Societies and the Whiskey Rebellion, it is clear that western Pennsylvania rebels and members of the societies had a common purpose. The whiskey rebels, by resorting to "extra-institutional" means—that is, armed resistance to obnoxious laws—also were raising very clearly for the Americans of 1794 the questions of how and in what form opposition should be manifested against the established authority in a republic, and what limitations there should be upon this opposition as well as upon the constituted authority itself.

Thus, both the rebels and members of the societies were exploring the functions, role, and limits of opposition to the government in a democratic society. And although virtually all the clubs, as well as most political leaders, denounced the violence in western Pennsylvania and there is no evidence that the Democratic-Republican societies as institutions fomented the outbreak, it is true that some members of the Washington County society in western Pennsylvania did actively participate in the insurrection.[25] Furthermore, the societies did agree with the westerners' assessment of the excise. Nonetheless, they argued that ''in a democracy a majority ought in all cases to govern.'' Therefore, since the Constitution ''emanated from the people,'' it was seen as essential that ''unjust and oppressive laws, and bad measures'' be remedied by constitutional means and ''that every other appeal but to the constitution itself, except in cases of extremity'' should be considered ''improper and dangerous.''[26]

Majority rule, members of the Democratic clubs argued, was an inviolable principle at the heart of the American political system. The Constitution, however, and the operation of the federal government under its authority, made no provision, created no machinery to implement and to insure ''majority rule.'' In fact, the checks and balances between governmental institutions, the indirect election of senators and the president, and the division of sovereignty between the state and national governments all worked against any kind of simple majority rule. But it was not clear from the writings of the club members how the sentiments of the majority were to be determined, let alone implemented. And other than eschewing extraconstitutional action ''except in cases of extremity,'' the societies were also rather vague on how a minority would gain redress under such a system of majority rule and did little to define ''cases of extremity.'' What they did seem to be saying was that the old deferential style of politics, where the gentlemanly elite, after being filtered ''through a federal sieve into political leadership''[27] and being responsible for formulating and defining the public good, was inadequate as a system of representation.

Some western Pennsylvania opponents of the whiskey rebels did, however, attempt to spell out when armed resistance to the constituted authority was justifiable. At a September, 1794, meeting of Fayette County citizens led by Albert Gallatin, among others, resolutions were drafted that declared ''resistance by force against oppression'' to be ''lawful only when no legal and constitutional remedy is within the reach of the people, and when the evils arising from the oppression are excessive, when they far surpass those that must ensue from the resistance.'' This is what gave moral legitimacy to both the French and American Revolutions, it was pointed out. The situation in western Pennsylvania, however, was seen as different because that constituency was represented in the legislature and ''every mode of redress'' in a ''republican form of government'' was available. Therefore, under such circumstances, it was avowed, the "violence and resistance" was no more than an "attempt of a minority to overrule, and . . . to oppress the majority of the people of the United States."[28]

By late fall 1794, amid an outpouring of popular support for his policy, Washington, obviously still deeply troubled by the Pennsylvania violence, renewed the controversy by publicly denouncing the Democratic-Republican Societies for encouraging the whiskey rebels. By linking the societies with the insurrection and equating peaceful opposition to governmental policy with armed rebellion, Washington extended and deepened the political dimensions of the conflict. In his annual address to Congress, the president condemned as hypocritical and self-serving the resolutions of the Democratic-Republican Societies critical of the insurrection.[29] Privately, he was even more outspoken. "My mind is so perfectly convinced," he wrote, "that, if these self-created societies cannot be discountenanced, they will destroy the government of this country." The great danger of the societies he saw as not so much their "design" but rather their "tendency" and proclaimed that he would "be extremely sorry . . . if Mr. M[adiso]n *from any cause whatsoever* should get entangled with them, or their politics."[30]

These public and private statements of Washington exhibited a dangerous inclination to connect indiscriminately the various modes of opposition to his administration. Thus the armed rebellion of the whiskey insurrectionists was viewed by Washington as merely a violent manifestation of the equally "subversive" ideas of the Democratic-Republican Societies. Even fellow Virginian James Madison, who had led the opposition in Congress to a number of administration proposals, did not escape suspicion. To the embattled chief executive, the whiskey rebels, the Democratic-Republican societies, as well as Madison and his congressional allies were all threatening the stability of the republic and challenging the authority of the federal government.

Washington's denunciation of the "self-created societies" set off a vigorous debate within the House of Representatives. Supporters of the president sponsored a resolution that condemned the societies as "misrepresenting the conduct of the Government, and disturbing the operation of the laws, and . . . by deceiving and inflaming the ignorant and the weak," having undoubtedly "stimulated and urged the insurrection." Washington's critics, wary of clashing openly with the popular chief executive and of defending the Democratic-Republican Societies, took the position that the House should ignore the societies because to condemn them would "raise them into much more importance than they possibly could have acquired if they had not been distinguished by a vote of censure from that House."[31]

One supporter of the motion to denounce the societies maintained that such organizations might be needed in France, "where Despotism, inpregnable to public opinion, had reigned—where no channel opened a sympathy by Representation with the great body of the nation." The United States, however, was a totally different case, he argued, for there was an "immense body of public functionaries . . . elected immediately by the people, or by their electors, in a Constitutional mode" and which included "every description of Legislators, Councils, Governors, Courts, Jurors, and Sheriffs." Thus, he concluded, the "whole country is full of well-constituted organs of the People's will."[32]

But how responsive these "public functionaries" were to the popular will was the key question. One defender of the societies pointed out that certain sections of the country were already the beneficiaries of more institutionalized forms of democratic expression, particularly New England with its town meetings. But while town meetings might be "the proper vehicles for communication of political ideas" and a means of facilitating the flow of information between voter and office holder in populated districts of the country, in other regions, such as the South, such institutions were impractical "because the population was too thin and too widely scattered." Therefore, Americans in the more rural and thinly settled areas needed institutions like the societies for they "had to make the best of it . . . and meet and deliberate, no matter where, whenever they found a convenient opportunity."[33]

The acerbic Fisher Ames, representative from Massachusetts, attacked the notion that the Democratic-Republican Societies had a legitimate role in representing the popular will and vigorously defended the concept of deferential representation. In an impassioned speech on the floor of the House, he denied that Democratic clubs might play the same role as New England town meetings. If the "people have grievances," he declared, were "they to be brought to a knowledge of them only by clubs? Clubs may find out more complaints against the laws than the sufferers themselves had dreamed of." It was absurd to suppose, Ames argued, that the clubs were useful as a vehicle for dispensing "political information." In addition to spreading "jealousies, suspicions and accusations of the Government" and fomenting "daring outrages against the social order and the authority of the laws," the societies, he charged, "have arrogantly pretended sometimes to be the people, and sometimes the guardians, the champions of the people," and to "affect to feel more zeal for a popular Government, and to enforce more respect for Republican principles, than the *real* Representatives are admitted to entertain."

Ames defended the deferential system of representation with its notion that a selfless elite was best able to divine the public good. The societies, on the other hand, the vitriolic Yankee charged, would not and could not provide a substitute for this kind of representation, and in fact since the total membership in the clubs was quite small, any action they took in the name of the majority was plain and simple usurpation. Thus, he went on, any suggestion that the societies were more representative of the people than the lawfully elected representatives was blasphemous. In the final analysis, Ames concluded, the societies were destructive to republican government, for the "continual contest of one organized body against another would produce the alternate extremes of anarchy and excessive rigor of Government.'' Therefore, Ames pleaded, it was essential that the members of the House of Representatives support the president in his efforts to enforce the law and to suppress insurrection.[34]

For the most part those who were opposed to the denunciation of the societies avoided the more general arguments about the nature of representative government. Instead the assertion that the societies were responsible for fomenting the insurrection was challenged for lack of evidence. Madison, however, after deferring to the president and declaring that Congress should not have entered into the discussion, maintained that the very nature of republican government required ''that the censorial power is in the people over the Government, and not in the Government over the people.'' And since he had great confidence in the ''good sense and patriotism of the people,'' no great harm would come from the societies' expression of opinion, since ultimately they would ''stand or fall by the public opinion.''[35] Finally, after lengthy debate the initial resolution condemning the societies was defeated, and a more moderate one, defending public order and expressing concern ''that any misrepresentations whatever, of the Government and its proceedings, either by individuals or combinations of men, should have been made,'' passed.[36]

Privately the opposition leadership was outraged by Washington's action and the support for it in the House of Representatives. Jefferson regarded the ''denunciation of the democratic societies'' as ''one of the extraordinary acts of boldness of which we have seen so many from the faction of monocrats.'' Madison believed that it was ''the greatest error of his [Washington's] political life.'' He particularly was alarmed by the attempt in Congress ''to connect the democratic Societies with the odium of the insurrection,'' and to link opponents of the administration ''in Congress with those Societies.''[37]

The same issues of representation that were being raised in the House debate also were being discussed at length in public throughout the winter and spring of 1794–1795. Essayists critically examined the nature of the representative system and questioned whether the will of the community was being adequately represented. The discussion of these questions indicated a growing awareness and appreciation, at least among those who were becoming increasingly critical of the Washington administration, of the pressing need for some sort of mediating institution between the people and the government, whether it be Democratic clubs or proto-political parties.

The ''Watchman,'' an essayist in the Philadelphia *General Advertiser*, defended the role of the Democratic-Republican Societies as communicators of political information. ''Tell me, if you can,'' he challenged, ''ye advocates for ignorance, in what manner you communicate information to the mass of people, but by forming them into town meetings or societies?'' Without such institutions the public will cannot be determined, he argued, and

government has no solid basis. It is not in the power, of one fourth of our citizens to obtain information, by ordinary means—but in a town meeting or society, every man may, at a very trifling expense, know and judge of the conduct of the agent he has entrusted—he will soon find out, from the votes of the house, the language of the debates—the strictures of the press—and the remarks of his neighbors—whether he is faithfully served or basely betrayed.[38]

Thus the "Watchman" as well as other commentators believed it was necessary for some intervening body or institution to be created to translate and transmit the public will to the legislator and to report the actions of the legislator to the public.

The German Republican Society of Philadelphia made perhaps the most eloquent and forceful statement in defense of the society as such an institution. "All governments," it argued, were

more or less combinations against the people; they are states of violence against individual liberty, originating from man's imperfection and vice, and as rulers have no more virtue than the ruled, the equilibrium between them can only be preserved by proper attention and association; for the power of government can only be kept within its constituted limits by the display of a power equal to itself, the collected sentiment of the people. Solitary opinions have little weight with men whose views are unfair; but the voice of many strikes them with awe. To obtain a connected voice, associations of some sort are necessary, no matter by what means they are designated. The checks and balances of government are inventions to keep the people in subordination, a reaction of some sort is necessary, therefore, to keep up the equipoise, between the people and the government.

And to maintain the "equipoise" or balance between the people and the government, the Philadelphia club contended that town or township meetings or associations like the Democratic Societies were needed.[39]

Thus by the spring of 1795 on the eve of the controversy over the soon-to-be released Jay's Treaty, there was a growing acceptance within the ranks of the opponents to the Washington administration of the necessity for some type of "extraconstitutional" organization to express and reflect the public's will. To Washington and many of his supporters, the idea was an anathema, for it was believed that institutions that were interposed between the people and their elected officials represented an intolerable threat to the government and the Constitution. Elected representatives, Washington and his followers felt, individually could best determine the will of their constituents and any interposing body was alien and hostile to the natural harmony and balance established by the Constitution. Thus, it was no accident that Washington and his supporters linked the whiskey rebels with the members of the Democratic-Republican Societies as well as with the congressional opposition to the administration. All, by different means and with varying degrees of intensity, seemed to be challenging the authority of the government and weakening its ability to govern.

Two studies, one written almost two decades ago by Jacob Cooke and the other a more recent one by Rudolph M. Bell, depict the Whiskey Rebellion as a concluding chapter of the American Revolution with its excess of liberty and political fragmentation.[40] The insurrection, according to Cooke, was fostered by "self-seeking politicians," and based on an unfortunate "literal reading of the Revolutionary creed which equated government with oppression, order with tyranny, rulers—even popularly elected ones—with despots."[41]

Bell maintains that the Whiskey Rebellion marked a dramatic shift in the "debate over limits of government authority." From the Declaration of Independence down to the insurrection, he claims, the discussion centered primarily on the question of "external restraints," with many Americans believing as well as acting on the premise that although "a community might form a civil government to meet common needs" it still "retained the right to alter, in fundamental ways . . . the government it had established." As a result, Bell finds, "anti-statism and suspicion of delegated power" to be "widespread in the 1780s," but after the Western Pennsylvania insurrection, "the balance shifted sharply," and Americans "abandoned the question of restraints on federal power (except through states' rights) in order to concentrate fully on attaining power, that is, on gaining control of a regime unfettered by external limits."[42]

There is no doubt that the Whiskey Rebellion and the debate that followed were tied to the American Revolution, with its undermining of all constituted authority. But, more important, the uprising was also a part of the American struggle to come to grips with republicanism and the nature of representative government. Gordon Wood writes that representation "explained the uniqueness of the American politics," and was, in fact, "the foundation of all of men's ideas about their relation to government."[43]

But the ratification of the Constitution did not end the debate. Americans in 1794, and afterwards, continued to hold different and conflicting notions about the nature of representation. Many citizens, perhaps, were beginning to fear that Benjamin Rush's conclusions drawn at the time of the writing of the Constitution were unhappily accurate. "It is often said that 'the sovereign and all other power is seated *in* the people.' This idea is unhappily expressed. It should be—'all power is derived *from* the people.' They possess it only on the days of their elections. After this, it is the property of their rulers, nor can they exercise it or resume it, unless it is abused.'"[44] Compounding the problem was the enduring legacy of suspicion many Americans continued to harbor against the new government and the Constitution. Despite the fact that the legitimacy of the Constitution was not seriously challenged, the warning issued by the anti-Federalist "Philadelphiensis" that the opposition was "against the fundamentals of the constitution itself" continued to haunt and influence the political debates of the 1790s.

Ironically, both the Federalists and the Republicans viewed one another as hostile to the Constitution and implacable enemies of republican government. Only after the Republicans had established political hegemony and the Constitution had survived the critical tests of the transference of political power from one proto-party to another and an unpopular and almost ruinous war, would politics be conducted within a framework of consensus and mutual trust. And only at that time could it be assumed that all political disputes would be resolved within the boundaries established by the Constitution.

Therefore the Whiskey Rebellion was part of the process Americans went through in search of a more democratic form of representation. This process continued well into the nineteenth century and beyond, and was characterized by insurrection, threats of secession, and the forming of proto-political parties. The establishment of a balanced, stable, two-party system during the Jacksonian Era did not, of course, end the search. Popular third parties, the reforms of the Progressives (initiative, referendum and recall), direct primaries, as well as the controversial political action committees all have been part of the quest for a more democratic polity.

NOTES

1. As quoted by James Thomas Flexner, *George Washington and the New Nation, 1783–1793* (Boston, 1970), 3:151.

2. See Carl Van Doren, *The Great Rehearsal, the Story of the Making and Ratifying of the Constitution of the United States* (New York, 1961), for an excellent discussion of the "Federal Procession." See esp. pp. 239–49.

3. Gordon S. Wood, *The Creation of the American Republic, 1776–1787* (Chapel Hill, N.C., 1965), pp. 164, 173.

4. Herbert J. Storing, *The Complete Anti-Federalist* (Chicago, 1981), 3:158.

5. *Ibid.*, 136.

6. William D. Barber, "Among the Most *Techy Articles of Civil Police*': Federal Taxation and the Adoption of the Whiskey Excise," *William and Mary Quarterly* 25 (January 1968), 60–61.

7. George Gibbs, ed., *Memoirs of the Administrations of Washington and John Adams, edited from the Papers of Oliver Wolcott, Secretary of State* (New York, 1846), 1:146–47; Henry M. Brackenridge, *History of the Western Insurrection in Western Pennsylvania Commonly Called the Whiskey Insurrection, 1794* (Pittsburgh, 1859), p. 17; Jacob E. Cooke in his "The Whiskey Insurrection: A Re-evaluation," *Pennsylvania History* 30 (July 1963), 316–46, plays down the economic factors as motives for the insurrection. The point should be made, however, that the excise was, in many ways symbolic—it symbolized to many the section's political impotence and reaffirmed the fears that not only would the section be neglected (as apparently borne out by the inaction of the government on the Mississippi question), but also discriminated against.

8. Leland D. Baldwin, *Whiskey Rebels: The Story of a Frontier Uprising* (Pittsburgh, 1939), pp. 71–72.

9. Harold C. Syrett, et al., eds., *The Papers of Alexander Hamilton* (New York, 1967), 12:308–09n.; Gibbs, *Memoirs* 1:146–48, emphasis added.

10. Alexander Hamilton to George Washington, September 1, 1792, and Hamilton to John Jay, September 3, 1792, in Syrett, ed., *Papers of Hamilton* 12:311–12, 316–17.

11. For an excellent account of the Washington administration's decision to use force against the whiskey rebels, see Richard H. Kohn, "The Washington Administration's Decision to Crush the Whiskey Rebellion," *Journal of American History* 59 (December 1972), 567–84.

12. Brackenridge, *History of the Western Insurrection*, pp. 79–151; Baldwin, *Whiskey*

Rebels, pp. 129–71; John C. Miller, *The Federalist Era, 1789–1801* (New York, 1963), p. 157.

13. Pauline Maier, *From Resistance to Revolution: Colonial Radicals and the Development of American Opposition to Britain, 1765–1776* (New York, 1972), pp. 4–5.

14. See, for example, John R. Howe, Jr., "Republican Thought and the Political Violence of the 1790s," *American Quarterly* 19 (Summer 1967), 148–65; Marshall Smelser, "The Jacobin Phrenzy: Federalism and the Menace of Liberty, Equality, and Fraternity," *Review of Politics* 13 (1951), 457–82; and Smelser, "Jacobin Phrenzy: the Menace of Monarchy, Plutocracy, and Anglophobia, 1789–1798," *Review of Politics* 21 (1959), 239–58. See also J. Wendell Knox, *Conspiracy in American Politics, 1787–1815* (New York, 1972), and, for a statement about a later period, see James Arthur Mumper, "The Jeffersonian Image in the Federalist Mind, 1801–1809; Jefferson's Administration from the Federalist Point of View," Ph.D. diss., University of Virginia, 1966. The most recent and best discussion of the Jeffersonians' perception of the politics of the 1790s is Lance Banning, *The Jeffersonian Persuasion, Evolution of a Party Ideology* (Ithaca, N.Y., 1978).

15. Kohn, "The Washington Administration's Decision," pp. 571–72.

16. George M. Dallas, ed., *Life and Writings of A. J. Dallas* (Philadelphia, 1871), p. 150.

17. Kohn, "The Washington Administration's Decision," pp. 575–76; Baldwin, *Whiskey Rebels,* p. 185.

18. As quoted in Baldwin, *Whiskey Rebels,* p. 198.

19. Philadelphia *General Advertiser,* August 12, 1794; Kohn, "The Washington Administration's Decision," p. 578.

20. Hamilton to Angelica Church, October 23, 1794, in Syrett, ed., *Papers of Hamilton* 17:340.

21. Philadelphia *General Advertiser,* November 1, 1794; see November 8, 1794, for similar resolutions; see also Baldwin, *Whiskey Rebels,* pp. 234–35, 262–64.

22. Philip S. Foner, *The Democratic–Republican Societies, 1790–1800: A Documentary Sourcebook of Constitutions, Declarations, Addresses, Resolutions, and Toasts* (Westport, Conn., 1976) p. 4. Eugene Perry Link, *Democratic Republican Societies, 1790–1800* (New York, 1942), pp. 19–35.

23. Link, *Democratic Republican Societies,* estimated that thirty-five societies were formed by the end of 1794, and forty-two by the end of the decade. See pp. 13–15 for a listing of the societies.

24. Philadelphia *General Advertiser,* May 16, 1794.

25. Foner, ed., *Democratic Republican Societies,* p. 29; see also Link, *Democratic Republican Societies,* pp. 145–48.

26. Foner, *Democratic Republican Societies,* pp. 88–89.

27. Wood, *Creation of the American Republic,* p. 615.

28. Declaration of the Committees of Fayette County, September, 1794, in Henry Adams, ed., *The Writings of Albert Gallatin* (Philadelphia, 1879), 1:6.

29. Sixth Annual Address to Congress, November 19, 1794, in John C. Fitzpatrick, ed., *The Writings of George Washington* (Washington, D.C., 1940), 34:29.

30. Washington to Edmund Randolph, October 16, 1794, in *ibid.* 34:2–4. See also William Miller, "The Democratic Societies and the Whiskey Insurrection," *Pennsylvania Magazine of History and Biography* 62 (July 1938), 334–36, for the president's position.

31. *Annals of Congress,* 3d Cong., 1793–1795, pp. 899–906; James Madison to

Thomas Jefferson, November 30, 1794, in Madison Papers, Library of Congress; Madison to James Monroe, December 4, 1794, in Gaillard Hunt, ed., *The Writings of James Madison* (New York, 1906), 6:219–27.

32. *Annals of Congress*, 3d Cong., 1793–1795, pp. 906–07.

33. *Ibid.*, pp. 913–14.

34. *Ibid.*, pp. 921–32, emphasis added.

35. *Ibid.*, pp. 911–12, 934–35.

36. *Ibid.*, p. 947. See Madison to Jefferson, November 30, 1794, in Madison Papers, Library of Congress, for a report on the debate and vote in the House of Representatives.

37. Jefferson to Madison, December 28, 1794, in Paul Leicester Ford, ed., *The Works of Thomas Jefferson* (New York, 1904–05), 8:156–59; Madison to Jefferson, November 30, 1794, in Madison Papers, Library of Congress; Madison to Monroe, December 4, 1794, in Hunt, ed., *Writings of Madison* 6:219–27.

38. Philadelphia *General Advertiser*, February 28, 1795.

39. *Ibid.*, December 27, 1794.

40. Cooke, "The Whiskey Insurrection"; and Rudolph M. Bell, *Party and Faction in American Politics, The House of Representatives, 1789–1801* (Westport, Conn., 1973).

41. Cooke, "The Whiskey Insurrection," p. 345.

42. Bell, *Party and Faction*, p. 53.

43. Wood, *The Creation of the American Republic*, pp. 596, 185.

44. As quoted in *ibid.*, pp. 373–74.

Philadelphia's Manufacturers and the Excise Tax of 1794: The Forging of the Jeffersonian Coalition

The Whiskey Insurrection in Pennsylvania is a familiar event. Supposedly, the insurrection, arising from opposition to the federal excise tax, was centered in the four western counties. Individualism, frontier spirit, and economic deprivation were the underlying causes for the uprising. The tax revolt is further regarded as an important chapter in the constitutional and economic history of the early republic. Other opponents of the excise in the other sections of the United States—Kentucky, western Virginia, Carolina backcountry and Georgia—are depicted in the same agrarian mold.[1] Historians have left the impression that the farmers of rural America were the only interest group to face economic hardship when the national government sought to develop revenues by the imposition of excise taxes in 1791 and 1794. Such an interpretation has prevailed because historians of the Federalist Era have not considered all of the provisions of the Revenue Acts of 1794. Most important, they have overlooked the existence of significant agitation in the seaboard towns over the extension of the excise.[2]

This chapter explores the contours of urban opposition to the introduction of indirect taxes in Philadelphia during the years 1794–1797. Because that protest differed in form and content from the excise rebellion in rural America, the administration of George Washington did not use military force in the spring and summer of 1794 to put down an urban insurrection. But the city's protests, including petition campaigns, meetings, and electioneering, generated consequences for the Federalist party that probably exceeded the political significance of the rural rebellion. Indeed, the agitation over the excise taxes in urban America helped to forge the Democratic-Republican movement in Philadelphia by allow-

This article was presented in a somewhat abbreviated form at the forty-ninth meeting of the Pennsylvania Historical Association held at Wilkes-Barre on October 17–18, 1980. The author wishes to thank Steven R. Boyd and Alfred F. Young for their helpful suggestions.

ing Republicans to draw on the support of self-conscious occupational groups who felt economically threatened by the excise tax placed on manufacturers.[3]

In 1789, Philadelphia was an important manufacturing center and promoter of mechanical arts, the hub of a regional economy and the principal commercial entrepot of the country.[4] The city contained large-scale manufacturers, small-scale manufacturers, and rank-and-file artisans. Exclusive of carpenters, masons, and other skilled workers, the city and suburbs of Northern Liberties and Southwark, with a total population in 1790 of 43,000, had some 2,200 persons (or one-quarter of the adult males) who might properly be identified as manufacturers—that is, individuals who were engaged in the production of such articles as beer, distilled spirits, carriages, flour products, hats, leather, pearl, ash, rope, shoes, sugar, textiles, timber, and tobacco products. At least one-half of these articles were produced locally and sold in both an internal and external market.[5]

The manufacturers' prominence came as the result of continuous growth and development since the 1760s. The nonimportation movements of the 1760s and 1770s stressed the development of household and other predominantly small-scale manufacturers. Before the American Revolution, Philadelphians depended upon England for the bulk of their manufactured goods, but during the immediate postwar years the "industrial sector" challenged the "commercial-maritime" sector for attention and sought the support and patronage of the Pennsylvania General Assembly for loans, subsidies, and other preferential treatment.[6] Many large-scale manufacturers also formed partnerships in order better to serve the needs of a growing urban center. This non-British capitalization—along with the state's aid of protective duties, use of water power, and the adoption of modern techniques of production and marketing—was most conspicuous in the brewing, carriage-making, distilling, snuff-making, sugar refining, and tanning industries.[7] The long struggle for economic independence coincided with the struggle for political independence.[8]

Before one analyzes how this economic group was tested in the 1790s, one must understand what is meant by the term "large-scale manufacturer." Laboring in the aforementioned industries and running a manufactory, the manufacturer either worked for himself or with a partner. He thus manufactured outside the small shop and garret, usually employed journeymen and workers for a wage, and where possible used newer methods and tools. The large-scale manufacturer who combined the functions of merchant and artisan was often required to make a considerable investment in plant and equipment. In the industries of snuff-making and sugar refining, for example, the leading manufacturers were retailers as well as wholesalers, filled orders at prearranged prices, and exposed themselves to foreign competition and to the risks of owning raw materials, stocking goods, extending credit, and operating in a modern marketplace subject to price and market fluctuations. In short, these were independent businessmen who needed capital to operate and who sought to improve their station by taking advantage of the buoyant economy of the leading seaport. By 1800, many of the large-scale manufacturers had become members of the economic elite of Philadelphia.[9]

These manufacturers increased their political participation when economic interests took sides on issues involving the nature and functions of the national government. For instance, on the eve of George Washington's inauguration as president of the United States in April 1789, Philadelphia's manufacturers stood solidly behind the Federalist party. They not only were an important voting bloc in favor of the Federal Constitution, but also had provided support for Federalist candidates in the first congressional and presidential elections. In joining the party of Federalism, the manufacturers demonstrated their belief that the new national government would advance the interests of home manufacturers and foster a self-sufficient American economy. Indeed, a strong national government would put an end to the conflicting legislation of separate states and offer manufacturers better protection against imports. There also was some anticipation of discriminatory duties on British tonnage and goods imported on foreign vessels.[10]

The buoyant enthusiasm of the manufacturers and their sense of the dawning of a "new era" under the banner of protection was evident on July 4, 1788, when Philadelphians commemorated the ratification of the Federal Constitution.[11] Figuring prominently in the "Federal Procession" of leading citizens and occupational groups were members of eighty-eight trades who organized and marched in separate groups, carrying "flags, devices and machines." One such machine was a large stage sponsored by the Manufacturing Society on which carding and spinning machines displayed the manufactory of cotton. Among the other groups present were ten brewers, one hundred and fifty coachmakers and their allied branches, twelve distillers, seventy tobacconists, and thirty-six sugar refiners. Outfitted in the dress of their vocations, the manufacturers carried slogans or mottos on banners that read: "Home-brewed is best"; "No tax on American carriages"; and "May government protect us." One of the ten toasts offered honored "the agriculture, manufactures, and commerce of the United States."[12]

The parade, considered by some observers the greatest spectacle in eighteenth-century Philadelphia, testified to the importance of manufacturing in Philadelphia's multifaceted economy. This grand celebration indicated how far the respective trades had come in both economic and political esteem and showed the ambitions and expectations of the various groups. Indeed, the parade could be viewed as part of the lobbying effort of Philadelphia's manufacturers who wanted a federal tariff shield to protect them from the British goods flooding the Philadelphia market. Aided by the well-organized Pennsylvania Society for the Encouragement of Manufacturers and the Useful Arts, an advocate since 1785 of duties on competitive imports and the admittance of scarce raw materials duty-free, the manufacturing community during the First Congress also lobbied for protection directly with "federal" representatives Thomas Fitzsimmons and George Clymer.[13]

Obviously, the expectations of the manufacturers had to be weighed against the complicated demands of other interest groups. Some sectors of the urban economy had long-standing ties to Britain, and others had developed newer markets to the Orient, France, and, by means of navigation of the Mississippi River, the West. Capitalization of economic activity and access to credit also varied among groups. Some individuals (the house carpenter, butcher, and baker) sold goods in the naturally protected local customer's market and others (hatters, ironmongers, shoemakers, sugar refiners, and tobacconists) competed with British imports. And, as Jacob Price has argued, certain occupations fell in both the industrial and service sectors and worked for the local and external markets.[14] Placed against such a background of economic diversity, one might well understand why the manufacturers experienced only modest success in protecting their interests.

The nation's first tariff act of 1789 epitomized the manufacturers' ambiguous position in the government's hierarchy of interests. The act enumerated a long list of specific duties, and five classes of goods carrying *ad valorem* rates. Among those articles listed for protection were beer, carriages, cordage, shoes, sugars, snuff, and tobacco products.[15] Manufacturers in the industrial sector immediately criticized the act's encouragement and protection clause as providing either not enough or the wrong type of protection. For instance, early in the second session of the First Congress, Philadelphia distillers complained that a "greater difference" of duties should be placed on imports of rum and molasses, and the manufacturers of tobacco products from Philadelphia and New York City petitioned about possible duties being placed on the articles they exported in order to produce revenue to pay for the assumption of state debts.[16] From Philadelphia alone members of at least five other native industries—coachmakers, cordage makers, mustard makers, shipwrights, and tanners—voiced their differences over the original legislation and the attempt to provide further increases in revenue by means of excises.[17] When the tariff law was later amended in the same session to provide for the effectual collection of duties and to increase them by only about 2.5 percent, revenue considerations took precedence over the encouragement and protection to manufacturers.[18]

During the third session of the First Congress, an excise tax, discussed even before the enactment of the tariff of 1789, followed as the "next logical step for the Federalists beyond the existing customs arrangements."[19] Still, during its first years, the Washington administration seemed prepared to favor manufacturers more than merchants and shopkeepers by relying more heavily on customs or tonnage duties than on excise taxes. Secretary of the Treasury Alexander Hamilton, in his 1791 "Report on Manufacturers," proposed to create a city of manufactories in New Jersey.[20] Help was received from Assistant Secretary Tench Coxe of Philadelphia, a merchant and a member of the local Society of Manufacturers.[21] In Philadelphia, however, the industrial experiment, commonly called the S.U.M., did not attract wide support.[22]

Although Hamilton's public image has been that of an advocate of American manufacturing,[23] Philadelphia's manufacturing community early questioned his economic stabilization program because it appeared to forsake a highly developed division of labor as the essence of social progress and economic independence. According to Drew McCoy, "The Report on Manufacturers seems to describe a society ominously reminiscent of the English system that Franklin and the Revolutionaries had rejected."[24] Gradually the worst fears of manufacturers were confirmed: protection against British competition proved inadequate, and reliance upon domestic taxation to produce income increased sharply.[25] At a time when American agriculture and commerce were very prosperous, Hamilton's economic stabilization program, which depended upon ties to British manufacturing power, left little room for support to America's manufacturers.[26] Seeking either more protection or the retention of existing schedules, certain classes of manufactures in 1794 faced instead the prospect of being burdened with excise taxes and of having protection subordinated to other national goals.

The first real test of the 1789 Federalist commitment to protect manufacturers, a test also of the political coalition molded during the ratification contest, came during the spring of 1794 when the Washington administration also faced an unexpected crisis in foreign affairs. News of the massive British depredations against American ships and of a British threat to renew Indian war on the western frontier angered many Philadelphians.[27] James Madison revived his proposals for discriminatory tonnage duties and restrictions on British trade policies that Federalists had sidetracked in 1789 and again in 1791.[28] Madison's 1794 "commercial resolutions" constituted Congress's response to Britain's failure to enter into a trade agreement with the United States. Thus, the resolves were aimed at forcing Britain to improve her ways, breaking the British monopoly of the import trade, and encouraging American manufacturing and shipbuilding.[29]

Anti-British views were warmly received in Philadelphia, and were echoed by import-export merchant John Swanwick at a series of well-attended mercantile meetings held in Philadelphia on March 8, 15, and 16, 1794.[30] The wealthy Swanwick, a business partner in the firm of Willing, Morris, and Swanwick and a member of the Pennsylvania General Assembly, did not act strictly out of political gain or economic interest. In mid-1790, while still a Federalist, Swanwick authored an article entitled "Thoughts on the Commerce of the United States," in which he insisted that commerce, navigation, agriculture, and manufacturing were mutually dependent.[31] Swanwick called for higher tariff barriers as a way to develop commercial reciprocity and for discrimination against foreign vessels. In 1794 the "merchant-Republicans" and the "manufacturer-Republicans" warmly supported Madison's resolves and they offered numerous alternatives to the policies pursued by the Federalists to American commerce and manufactures.[32]

In addition to the call for commercial retaliation, both state and federal governments responded to the Anglo-American crisis. In Pennsylvania Governor Thomas Mifflin demanded that the harbor along the Delaware River be fortified, stationed an artillery company at Mud Island, and readied the state militia.[33] The Washington administration sent John Jay as a special envoy to Great Britain to seek ways to improve relations, and, with the approval of Congress, authorized an expensive national defense program, including the construction of six frigates, the raising of an army of 15,000, and the placing of 80,000 militia in a state of readiness.[34] These expenditures, along with the possible drying up of import duties owing to dislocations in trade, raised the prospect of a federal deficit unless new taxes were levied.

If the Washington administration asked Congress to raise revenues to pay for the new defense programs and the interest on the public debt, it faced major difficulties. Five years of experience had shown that tax measures were neither easily written into law nor administered, since the choices were limited to direct taxes (those on real estate, general assessments on property of all kinds, and on polls) and indirect taxes (excises and custom duties). Taxes were also still a battleground between federal and state governments.[35] The issue was drawn, however, when Secretary Hamilton, siding with those who believed existing revenues would be inadequate by at least $621,000, recommended the enlargement of excise taxes.[36]

The Revenue Act of 1794, which passed in the House of Representatives as a series of separate tax bills during the first nine days of June, is an overlooked piece of tax legislation.[37] Specifically, a duty of eight cents per pound upon all snuff manufactured for sale and a duty of two cents per pound was placed upon all refined sugar. Drawbacks equal to the duty paid were allowed on all snuff and refined sugar exported, provided the quantity exported was not worth less than twelve dollars in value. On account of the duties paid on raw sugar imports, three cents per pound was added to the drawback allowed on refined sugar.[38] There also was a carriage duty or rate that ranged from two to ten dollars, depending upon the type of vehicle.[39] Other legislation in 1794 reduced import duties on carriages and parts of carriages by nearly 70 percent from 15 to 4.5 percent *ad valorem*.[40] Duties were placed on wines and foreign distilled spiritous liquors sold by retailers, who also had to obtain a five-dollar license.[41] Likewise, property sold at auction received a levy based on a schedule of rates for all auction sales, and the auctioneers had to obtain a license.[42] Warmly debated but not favorably acted upon were proposals to tax stock transfers, to adopt a stamp tax, and to increase tonnage duties.[43]

The manner in which the duties were to be levied and collected by federal revenue officials, a continuation of procedures begun in 1791, troubled the manufacturers. In most cases manufacturers had to give a $5,000 bond as a way to ensure accurate reporting of the daily quantity of production of the article. Forfeiture of a bond would result if the manufacturer omitted an entry or neglected to pay the required duties. Inspectors also were to be given six hours' notice when the article was to be exported. The large-scale manufacturers characterized as excessive and expensive regulation the inspection of exports, along with the oaths, fines, court costs, and so forth.[44] Finally, while the revenue bill of 1794 did not cover all of the goods or articles manufactured in Philadelphia, there existed a possibility that in the future other articles could be taxed under this system.[45] Remembering the Boston port bill of 1774, the opponents to the excise legislation argued that "if the system of excise is not early checked, it will hamstring, in turn, every manufacture in America."[46]

Philadelphia's manufacturers considered the excise system a "real grievance" because it represented a revised policy. Manufacturers believed that they should receive special encouragement (protection) from state and national government in order to insure the nation's economic independence from England. They were also not convinced of their ability to pass on the extra cost to the consumer. Certainly they were not about to remain in a political alliance that provided direct benefits to merchants and not to manufacturers. Thus, because the excise threatened, either directly or potentially, the interests of virtually every manufacturer in Philadelphia, the subject of the enlargement of the excise law proved controversial. In responding to the apparent economic threat and the lack of commitment to develop manufactures, the large-scale manufacturers advanced the same arguments as the opponents of the excise tax placed on distilled spirits in 1791 (namely, that they were being made victims of unconstitutional, discriminatory, and confiscatory taxes).[47] They argued that the state should levy indirect taxes and that the federal excise was more than revenue producing. Drawing upon the 1791 debates of Pennsylvania's General Assembly,[48] the urban critics also concluded that they would never have ratified such a provision in the federal Constitution if they had realized that excise taxes were to "become one of the first, and favorite resources of government."[49] The protest of 1794 took on additional significance because its organizers tied it with other antiadministration protests through the Democratic-Republican clubs, and they abandoned traditional restraints on electioneering by openly campaigning for candidates opposed to the excise. In doing so, they left behind the deferential politics of an earlier age as the manufacturers of Philadelphia sought to participate in society and government as equals of the gentry.[50]

The principal leaders of the excise protest in Philadelphia consisted of a handful of large-scale tobacconists (Gavin Hamilton, Thomas Leiper, and John Hankart) and sugar refiners (Jacob Morgan, J. Dorsey, Frederick A. Muhlenberg, and Isaac and Edward Pennington). Serving together on the local committee that organized the several public meetings held in Philadelphia during May 1794, they also prepared the series of memorials directed to the House, Senate, and President Washington in which Philadelphia's manufacturers of tobacco products and sugar asserted that the excise tax would prove economically destructive to the reasonable profits of their industries and a detriment to the growth of manufacturing throughout the country. A select committee formed to meet with a committee from the Senate to explore tax alternatives. Finally, the city's manufacturers of tobacco and sugar tried to organize a national petition campaign against the excise tax.[51] They attempted to communicate with the manufacturers in New York City, but for unknown reasons a concerted national effort never materialized.

In entering the political arena, these manufacturers demonstrated close and intelligent attention to detail. For instance, the meetings of May 2, 7, and 8 were held at 5 P.M., a time calculated to be most convenient to the journeyman manufacturers or tradesman who labored for about eight to ten dollars per week in these industries. Believing that the only way to defeat the administration's revenue plans was to organize all the manufacturers in and around the city and county of Philadelphia, the organizers drew up an address entitled "EXCISE— Citizens Attend!" which requested the city's large- and small-scale manufacturers to attend a general meeting to be held in the State House yard on 8 May 1794. A special invitation was extended to the manufacturers of malt, hops, beer, ale, cider, starch and hair powder, chocolate, cocoa paste, vinegar, glass, candles, soap, paper and paste board, leather and skins, iron, and all who opposed the excise. Those who gathered at Independence Square unanimously adopted a set of resolves, which condemned the excise and proclaimed "republicanism."[52]

We are fortunate to have a contemporary account of this Philadelphia protest meeting written by Samuel Hodgdon, an army storekeeper for the War Department:

By six o'Clock about three hundred of the lower class of people were assembled, when for want of more respectable characters Colonel Morgan, Mr. Leiper, Neddy Pole and Mr. Pennington wer[e] called on to preside. The meeting being thus organized, without further ceremony the Moderator, Morgan, handed to the Secretary Pennington, a number of resolutions cut and dried—and asked the Mob whether they should be read, all vociferated yes. The Secretary after making apologies for want of better lungs, read the resolutions (which were lengthy) through. Leiper then came forward to address the rable, his speech was worthy of such an orator—he attempted to explain, and then bitterly complained of the meditated tobacco and snuff excise as he was taught by the resolution-writer to call the duty. He said the whole fraternity were not able to raise the money, or give the requested security. Pole next came forward to complain of the injuries intended on the Auctioneers, having finished his reading and speech, without one word of debate the question on the resolutions were called for. The Moderator desired to be informed whether they would take them up separately or together, all being satisfied with the debates and fully understanding the merits of the resolutions they agreed to pass them in gross; which was instantly done—and three cheers ended the meeting. The spectators of the farce whom I took to be more than two thirds of the persons present, were distress'd to see with what facility a few demagogues could mislead and abuse an ignorant but harmless people. I shall say nothing of the resolutions more than they were well wrote, impertinent and insidious.[53]

The eyewitness account offers some clues as to the class of citizen who attended the meeting as well as who led the proceedings. Hodgdon described the crowd as "lower class" and "ignorant but harmless people." The leaders were characterized as misguided demagogues only a bit more respectable than their audience.

Hodgdon's characterization of the event reflects his inherited Federalist outlook of deferential expectations. He minimized the status of the leaders involved in the protest and the substance of the interests they represented. The manufacturers of tobacco products and sugar were clearly of a higher socioeconomic group than Hodgdon assumed, largely because occupational classifications in Philadelphia were changing in this "age of merchant-capitalism" (see table 1). In fact, the manufacturers who led the excise protest compare favorably to many of the persons who led and dominated the Federalist party.[54] Compared to Federalist leaders, fewer manufacturers owned a chair or sulky and held fewer servants, livestock, and ounces of plate. Still, such protest leaders as Gavin Hamilton, Sr. (Chestnut Ward and Blockley), John Hankart (North Mulberry Ward and Bristol), Thomas Leiper (Middle Ward and North Market Ward), Jacob Lawerswyler (South Mulberry Ward), Jacob Morgan (South Mulberry Ward), and F. A. Muhlenberg (South Mulberry Ward) were on an average but one or two steps below the import or export merchant on the economic ladder. The median assessed personal tax of these six manufacturers was £150. The 1794 personal tax of Philadelphia's three Federalist members to Congress was £166.[55] Far from being among the ignorant propertyless, these manufacturers would soon come to dominate the economy of the city of Philadelphia and they were far more successful than their numbers might suggest.

The life of Thomas Leiper, a manufacturer who achieved economic prominence and political fame, is representative of the ambitious, aspiring manufacturers. After emigrating from Scotland to the United States in 1763, Leiper soon came to Philadelphia to work for his cousin Gavin Hamilton, a pioneer in the snuff business in the country. This relationship turned into a business partnership, which was dissolved by mutual consent sometime during or after the American Revolution in order to bring their sons into the business. Leiper, who married well—Elizabeth Gray, daughter of George Gray of Gray's Ferry—became a prominent member of the First Troop, Philadelphia City Cavalry, St. Andrews Society, and the Democratic Society of Pennsylvania.[56] By 1794 the Leipers and Hamiltons were among the principal wholesale and retail merchants in the city. Leiper, although he started later, actually prospered more than his kinsman. He accumulated a considerable fortune based on snuff mills, stone quarries, public securities, and numerous pieces of urban real estate. In 1794 he had an assessed evaluation of nearly £20,000 for his properties in Philadelphia City and Delaware County.[57] His finest urban dwellings were rented to distinguished persons, such as French merchant Theophiles Cazenove, Secretary of the Commonwealth Alexander James Dallas, Supreme Court Justice James Wilson and Secretary of State Thomas Jefferson.[58] Leiper, who had supported the American Revolution by contributing large sums of money and participating in the First City Troop's active field service, had become by 1789 one of the leading advocates of government support to promote, defend, and protect, individually and collectively, manufacturing enterprises and to sustain a self-sufficient American economy.[59] He was a firm believer in what historian Louis Hartz describes as mixed enterprises.[60] Tobacconists Jacob Benninghove, John Hankart, Isaac Jones, and Philip Stimmel also were parvenus who took advantage of free and mixed enterprise

TABLE 1

INDEX OF ASSESSED TAXES PAID BY MAJOR PHILADELPHIA MANUFACTURERS, 1794

Value in Pounds	Tobacconists/ Snuffmakers		Sugar Refiners		Brewers & Distillers		Coachmakers	
	Property	Personal	Property	Personal	Property	Personal	Property	Personal
0-25	12	12	4	3	3	7	6	14
26-50	0	15	1	5	1	3	1	4
51-100	2	5	0	7	1	7	2	2
101-250	4	3	2	1	2	3	6	0
251-500	9	0	1	0	2	0	2	0
501-1,000	5	0	2	0	3	0	2	0
1,001-2,000	1	0	3	0	7	0	1	0
2,001-2,500	0	0	1	0	0	0	0	0
Over 2,500	2	0	2	0	0	0	0	0
Unidentified	33	33	4	4	2	1	33	33

Source: Tax Assessment Ledgers, 1794, Philadelphia City, Archives of the City and County of Philadelphia. National Archives and Records Service, U.S. Direct Tax of 1798: Tax Lists on Microfilm for Pennsylvania (Washington, D.C., 1963).

and experienced occupational mobility.[61] In battling with state and national governments over taxation and tariff protection they acted to ensure that they would not long remain second-class citizens in the new republic.

The leading sugar refiners also possessed wealth. Jacob Morgan, F. A. Muhlenberg, and Jacob Lawerswyler, Isaac and Edward Pennington, Charles Schaffer, John Corman, Matthew Lawler, John Bartholomew, J. Dorsey, and Peter and Henry Miercken were well-to-do, and were among the economic leaders of Philadelphia's manufacturing community. Most of them owned their own homes and possessed horses, cows, plate, and riding chairs. Like the tobacconists, they had benefited from the city's increased wealth and enjoyed many of the new luxuries in life.

Two conclusions can be drawn about the size and wealth of this group. If the manufacturers of sugar and tobacco appear to have been small in number, totaling under 100, they were vocal and certainly possessed the potential to rouse the entire manufacturing community and the laborers dependent upon those industries. Of the approximately 2,200 manufacturers in Philadelphia, the new excise taxes directly affected at least 15 percent, including the producers of ale, beer, cider, hops, malt, chocolate, cocoa, paste, vinegar, candles, glass, soap, paper and paste board, starch and hair powder, leather and skins, and iron.[62] Perhaps the indirect or potential effect of these taxes mobilized other manufacturers, as well as auctioneers, brokers, cardmakers, coachmakers, innkeepers, and stationers. The ability of this core group, highly concentrated in a few wards, to merge the interests of the manufacturers with the city's Democratic Republican societies, heightened their political impact.

Although the city's two Democratic Societies—the German Republican Society and the Democratic Society of Pennsylvania—formed before the spring of 1794, the protest of the manufacturers provided the clubs with an issue and a source for new support. The societies apparently enjoyed greater unity and momentum as a result of the enthusiastic support they received from the manufacturers.[63] Little is known about the activities of the German Republican Society during the year 1794. The society's April 1793 constitution reveals that its members planned to concern themselves with maintaining a Republican government and searching for ways to improve themselves.[64] Only persons of German "blood" could join; officers were elected the first Wednesday in January.[65]

The constitution and circulars of the Democratic Society of Pennsylvania, suffused with international republicanism and an emphasis on the cultivation of "rational liberty," explicitly endorsed the promotion of the country's infant industries and the exclusion of British goods.[66] On April 10, 1794, before the excise was debated in Congress, the Philadelphia Society had resolved:

That this society considering and believing that the general welfare of our country is involved in promoting necessary manufacturers as far as is consistent with our situation in giving full employment and comfortable support to our fellow citizens; it is expected that the members of the Democratic Society will have sufficient patriotism to prefer and make use of the manufacturers of their own country, confident that by creating a demand for them we shall afford them that substantial encouragement and support particularly necessary at this time.[67]

In appealing to the nation's general welfare, full employment, and patriotism, the Democratic Society attracted manufacturers, especially the producers of snuff, tobacco, and sugar. Of the 315 members of the society, more than a quarter can be identified as craftsmen. Signers of the memorials and resolutions protesting the excise on tobacco and sugar are listed on the membership rolls of the two societies. Among the tobacconists and snuffmakers in the Philadelphia society were George Brown, Michael Lawler, Thomas Leiper, Christian Schaffer, and William Watkins; the sugar refiners were Matthew Lawler, Jacob Morgan, Isaac Pennington, and Conrad and Peter Sybert.[68] Although the occupations of the general membership in the German Republican Society remains a great mystery, Eugene P. Link argues that urban support for the club came from manufacturers, and we do know that manufacturers dominated its leadership. Henry Kammerer (papermaker) was president; Jacob Lawerswyler (sugar refiner) was vice president and Christopher Kucher (sugar refiner) was treasurer. The meetings of the Democratic Society of Pennsylvania, usually held at 8 P.M. at the German Lutheran schoolhouse, often followed the scheduled 5 P.M. excise protest gatherings. "Doubtless these men [protestors]," writes Link, "were responsible for introducing resolutions passed by the two Philadelphia organizations condemning excise taxes and pledging devotion to the American manufacturing interests."[69]

Because the formation of the Democratic Society of Pennsylvania occurred two years after the passage of the 1791 excise on distilled liquors, one should not draw any firm conclusions about any position that the society might or might not have taken before 1794. The excise tax was a small issue in the local elections of 1792.[70] Once the report to enlarge the number of products to be covered under law came before the House of Representatives in the spring of 1794, the society wasted no time in identifying with the manufacturers' grumblings over the proposed excise taxes. On May 8, for instance, the organization issued resolves declaring that its membership opposed excises "on salt and coal, on sugar and snuff, on boots and shoes, on spirits, coffee, carriages and cheese."[71] Declaring that these infant industries required the "fostering care of government" and would be ruined by the burdens of taxation, the society argued that an excise system would lead to fraud, great expense for collection, and the unnecessary appointment of placemen whose salaries and other requisites would be greater than the tax itself. The manufacturers faced reluctantly the prospect of having to pass on this tax to the consumer, but, more important, they preferred "republican taxes" which were direct in their object, equal in assessment, and economical in collection.[72]

The aforementioned declarations were, of course, drawn up to win the support of the manufacturing community. New members were attracted to the society with some success. After the club issued the so-called infant industries resolution, at least forty new persons joined between May and July 1794, including manufacturers James Burges McCoy, Conrad Seyfert, Robert Cochran, Henry Bellegeau, Samuel Johnson, Michael Lawler, Robert McGee, David Ogden, Jacob Morgan, and George Rehn (Rein).[73]

Contemporaries, though, such as James Madison, Oliver Wolcott, Jeremiah Smith, and Fisher Ames, attributed the societies' opposition to the excise to base political motives and an attempt to embarrass the Washington administration. "The discontent as to the excise law has probably been stirred up for some electioneering purpose, and will subside, of course," wrote James Madison on May 19, "unless fostered by other excises now in agitation here, to wit, on manufactured tobacco and refined sugar."[74] The political unrest was widely reported in the Philadelphia press.[75] The Democratic-Republicans in and out of Congress, however, failed in their effort to organize a successful campaign, although they succeeded in having the stamp tax bill rejected. "All opposition to the new excises, though enforced by memorials from manufacturers," wrote Madison, "was [in] vain."[76]

Although the manufacturers, the societies, and Republican party could not defeat the excise tax, they did not give up the battle. Republicans in particular, knowing that the manufacturers of tobacco products, sugar, distilled spirits, and carriages resented the excise tax and that other manufacturers in the city feared coverage extended on other articles or products, moved to draw this important following solidly into their ranks. Alexander Graydon observed that "a handle was made of the excise law."[77] In order to rekindle the body politic, the Democratic-Republican clubs made the inflexible Thomas Fitzsimmons, who had voted in favor of the administration's six indirect tax measures and who stood during his two terms in Congress as the champion of Secretary Hamilton's stabilization program, their bête noire.[78]

The strategy to unseat Fitzsimmons developed in early June. At meetings held on June 5 and 12, 1794, the Democratic Society defended the right of an individual to criticize government actions which tampered with constitutional liberty, and reminded the people that in times of peace interest in public concerns often lagged. Joining hands with the German Republican Society in the cause of liberty and in the anti-Fitzsimmons movement, the Democratic Society of Pennsylvania formed a task force on the excise and taxation. It also resolved to organize an election committee for the purpose of deciding "how far their Representatives are entitled to public confidence, by approving the good and dismissing the bad."[79] The tone of the fall political campaign was symbolically set forth during the Independence Day Dinner of 4 July 1794, when party revellers offered the toast: "EXCISE, may this baneful exotic wither in the soil of freedom."[80] In honor of Bastille Day, July 14, 1794, shipwrights and mariners, some of whom were members of the clubs, drank toasts to celebrate French independence.[81] These events reinforced the view that on matters of taxation and foreign policy Fitzsimmons no longer represented many interests in Philadelphia.

During the summer and fall months of 1794, the manufacturers in need of protective duties and opposed to excise taxes played a substantial role in the city's politics. No longer prepared to recognize the mercantile community as the city's natural leaders, they moved to ameliorate the provisions of the act of 1794 and to defeat one of its principal spokesmen. There was new involvement in ticket making to support their economic aspirations.[82] This process was complicated by the unanticipated acts of the insurgents at Braddock's field in western Pennsylvania in late July, which divided political ranks between moderates and radicals in Philadelphia and disrupted the activities of the city's two democratic societies.[83] The majority of the manufacturers and the members of the society held an ambivalent position. They could not condone the intemperate actions of the western insurgents because they believed that change had to be carried out through legal, constitutional channels. At the same time they also disapproved of the federal government's taxation program because they believed "excise systems to be oppressive, hostile, to the liberties of the Country."[84]

While events were in progress to quell the rebellion in the four western counties of Pennsylvania, the manufacturers of tobacco products and sugar took their case to the Pennsylvania General Assembly which Governor Thomas Mifflin convened to deal with the crisis.[85] The manufacturers' memorial of 5 September 1794 carried the signatures of twenty-three snuffmakers and thirteen sugar refiners.[86] The thirty-six memoralists sought the "interposition" and "influence" of the state legislature on the excise question as "the more immediate guardian of the rights and liberties of the citizens of Pennsylvania."[87] As precedent they cited the action taken by the Pennsylvania General Assembly on the original excise law on January 22, 1791, and they requested that body to exercise again its right to review the proceedings and acts of the United States Congress.[88] Because the excise law was never popular in Pennsylvania, either among Federalists or anti-Federalists, there was reason to expect a favorable legislative response.[89] Yet for some unexplained reason, the memorial was never seriously taken up a second time by the General Assembly.

Unable to get the desired support in the legislature to exercise its right to review the law, the manufacturers and local political leaders now found it necessary to seek national as well as state and local ties. Reaping the benefits of the failure of the Federalists to be responsive to manufacturers' needs and sentiments were, of course, the Democratic-Republicans. The manufacturers did not select one of their own to challenge Fitzsimmons, but they found an antiexcise spokesman in John Swanwick, who had joined the Democratic Society on May 15.[90] To become the candidate of the Democratic-Republican party, of the societies of "moderate" Federalists, of disgruntled merchants, of manufacturers and tradesmen, and in general of the city's immigrants, Swanwick broke with existing political practice and openly sought the seat in Congress. His early Federalism, wealth, and status, and espousal of the interests of banking, insurance, and freer enterprises for the "arriviste," made Swanwick an ideal opponent to Fitzsimmons.[91]

Swanwick defeated Fitzsimmons by 248 votes (see tables 2 and 3). His triumph

TABLE 2
CONGRESSIONAL DISTRICT ELECTION, 1794
BY WARD AND PARTY

Ward	Republican Swanwick	Federalist Fitzsimmons	Majority for Swanwick	Majority for Fitzsimmons
New Market	166	165	1	—
Dock	76	125	—	49
South	43	49	—	6
Walnut	17	34	—	17
Middle	120	114	6	—
Chestnut	22	37	—	15
Lower Delaware	43	32	11	—
Upper Delaware	46	35	11	—
North	160	128	32	—
High Street	35	36	—	1
South Mulberry	217	80	137	—
North Mulberry	177	59	118	—
Total	1,122	894	316	88

Source: Philadelphia Gazette, November 7, 1794.

met with a mixed response and contemporaries offered a variety of comments on it. According to James Madison, Swanwick's election represented "a standing change for the aristocracy." Subsequently, he wrote James Monroe that the election of a Republican at the commercial and political metropolis of the United States was "of itself, of material consequence," and it was so considered by the Federalists.[92] Federalist William Bradford thought the "contemptible" Swanwick owed his success "more to resentment against Fitzsimmons than to his own merits." "Many refused," he revealed, "to vote for either candidate and many voted for S[wanwick] in order to vote against F[itzsimmons]."[93] Perhaps Vice President John Adams best summed up the results of the election when he wrote, "Swanwick may be for anything that I know as federal as his Rival."[94]

More specifically, Swanwick owed his election to Congress from the country's largest city to the events of 1794. Certainly, if any two issues hurt arch-Federalist Fitzsimmons above all others, they were his conduct during the spring embargo and his vote for excise taxes. Especially damaging was the Republicans' cry, "Swanwick and no Excise."[95] Edmund Randolph reported that Fitzsimmons's conduct cost him support in the mercantile community and that the tax slogan gained support for Swanwick among the "less informed classes of men." In addition, Randolph noted that Chief Justice Thomas McKean, who had openly campaigned for Swanwick, remarked that at the last moment "the gentlemen" decided to vote the "merchant-Republican."[96]

TABLE 3
CONGRESSIONAL DISTRICT ELECTION, 1794
BY WARD AND PARTY

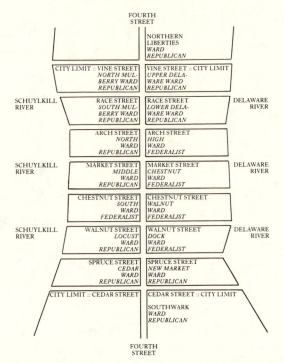

Swanwick won in Philadelphia City not because of any great upsurge of voters of little or no property, but because Fitzsimmons was unable to hold onto the traditional votes of merchants and large-scale manufacturers.[97] In particular, Swanwick found support among manufacturers hurt by the enlargement of the excise law and those in support of protective duties. The Democratic-Republicans clearly did not win over the votes of all manufacturers or artisans. An analysis of the returns by ward reveals that Swanwick carried seven of the twelve wards and that his greatest support came from the newer and middling-class wards of the city of Philadelphia (see table 3). One recent authority has concluded that, while Philadelphia had a striking inequality of wealth distribution, the wards were marked by considerable occupational diversity.[98] The 255-vote majority piled up by Swanwick in the peripheral wards of North and South Mulberry, the home of the German manufacturers hurt by the excise and threatened by foreign competition, proved decisive in overcoming Fitzsimmons's support in the core wards of Walnut and Chestnut and among the militia forces. (The late returns of the militia reduced Swanwick's winning margin to fifty-eight). Similarly, Swanwick proved he could hold his own against the incumbent in New Market, North, and Dock wards, which contained the highest concentration of

Irish.[99] Basic to the Federalists' defeat was their inability to recognize the self-esteem of merchant-manufacturers gained by their role in the Revolution and their support of the federal Constitution in 1787.

The political results were similar in the second congressional district, composed of Philadelphia and Delaware Counties, where F. A. Muhlenberg defeated Samuel Miles by 146 votes.[100] Since the two candidates were sugar refiners by trade and had contacts in both political parties, the contest pitted an antiexcise candidate against a proexcise candidate. Not only had Muhlenberg opposed the extension of the system as the Speaker of the House, but he also had signed a number of memorials of remonstrance, circulated in the city's counting houses and taverns, which were eventually forwarded to Congress. His business partner, Jacob Lawerswyler, was a consistent opponent to the excise tax. Samuel Miles's signature, on the other hand, was not found on any of the memorials. Benjamin Franklin Bache, editor of the *General Advertiser*, called for Muhlenberg's re-election because he had voted against the extension of the excise tax system. The Republican party editor remarked that this vote would "procure him the warm support of his former friends [Federalists] and indeed of every Republican."[101]

The election for seats in the General Assembly in Philadelphia and Delaware Counties also showed Republican gains and support from the manufacturers. In Philadelphia County the entire Republican slate of candidates, sponsored at a meeting chaired by George Egert on October 8, was elected. Jacob Morgan, one of the principal protest leaders among the sugar refiners and a member of the Democratic-Republican Society, received the highest numbers of votes.[102] In Delaware County John J. Preston and William West, alleged Republicans, won.[103] It is noteworthy that tobacco was raised and manufactured extensively in both counties. Bristol contained ten tobacconists or snuffmakers and there were ten more in the twin suburbs of Northern Liberties and Southwark. Leiper, certainly one of the principal spokesmen for support of manufacturers, lived in Delaware County as well as Philadelphia.[104]

The elections of 1794 in Philadelphia City and Philadelphia and Delaware counties were significant. With the exception of the races for the state Senate, which remained solidly Federalist,[105] the vote revealed that the newer mercantile and manufacturing interests, demanding expansion and diversification of the economy, were a growing political and economic force in an area becoming more urban and industrialized. Although their years of political and economic dominance were still in the future, the manufacturers had nevertheless used the issue of the excise taxes to rally the "interest." A "correspondent" summed up the 1794 election as follows:

From the state of the poll at our late election for a city member of Congress, the opinion of the people with regard to excise laws is clearly manifested. They have given a decided proof of their abhorrence of those revenue systems by excluding one of its most strenuous advocates . . . in the Federal legislature, and supplying his place with an acknowledged enemy to excises. The same reasons actuated the electors of the county in their choice of a Federal representative, and we have no doubt the same spirit prevailed in the Delaware State.[106]

When the second session of the Third Congress convened on November 3, 1794, the issues of the first session were still very much on the minds of the representatives. Although House members were preoccupied with a resolution denouncing the "self-created" societies designed to place the "Republican interest" on the defensive, the most significant domestic issue was the raising of revenues to reduce the public debt. The call by some representatives that the excises be continued through 1801 sent shock waves through the manufacturing community. It was further stunned by Congressman William L. Smith, who, scoffing at the excise protestors, stated on December 23, 1794, that "there had been no petition or complaint against the snuff or sugar excises. They appeared as popular as any taxes could be expected to be."[107]

The tobacconists (snuffmakers) and sugar bakers answered Congressman Smith's assertion almost immediately by a petition.[108] They called for either the repeal or revision of the excise tax on refined sugar and tobacco products because excises placed on a domestically produced luxury brought foreign competition, oppressed the poor, and caused an increase in wages; the petitioners further explained that the public had resorted to white sugars of an inferior quality and that the manufacturer and not the consumer paid the excise. Taxing industry rather than wealth or property, they concluded, was contrary to the social compact of 1789. The manufacturers reasoned that extinguishing the public debt would be more cheerfully and effectively brought about through a general system of taxation on property of all descriptions. They regarded raising a tax on landed or personal property as neither "unjust" nor "impossible," but as the safest way to pay off the interest on the debt to 1801.[109]

The manufacturers added weight to their argument by demonstrating that the excise system had proven troublesome and costly. Not only had it failed to generate the expected new revenues, but also there was every reason to conclude that the revenues had not equaled the expenses of a system that required a large force of revenue officers to maintain adequate surveillance over the country's manufacturers.[110] Congress was informed that six of the seven snuff mills in Pennsylvania closed at one time or another because of the 1794 excise taxes, while the seventh mill was open but remained on a precarious footing. Evasion of the taxes was easy, the petitioners added, if one either worked in his cellar and bolted his door or smuggled snuff by using a hand mill. Both methods were used in Philadelphia. Testimony before the 1795 select committee also indicated that the "excise had 'shut up the workhouses' " and that a number of sugar bakeries had been taxed out of business. In summary, the manufacturers contended that the excise law was "oppressive, unequal and consequently unjust."[111]

Congress debated the subject of extending revenues to reduce the public debt during the early months of 1795. The manufacturers of tobacco products and sugar in New York City, Baltimore, and Philadelphia were regarded as the principal complainers but none were more vociferous than the Philadelphians.[112] Congressman Fitzsimmons, serving out his term, not only remained adamantly opposed to any changes in the present system, but also led the supporters of the present system.[113] Still, a House bill calling for changes in the taxing procedures was approved by the United States Senate on March 2, and the House concurred in the amended Senate version on March 3, 1795.[114] The fourteen-part act, which altered the provision of "An Act Laying Certain Duties Upon Snuff and Refined Sugar," essentially repealed the previous pound weight duties (eight cents duty on snuff) and laid them instead upon all mills employed in the manufacture of snuff at annual rates that varied according to the mode of production. The law required entries of the mills and a license before commencing business. If a person exported in quantities of not less than 300 pounds at one time, the duties on refined sugar were not altered.[115] He continued to receive the drawbacks of six cents per pound. The new law had minimized the so-called evils of the excise system by eliminating the visits of excisemen and removing the dangers of false and erroneous swearing as to the weight of the product, which varied in the snuff industry according to the day's temperature.

Even though the tobacconists and snuffmakers were instrumental in modifying the revenue law of 1794, they were still not fully satisfied, probably because the principle of excise taxation remained intact. "This law is a lesser evil than its predecessor, from which it differs as one broken leg differs from two; and this is," summed up an apologist for the antiexcise interest, "the utmost which can be said in defence of it."[116] And while Philadelphians debated the merits of John Jay's mission to England and the subsequent treaty, the city's manufacturers of tobacco products continued to work feverishly to regain their pre-1794 status. Because the issue had to compete for public attention with the controversy over Jay's Treaty, the manufacturers paid James Thompson Callender to write a pamphlet entitled *A Short History of the Nature and Consequences of Excise Laws; including Some Account of the Recent Interruption to the Manufactories of Snuff and Refined Sugar* (Philadelphia, December 7, 1795). The 116-page pamphlet, released to all members of the two houses of Congress and to the principal officers of the federal government, coincided with the opening of the Fourth Congress.[117] The tract spelled out the so-called ruinous effects of the previous revenue measures, incorporating all of the memorials prepared on the subject, and contained as preface a short history of the nature and consequences of excise laws in England and Ireland.

In seeking alternatives to the excise, the snuff and sugar manufacturers found an able and articulate spokesman in John Swanwick, who was reelected to the Fifth Congress over Edward Tilghman. Philadelphia and Delaware Counties, a key region in the country for tobacco and sugar manufactories, had as representatives Swanwick and F. A. Muhlenberg (Fourth Congress) and Swanwick and Blair McClenachan, former president of the Democratic Society of Pennsylvania (Fifth Congress).[118] Between December 1795 and May 1797, the urban representatives busied themselves with presenting the memorials of snuff makers and sugar refiners, calling for the repeal of the original legislation.[119] As a member of the Committee of Commerce and Manufacturers, Swanwick worked particularly hard for the repeal of the revenue law on tobacco products, including the eventual elimination of drawbacks (bounties), and voiced the general concerns of protectionist-minded manufacturers and direct tax advocates. Bounties, described as favored by Hamilton, were considered unrepublican. The actions of the memorialists, referred to as the "rebellious men," and the Philadelphia area representatives troubled other members of the House of Representatives. One of them sarcastically asked, would the public be satisfied after learning that the important object of reducing the public debt "had been defeated by the means of half a dozen manufacturers of snuff and loaf sugar?"[120]

The chief argument for repeal was that the law seemed to defeat its own purposes—drawbacks being greater than the revenues. For instance, it was reported that large commercial mills that exported snuff, such as the Richard Gernon and Company, received drawbacks ten times as great as the taxes paid. In any event, after three years of detailed examination, countless memorials, and local pressure, a majority in Congress finally yielded to the demands of the Philadelphians and decided that it was too difficult to make the excise tax equal and just, and to prevent fraud. The act had never produced, according to John Swanwick, "anything but uneasiness and dissatisfaction in whatever way the tax might be collected."[121] For Congress, repeal of the law eventually brought a negligible loss of funds to the union, and the vexatious tax experiment that had produced a sinking fund rather than revenue was terminated.[122] Swanwick and others argued that additional stop-gap revenues might be more easily acquired through a national lottery system.[123]

The excise repealers in Congress, who were led by the Pennsylvania and Virginia delegations, were not yet able to overcome the strong objections of Congressman William L. Smith and other members of the House Ways and Means Committee.[124] Being forced to compromise, the Committee of Commerce and Manufacturers resolved to suspend rather than repeal the 1795 Act. On May 21, 1796, a suspension bill passed that terminated provisions of the act of March 3, 1795, until the end of the second session of the Fourth Congress (March 4, 1797).[125]

In 1796 and 1797 Philadelphia manufacturers of tobacco products and sugar again fell short of their objective: repeal of the Revenue Act of 1794. Instead, their petitions for repeal were met with suspension of the act. As the members of the House developed new tax schemes and perfected the collection of old ones, the battle in Congress between the direct and indirect tax forces became more intense.[126] Pennsylvania's congressional delegation and its manufacturers were especially involved in this process. Writing from Philadelphia, Fisher Ames complained, "The silly reliance of our coffee house and Congress prattlers on the responsibility of members of the people etc., is disgraced by every page of the history of popular bodies."[127]

The repeal forces, led by Albert Gallatin and John Swanwick, demanded that the federal government shift its revenue base from import duties and stop-gap indirect taxes to a domestic land tax. A land tax would break the national government's dependence upon the commercial interests and allow for a foreign policy devoted to national needs rather than the payment of public creditors. The snuffmakers' petition of February 9, 1796, calling for the repeal of the law, was once again answered by suspending the act. The suspension was to run through the end of the first session of the Sixth Congress (May 14, 1800).[128] By the subsequent act of April 24, 1800, the tax on tobacco products was finally repealed.[129] A similar measure, dated April 6, 1802, repealed the legislation of 1795 relating to sugar.[130] With the passage of these two acts, the eight-year controversy over the excise taxes ended.

The enlargement of the excise tax in 1794 had a substantial impact on the politics of Philadelphia. The manufacturers and tradesmen, who made up a majority of the city's population, ranged from journeyman to master artisans to affluent manufacturers. Solidly behind the Federalists in supporting the Constitution in 1789, many—although not all of the manufacturers of products affected by the excise tax—gradually shifted to the Republicans during the middle years of the 1790s. Led by the more wealthy sugar and tobacco manufacturers, and working initially through the Democratic Societies, the shift into the Republican camp between 1794 and 1800 in part can be attributed to dissatisfaction with Federalist tariff and excise policies. The Democratic-Republicans of Philadelphia became the spokesmen for the self-conscious occupational groups or the antiexcise interest. The Republicans presented the manufacturers with an ideology that placed them on an equal footing with their counterparts in commerce and supported their claim to a share in political power. The Federalists, on the other hand, refused to adopt a political response that supported all of the demands of the manufacturers and that accepted the older justification for formed opposition to the policies of the Washington administration.[131]

If Philadelphia is to be considered a test case, this chapter confirms the recent revision by Alfred F. Young and others of the traditional view of Jeffersonian Republicans as either exclusively agrarian or as the poorer elements in the urban manufacturing interest.[132] To be sure, opposition to the Federalist system, consisting of funding, assumption, banks, and indirect taxes, was never limited to agrarian-minded ideologues. While in theory there was an abiding faith in the superiority of agriculture, in practice the Jeffersonians early abandoned free trade and often adopted full-fledged mercantilist ideas before 1800. Federalist foreign policy and restrictions upon non-British commerce alienated Federalist merchants such as John Swanwick, Blair McClenachan, Stephen Girard, and Charles Pettit in a way that led to "merchant-Republicanism."[133] Similarly, the larger, entrepreneurial-minded manufacturers such as Gavin Hamilton, Thomas Leiper, and Jacob Morgan opposed Hamilton's political economy that favored import merchants of British industrial goods at the expense of export merchants and domestic manufacturers. Contrary to Drew McCoy, the Jeffersonians did not support only small-scale manufacturers because they were appropriate to a predominantly agrarian stage of society.[134] Instead, the evidence presented here documents the response of the large-scale manufacturers to Hamilton's taxation policies. Their opposition was not only limited to excise taxes placed on domestic manufactures but also involved protection to compete favorably in the international market and economic independence from Great Britain. Thomas Jefferson, taking his cues from early promoters like Tench Coxe, Albert Gallatin, and James Madison, wrote in 1816 to Benjamin Austin, "Experience has taught me that manufacturers are now as necessary to our independence as to our comfort."[135] There were, in short, entrepreneurial sources of Jeffersonianism. The urban variant of republicanism did not represent the main thrust of party strength, but it was a significant component.

NOTES

1. For a comprehensive study of the rebellion in Pennsylvania, see Leland D. Baldwin, *Whiskey Rebels: The Story of a Frontier Uprising* (Pittsburgh, 1939). Jacob E. Cooke, "The Whiskey Insurrection: A Re-Evaluation," *Pennsylvania History* 30 (July 1963), 316–346, is still the best summary of what has been written on the subject. Forest McDonald, *Alexander Hamilton, A Biography* (New York, 1979), pp. 255–256, 297–303, restates the traditional view of the event.

2. This subject was not developed either in Harry M. Tinkcom, *The Republicans and Federalists in Pennsylvania 1790–1801: A Study in National Stimulus and Local Response* (Harrisburg, 1950), ch. 6; or in Richard G. Miller, *Philadelphia—The Federalist City: A Study of Urban Politics, 1789–1801* (Port Washington, N.Y., 1976). Passing references to an urban response to the excise tax exist, however, in the earlier studies of William Miller, "The Democratic Societies and the Whiskey Insurrection," *The Pennsylvania Magazine of History and Biography* 62 (July 1938), 324–349; Eugene P. Link, *Democratic-Republican Societies, 1790–1800* (New York, 1942), pp. 76–78.

3. These views were originally presented in Roland M. Baumann, "The Democratic-Republicans of Philadelphia: The Origins, 1776–1797," Ph.D. diss., Pennsylvania State University, 1970, ch. 10.

4. According to one English traveler, Philadelphia was "the London of America" (Henry Wansey, *An Excursion to the United States of North America in the Summer of 1794*, 2d ed. [Salisbury, 1798], p. 57). For an excellent secondary description of Philadelphia, see Ethel M. Rasmusson, "Capital on the Delaware: the Philadelphia Upper Class in Transition, 1789–1801," Ph.D. diss., Brown University, 1962, ch. 3.

5. Thomas J. Scharf and Thompson Westcott, *History of Philadelphia, 1609–1884*. (Philadelphia, 1884), 3:2230, 2251, 2285. To understand the occupational structure of Philadelphia by wards, I have depended upon the little-used November 1793 Septennial Census Returns, RG 7, Records of the General Assembly, Div. of Archives and Manuscripts (State Archives), Pennsylvania Historical and Museum Commission.

6. For this story, see Charles S. Olten, *Artisans for Independence, Philadelphia Mechanics and the American Revolution* (Syracuse, N.Y., 1975). Robert L. Brunhouse, *The Counter-Revolution in Pennsylvania, 1776–1790* (Harrisburg, Pa., 1942), pp. 115–116, 134–135, 142, 151–152, 172–173, 181–182, 195.

7. On the formation of business partnerships to raise capital, see John R. Commons et al., *History of Labour in the United States* (New York, 1918–1935), 1: ch. 3; Curtis P. Nettels, *The Emergence of a National Economy, 1775–1815* (New York, 1962, 1969), pp. 69–75. The manufacturers used mercantile models: see Harry D. Berg, "The Organization of Business in Colonial Philadelphia," *Pennsylvania History* 10 (1943), 155–177.

8. Olten, *Artisans for Independence*, pp. 117–119. See also the insightful analysis of this struggle in Eric Foner, *Tom Paine and Revolutionary America* (New York, 1976), ch. 2.

9. Philadelphia's economic elite lacked cohesion and distinctiveness, often engaged in economic conflict, and its members came from all social groups (Robert Gough, "Towards a Theory of Class and Social Conflict: A Social History of Wealthy Philadelphians, 1775 and 1800," Ph.D. diss., University of Pennsylvania, 1977, pp. 285–287, 564–567, 621–642). Gough also rejects the view that a struggle existed between competing economic elites. I contend that Gough's study supports, on an individual basis, the significance of the large-scale manufacturers as wealthy and prominent members of Philadelphia society.

10. The 1789 debate in the House of Representatives is reported in *The Debate and Proceedings in the Congress of the United States, 1789–1824*, comp. Joseph Gales (Washington, D.C., 1834–56), 1:183–199, 294–302, *et passim* [*Annals of Congress*]. The best study of the nation's attempt at commercial independence and regulation is Vernon G. Setser, *The Commercial Reciprocity Policy of the United States, 1774–1829* (Philadelphia, 1937), esp. ch. 4.

11. Francis Hopkinson, "Account of the Grand Federal Procession in Philadelphia, July 4, 1788," *American Museum* 4 (July 1788), 55–78.

12. *Ibid.*, esp. pp. 60–61, 65, 68–69; L. H. Butterfield, ed., *Letters of Benjamin Rush* (Princeton, N.J., 1951), 1:470–477.

13. Thomas Fitzsimmons to Benjamin Rush, April 20, 1789, in Gratz Collection, Historical Society of Pennsylvania; *Annals of Congress* (1st Cong., 1st & 2d sess.), *passim*; Linda Grant DePauw et al., eds., *Documentary History of the First Federal Congress, 1789–1791*. (Baltimore, 1977), 3:60, 72, 350, 370, 388, 395, 451, 458.

14. Jacob Price, "Economic Function and the Growth of American Port Towns in the Eighteenth Century," *Perspectives in American History*, ed. Donald Fleming and Bernard Bailyn (Cambridge, Mass., 1974), 7:132–133. Large-scale manufacturers were proto-merchants. A sugar house, for instance, required some $16,000 worth of sugar-baking apparatus, plus capital of at least $50,000 and a good measure of credit. To engage in the manufacture of snuff for a profit required £5,000 to purchase and stock the materials, plus monies for house rent, machinery, wages for journeymen, and the frequent repair of mill dams damaged by flood waters. James T. Callender, *A Short History of the Nature and Consequences of Excise Laws* (Philadelphia, 1795), pp. 107, 112 [*History of the Excise Laws*].

15. "An Act for laying a Duty on Goods, Wares, and Merchandises imported into the United States," in Richard Peters, ed., *The Public Statutes at Large of the United States from . . . 1789 to March 3, 1845* (Boston, 1848–1850), 1:24–27 [*U.S. Statutes*].

16. The memorial is cited in DePauw, ed., *Doc. Hist. of 1st Federal Congress*, 3:60, and n.

17. *Ibid.*, 3:72, 370, 388, 395, 451, 458.

18. "An Act to provide more effectually for the collection of the duties," in Peters,

ed., *U.S. Statutes*, 1:145–178 *Annals of Congress* (1st Cong., 2d sess.), 1:1721–1722, 1724.

19. *Ibid*. (1st Cong., 3d sess.), 2:2321–2322, 2339–2340. Quote in William D. Barber, "Among the Most Techy Articles of Civil Police: Federal Taxation and the Adoption of the Whiskey Excise," *William and Mary Quarterly*, 3d ser., 25 (Jan. 1968), 70.

20. Prospectus of the Society for Establishing Useful Manufactures, August 1791, Report on Manufacturers, and Hamilton's Final Version (Dec. 5, 1791), in Harold C. Syrett, et. al., eds., *The Papers of Alexander Hamilton* (New York, 1961–1977), 9:145–147; 10:266, 295–296.

21. Jacob E. Cooke, *Tench Coxe and the Early Republic* (Chapel Hill, N.C., 1978), 182–189; and "Tench Coxe, Alexander Hamilton and the Encouragement of American Manufacturers," *William and Mary Quarterly*, 3d ser., 32 (July 1975), 369–392.

22. "A Mechanic," *Independent Gazetteer* (Philadelphia), Aug. 18, 1792. For the reply and rebuttal, see also "Detector" and "A Manufacturer," in *ibid.*, Sept. 1, 1792; Frederick B. Tolles, *George Logan of Philadelphia* (New York, 1953), pp. 116–122; Baumann, "Democratic Republicans of Philadelphia," pp. 344–345, 370–372.

23. This view is well established in the literature of the period. Less well known is the fear held by citizens of economic decline and ruin, and of the need to expand employment opportunities and the urban economy; see John K. Alexander, *Render Them Submissive: Responses to Poverty in Philadelphia, 1760–1800* (Amherst, Mass., 1980), pp. 6, 13–15, 33, 77–78; Billy G. Smith, "The Material Lives of Laboring Philadelphians, 1750 to 1800," *William and Mary Quarterly*, 3d ser., 38 (April 1981), 163–202.

24. Drew R. McCoy, *The Elusive Republic: Political Economy in Jeffersonian America* (Chapel Hill, N.C., 1980), p. 153.

25. Rudolph M. Bell, *Party and Faction in American Politics, The House of Representatives, 1789–1801* (Westport, Conn., 1973), ch. 5, esp. pp. 96–100, 104.

26. John R. Nelson, Jr., "Alexander Hamilton and American Manufacturing: A Reexamination," *Journal of American History* 64 (March 1979), 971–995, offers a corrective to the idea that Hamilton was a strong advocate of American manufacturing.

27. Baumann, "Democratic Republicans of Philadelphia," ch. 9, esp. pp. 452–469.

28. See James Madison's speech in the first session, Third Congress, *Annals of Congress* 4:155–156, and appendix, p. 1417. The resolves were actually based on a report, dated Dec. 16, 1793, prepared by Thomas Jefferson and Tench Coxe; it will be found in Paul L. Ford, ed., *The Writings of Thomas Jefferson* (New York, 1892–99), 6:470–484.

29. See the discussions in Irving Brant, *James Madison: Father of the Constitution, 1787–1800* (Indianapolis, 1950), pp. 389–393; Dumas Malone, *Jefferson and the Ordeal of Liberty* (Boston, 1962), pp. 154–160.

30. The meetings were reported in the Philadelphia newspapers: *Gazette of the United States*, Mar. 24, 25, 31, Apr. 10; *General Advertiser*, Mar. 10, 11, 13, 18, 21, 1794. For an analysis, see Roland M. Baumann, "John Swanwick: Spokesman for 'Merchant-Republicanism' in Philadelphia, 1790–1798," *Pennsylvania Magazine of History and Biography* 97 (April 1973), 159–161.

31. The pamphlet appeared in the *Universal Asylum and Columbian Magazine* (Philadelphia) 5 (July 1, 1790), 24–26. When reprinted in Mathew Carey's *American Museum* 12 (August 1792), 89–97, it included a reply by Dr. Thomas Ruston and a defense by

Swanwick. Swanwick to Carey, [undated], Lea & Febiger Collection, 1785–1796, Historical Society of Pennsylvania.

32. These alternatives are summarized in Baumann, "John Swanwick," pp. 160–161.

33. The *Pennsylvania Archives* (ser. 1–9) ed. Samuel Hazard et al., (Harrisburg, Pa., 1838–1935), ser. 9, 1:767–768, 772–777; Scharf and Westcott, *Philadelphia* 1:476–477.

34. *Annals of Congress* (3d Cong., 1st sess.), 3:485–504; *Gazette of the United States* (Philadelphia), Apr. 26, 1794.

35. The controversy was best captured in the Philadelphia newspapers. See in particular the exchange between "Warren" (pro–excise tax) and "Pluma" (anti–excise tax) appearing in the *General Advertiser*, May 17, 24, 26, June 3, 9, 1794, and elsewhere. Also see "From a Correspondent," May 7, 9, 16; in *ibid.*, and "Hancock," June 6, "Pluto," June 12, 1794, in *ibid.*; unsigned article, April 26, and "A Plain Spoken Man," *American Daily Advertiser*, May 10, 1794.

36. Syrett, ed., *Papers of Hamilton* 16:4. *Annals of Congress* (3d Cong., 1st sess.), p. 597; appendix, pp. 1307–1311. The debate was started on May 1, 1794, and it lasted for five weeks.

37. The best summary of the passage of these bills is to be found in Bell, *Party and Faction*, ch. 5.

38. "An Act laying certain duties upon Snuff and Refined Sugar" (June 5, 1794), in Peters, ed., *U.S. Statutes* 1:384–390.

39. "An Act laying duties upon Carriages for the conveyance of Persons," (June 5, 1794), in *ibid.* 1:373–376.

40. "An Act laying Duties of Goods, Wares and Merchandise imported into the United States" (June 4, 1794), in *ibid.* 1:391–392.

41. "An Act laying duties on licenses for selling Wines and foreign distilled spirituous liquors by retail," (June 5, 1794), in *ibid.* 1:376–378.

42. "An Act laying duties on property sold at Auction," (June 9, 1794), in *ibid.*, 1:397–400.

43. *Annals of Congress* (3d Cong., 1st sess.), 4:666, 670, 699, 726, 740–741; Bell, *Party and Faction*, pp. 104–107.

44. These views are best summarized in Callender, *History of the Excise Laws*, sec. 2, pp. 56–116.

45. *American Daily Advertiser* (Philadelphia), Apr. 26, 1794.

46. James Thompson Callender, *History of the United States for 1796* (Philadelphia, 1797), p. 8. See also the remarks by Samuel Smith, *Annals of Congress* 4:1115–1117.

47. These arguments are ably summarized in Barber, "Most Techy Articles of Civil Police," pp. 58–84; Callender, *History of 1796*, p. 202.

48. The 1791 resolves denouncing the excise tax, although primarily written by Albert Gallatin, were actually introduced in the General Assembly by Francis Gurney, a Philadelphia merchant. *Journal of the First Session of the House of Representatives* (Philadelphia, 1791), pp. 94–95, 98, 101, 104, 107–109, 112–113, 138, 142–149.

49. Gavin Hamilton and Thomas Leiper were embittered by the course of events during the framing of the excise bill. Apparently Alexander Hamilton had invited the tobacconists to his office to discuss the subject of the manufacture of tobacco so as not to injure the industry. But the original draft, which contained an excise of four cents per pound on tobacco, was expunged by the House Ways and Means Committee and increased

to eight cents before the bill was reported to the whole House (Callender, *History of the Excise Laws*, p. 48).

50. The breakdown of deference in politics was speeded up by the American Revolution (Richard A. Ryerson, *The Revolution Is Now Begun: The Radical Committees of Philadelphia, 1765–1776* [Philadelphia, 1978], pp. 3–4, 77–88, and ch. 8). See also Ronald P. Formisano, "Deferential-Participant Politics: The Early Republic's Political Culture, 1789–1840," *American Political Science Review* 68 (1974), 473–487.

51. Callender, *History of the Excise Laws*, pp. 70–75, 86–88. On the national campaign, see the exchange of letters, dated April 24 and 29, 1794, cited as "A.Z.," in the *American Daily Advertiser* (Philadelphia), May 2, 1794. A reading of the *Annals of Congress* in 1794 also suggests that cooperation existed among the manufacturers in the seaboard towns. Reference is also made to communications in the minutes of the Democratic Society of Pennsylvania, pp. 60–63, typescript, Historical Society of Pennsylvania.

52. My recounting of this event is based on Callender, *History of the Excise Laws*, pp. 66–75, and a reading of the Philadelphia newspapers cited below.

53. Hodgdon to Hamilton, May 9, 1794, in Syrett, ed., *Papers of Hamilton* 16:397. The resolutions appear in the *Gazette of the United States* (Philadelphia), May 10, 1794. See also *General Advertiser* (Philadelphia), June 3, 1794; there is a response by "Pluma" in *ibid.*, June 9, 1794. "Anti-Protextus" also poked fun at these well-to-do manufacturers for not being willing to pay their fair share of the taxes (*ibid.*, May 26, 1794).

54. This view is based on my reading and study of the Philadelphia County Tax Assessment Ledgers, 1770–1854, RG 1, Archives of the City and County of Philadelphia. By 1820, for example, the tobacconists ranked third behind merchants and physicians on an occupational rank order based on mean wealth (Stuart M. Blumin, "Mobility in a nineteenth-century American City: Philadelphia, 1820–1860," Ph.D. diss., University of Pennsylvania, 1968, p. 66). My own survey of the tax assessment books leads me to conclude that by 1794 the tobacconists, sugar refiners and distillers or brewers had already moved up the occupational rank order behind the "Gentlemen," merchant, doctor and/ or lawyer. Other occupations in the manufacturing community, such as watchmakers, tinsmiths, tanners, iron mongers and shipwrights, also ranked high.

55. Tax Assessment Ledgers, 1770–1854, RG 1, Archives of the City and County of Philadelphia, *passim*. The 1794 personal taxes for the Federalists were as follows: Robert Morris (£100); George Clymer (£100); and Thomas Fitzsimmons (£200). Social status, though closely related to wealth or occupation, was a very important independent variable. See also Gough, "Towards a Theory of Class and Social Conflict," chs. 6, 13.

56. John H. Frederick, "Thomas Leiper," *DAB* 11:154. This theme is presented in Carl Bridenbaugh, *The Colonial Craftsman* (New York, 1950), p. 165; and in Sam Bass Warner Jr., *The Private City: Philadelphia in Three Periods of its Growth* (Philadelphia, 1968), ch. 1.

57. Tax Assessment Ledgers, 1794, Philadelphia City, Archives of the City and County of Philadelphia. Searches were also made in Philadelphia City and Delaware county in the National Archives and Records Service, United States Direct Tax of 1798; Tax Lists for the State of Pennsylvania, microcopy no. 372 (Washington, D.C., 1963).

58. *Ibid.*, reel 1, frames 109, 262, 418, 420, 423, 426, 477–478; Tax Assessment Book, Middle Ward, 1794, 44, 46–47, Archives of the City and County of Philadelphia.

59. *DAB* 11:154; Henry Graham Ashmead, *History of Delaware County, Pennsyl-*

vania (Philadelphia, 1884), pp. 661–663, 742, 751–753; Henry Simpson, *The Lives of Eminent Philadelphians, Now Deceased* (Philadelphia, 1859), pp. 648–650.

60. Louis Hartz, *Economic Policy and Democratic Thought: Pennsylvania, 1776–1860* (Cambridge, Mass., 1948), pp. 3, 7, 82ff.

61. An assessment of their tax records suggests that these persons were successful entrepreneurial-minded manufacturers who hoped to achieve upper-class standing in Philadelphia.

62. The figure used here for the number of manufacturers in Philadelphia is the one cited in Tench Coxe, *A View of the United States of America* (Philadelphia, 1794), subsequently reported in Davies, *Some Account of the City of Philadelphia*, p. 82, and later in Scharf and Westcott, *Philadelphia* 3:2230.

63. Baumann, "Democratic Republicans of Philadelphia," pp. 448–449.

64. Link, *Democratic Republican Societies*, p. 608.

65. *Neue Philadelphische Correspondenz* (Philadelphia), April 9, 16, 1793. I am indebted to Kenneth Keller for this information.

66. Link, *Democratic Republican Societies*, pp. 11–12.

67. Minutes, Democratic Society of Pennsylvania, p. 74, Historical Society of Pennsylvania.

68. Baumann, "Democratic-Republicans of Philadelphia," appendix 1, table 3, "Democratic Society Membership by Occupation," pp. 598–601. My analysis of the membership, based on a reading of the manuscript minutes of the society, has recently been confirmed by Philip S. Foner, *The Democratic-Republican Societies, 1790–1800: A Documentary Sourcebook of Constitutions, Declarations, Addresses, Resolutions, and Toasts* (Westport, Conn., 1976), pp. 7, 42.

69. Link, *Democratic Republican Societies*, p. 90. The quote is on p. 78.

70. Baumann, "Democratic-Republicans of Philadelphia," pp. 344–347, 370–374.

71. The original minutes of the May 8, 1794, meeting of the Democratic Society of Pennsylvania are incomplete. Quoted words in John Bach McMaster, *A History of the People of the United States* (New York, 1883–1913), 2:188. The full minutes are printed in the *American Daily Advertiser* (Philadelphia) May 12, 13, 1794.

72. *Ibid.*, unsigned article, April 26; "A Plain Spoken Man," May 10, 1794, in *ibid.*

73. The number was probably greater than forty. Unfortunately, the manuscript minutes of the two key meetings held by the society on April 17 and May 1, 1794 (pp. 77–84 and 89–94), are missing. The society, which admitted new members only when they were sponsored by another member, had averaged about nine new members per meeting. On May 1, 1794, when the society celebrated St. Tammany's Day at the house of Israel Israel, treasurer of the Democratic Society, some 800 persons attended. *General Advertiser* (Philadelphia), Apr. 24, May 3, 16; *Gazette of the United States* (Philadelphia) May 9, 1794. References to the celebration can also be found in the minutes, Democratic Society of Pennsylvania, pp. 85–86, Historical Society of Pennsylvania.

74. James Madison to James Madison, Esq., May 19, 1794, United States Congress edition, *Letters and Other Writings of James Madison* (Philadelphia, 1865), 2:16.

75. The accounts of the excise can be found in all of the major party newspapers. See Donald H. Stewart, *The Opposition Press of the Federalist Era* (Albany, N.Y., 1969), pp. 83–86, 89–90, 523.

76. Madison to Jefferson, May 11, June 1, 1794, in *Letters of James Madison* 2:14,

18; quoted material on p. 14; Baumann, "Democratic-Republicans of Philadelphia," pp. 480–481.

77. Alexander Graydon, *Memoirs of His Own Time* (Philadelphia, 1846), p. 390.

78. Bell, *Party and Faction*, p. 107; Baumann, "Swanwick," p. 163. With the exception of the sketch in the *DAB* 6:444–445, the only biography of Fitzsimmons is James A. Farrell, "Thomas Fitzsimmons, Catholic Signer of the American Constitution," *American Catholic Historical Society Record* 39 (Sept. 1928), 175–224.

79. Minutes, Democratic Society of Pennsylvania, pp. 106–115, 117, Historical Society of Pennsylvania.

80. *General Advertiser* (Philadelphia), July 8, 9, 10, 1794.

81. *American Daily Advertiser* (Philadelphia), July 16, 1794.

82. Minutes, Democratic Society of Pennsylvania, p. 117, Historical Society of Pennsylvania. See also Baumann, "Democratic-Republicans of Philadelphia," pp. 483–484, 488ff. A battle was being waged over whether the election would be by districts. Tinkcom, *Republicans and Federalists*, pp. 138–139.

83. For a discussion, see Miller, "The Democratic Societies and the Whiskey Insurrection," pp. 324–349; Link, *Democratic Republican Societies*, pp. 45–49.

84. Resolve of July 31, 1794, in Minutes, Democratic Society of Pennsylvania, p. 131, Historical Society of Pennsylvania.

85. *Pennsylvania Archives*, 2d ser., 4:122–123; *ibid.*, 4th ser., 4:288–310.

86. A copy of the memorial, with accompanying signatures, can be found in the *Gazette of the United States* (Philadelphia), Sept. 8, 1794. Subsequently, Henry and Peter Miercken asked that their names be removed from the memorial (*Gazette of the United States* [Philadelphia], Sept. 12, 1794; *Annals of Congress*, 3d Cong., 2nd sess., 5:1191–1192).

87. *Gazette of the United States* (Philadelphia), Sept. 8, 1794. For a general discussion of deliberations during the special session, see Baumann, "Democratic-Republicans of Philadelphia," pp. 492–493.

88. The Pennsylvania House of Representatives passed a resolution denouncing the first federal excise tax in February 1791 and the doctrine of instruction had been advanced during the debate over funding in 1790 (William Maclay, *The Journal of William Maclay, United States Senator From Pennsylvania, 1789–1791* [New York, 1890], pp. 193, 199, 212, 220). See also above, note 48.

89. On the general opposition to the excise, see William Findley to Thomas Mifflin, Nov. 21, 1792, *Pennsylvania Archives*, ser. 2, 4:50; Charles Biddle, *Autobiography of Charles Biddle, 1745–1821*, ed. James S. Biddle (Philadelphia, 1883), p. 262; Tinkcom, *Republicans and Federalists*, pp. 91–94.

90. Minutes, Democratic Society of Pennsylvania, p. 97, Historical Society of Pennsylvania; Baumann, "Swanwick," pp. 161–163. Harry M. Tinkcom claims that Swanwick joined the society for business reasons in order to protest British interference with American commerce (Tinkcom, *Republicans and Federalists*, p. 85).

91. *Ibid.*, pp. 148ff., 156–163.

93. Bradford to Elias Boudinot, Oct. 17, 1794, in Wallace Collection 2:101, Historical Society of Pennsylvania. Fisher Ames wrote, "Here the supine good men let Swanwick get a nominal majority" (Ames to Christopher Gore, Nov. 18, 1794, in Seth Ames, ed., *The Works of Fisher Ames* (Boston, 1854), 1:152).

94. Adams to Abigail Adams, Nov. 11, 1794, in Adams Microfilm, reel 377, Massachusetts Historical Society.

95. Edmund Randolph to George Washington, Oct. 15, 1794, in Washington Papers, Library of Congress (DLC).

96. Randolph To George Washington, Oct. 16, in *ibid*. See also William Bradford to Washington, Oct. 17, 1794, in *ibid*.

97. "A Mechanic," *Gazette of the United States* (Philadelphia), Sept. 27, 1794. The Democratic Republicans had nearly overturned the candidacy of Fitzsimmons during the ticket making (*General Advertiser* [Philadelphia], Oct. 14, 1794).

98. Miller, *The Federalist City*, pp. 8–13.

99. Baumann, "Swanwick," pp. 162, 165–166; for the late militia returns from western Pennsylvania, see the *General Advertiser* (Philadelphia), Oct. 21, 31, Nov. 5, 6, 8, 10, 1794.

100. *Gazette of the United States* (Philadelphia), Oct. 8, 14; *General Advertiser* (Philadelphia), Oct. 13, 16, 1794. Samuel Miles and Col. Jacob Morgan operated a sugar refinery together at 77 Vine Street (C. A. Browne, "Early Philadelphia Sugar Refiners and Technologists," *Journal of Chemical Education* 20 [1943], 522).

101. *General Advertiser* (Philadelphia), Oct. 13, 1794.

102. *Gazette of the United States* (Philadelphia), Oct. 8, 13, 1794.

103. *General Advertiser* (Philadelphia), Oct. 16, 1794.

104. The count of tobacconists is based on a reading of the Philadelphia County Septennial Census, RG 7, Records of the General Assembly, Pennsylvania Historical and Museum Commission. On Thomas Leiper, see Ashmead, *Delaware County*, pp. 661–662.

105. *General Advertiser* (Philadelphia), Oct. 16; and *Gazette of the United States* (Philadelphia), Oct. 30, 1794; Tinkcom, *Republicans and Federalists*, pp. 141–142.

106. *General Advertiser* (Philadelphia), Oct. 17, 1794.

107. Callender, *History of Excise Laws*, p. 91. See also *Annals of Congress* (3rd Cong., 2d sess.), 4:1016. Congressman Smith's role in these proceedings is overlooked by George C. Rogers, Jr., *Evolution of a Federalist: William Loughton Smith of Charleston (1758–1812)* (Columbia, S.C., 1962), ch. 12.

108. *Annals of Congress*, (3d Cong., 2d sess.), 4:1023. A copy was received by Tench Coxe, which he forwarded to Secretary Hamilton in a letter dated December 26, 1794, in Syrett, ed. *Papers of Hamilton* 17:483–486.

109. Callender, *History of the Excise Laws*, pp. 92, 95–98.

110. *Annals of Congress* (3d Cong., 2d sess.), 4:1184.

111. Callender, *History of the Excise Laws*, pp. 101, 103.

112. *Annals of Congress* (3d Cong., 2d sess.), 4:1191.

113. *Ibid*. 4:1104; Baumann, "Swanwick," p. 166.

114. *Annals of Congress* (3d Cong., 2d sess.), 4:843–844, 847, 849, 1281.

115. "An Act to alter and amend the act entitled 'An Act laying certain duties upon Snuff and refined Sugar,' " in Peters, ed., *U.S. Statutes*, 1:426–430; J. Leander Bishop, *A History of American Manufactures from 1608 to 1860* (Philadelphia, 1864), pp. 61–62.

116. Callender, *History of the Excise Laws*, p. 104.

117. Callender, *History of 1796*, p. 198; *Annals of Congress* (3d Cong., 2d sess.), 4:1410. James Thompson Callender's 1795 pamphlet on the *History of the Excise Laws* has generally been overlooked by scholars.

118. *Aurora* (Philadelphia), Oct. 13; *Philadelphia Gazette* (Philadelphia), Oct. 12, 1796; Baumann, "Swanwick," pp. 166–167, 173–178.

119. *Annals of Congress* (3d Cong., 2d sess.), 4:171; (4th Cong., 1st sess.), 5:381, 636, 1406–1418; (4th Cong., 2d sess.), 6:2074.

120. Quoted words by Congressman Uriah Tracey, in *ibid.* 4:1186.

121. *Ibid.*, (4th Cong., 1st sess.), 5:1406, 1409. See references to the Richard Gernon and Co. and the method of drawbacks in Callender, *History of 1796*, pp. 199–202.

122. *Annals of Congress* (4th Cong., 1st sess.), 5:1409.

123. *Ibid.* 5:1412.

124. *Ibid.* 5:1415, 1417–1418.

125. *Ibid.* 5:1417.

126. This story has never been adequately told. See Henry C. Adams, "Taxation in the United States, 1789–1816," *Johns Hopkins University Studies in Political Science* 2, nos. 5–6 (Baltimore, 1884), 5–79. Rudolph M. Bell, *Party and Faction in American Politics* is limited to analysis of what happened in the House of Representatives.

127. Ames to Alexander Hamilton, Jan. 26, 1797, in Syrett, ed., *Papers of Hamilton* 20:487.

128. *Annals of Congress* (4th Cong., 2d sess.), 6:1562, 1565, 1569 [Feb. 27, 1797]. The petition of the manufacturers of snuff is in Callender, *History of 1796*, pp. 197–203. This meant that the suspension ran through the second and third sessions of the Fifth Congress as well as the first session of the Sixth.

129. *Annals of Congress* (6th Cong., 1st sess.), appendix, 1495; "An Act to repeal the act laying Duties on mills and implements employed in the manufacture of Snuff," in Peters, ed., *U.S. Statutes* 2:54.

130. "An Act to repeal the Internal Taxes," *ibid.* 2:148–150. For John Swanwick's role in the tax repeal struggle on sugar, see *Annals of Congress* (4th Cong., 2d sess.), 6:1885–1890, 2260–2262.

131. This theme can be found in Richard Buel Jr., *Securing the Revolution: Ideology in American Politics, 1789–1815* (Ithaca, N.Y., 1972). According to Lance Banning, Hamilton's economic program and President Washington's courtly formality offered the Republicans a foil for "country" symbolism (*The Jeffersonian Persuasion: Evolution of a Party Ideology* [Ithaca, N.Y., 1978]).

132. Alfred Young, "The Mechanics and the Jeffersonians: New York, 1789–1801," *Labor History* 5 (Fall 1964), 247–276; Staughton Lynd, *Class Conflict, Slavery, and the United States Constitution* (Indianapolis, 1967), p. 267; Foner, *Paine and Revolutionary America*, pp. 98–103; Baumann, "John Swanwick," pp. 131–182; Howard B. Rock, *Artisans of the New Republic: Tradesmen of New York City in the Age of Jefferson* (New York, 1979); Nelson, "Alexander Hamilton and American Manufacturing," pp. 971–995; Aleine Austin, *Matthew Lyon: 'New Man' of the Democratic Revolution, 1749–1822* (University Park, Pa., and London, 1980).

133. This point is developed in Baumann, "John Swanwick," pp. 131–182.

134. McCoy, *The Elusive Republic*, pp. 1077ff.

135. Jefferson to Austin, Jan. 9, 1816, in Albert E. Bergh, ed., *The Writings of Thomas Jefferson* (Washington, D.C., 1903–04), 14:392.

Treason in the Early Republic: The Federal Courts, Popular Protest, and Federalism During the Whiskey Insurrection

"The Storm in the west was brewing, or rather ready to burst when you left us."[1] St. George Tucker's letter to his friend James Monroe on the outbreak of the Whiskey Insurrection aptly describes the state of affairs in the western counties of Pennsylvania in the summer of 1794. The inhabitants of the four counties of Allegheny, Washington, Westmoreland, and Fayette had opposed the federal excise tax on distilled spirits since its introduction in 1791.[2] Even with the outbreak of widespread rioting in the four counties in 1794, however, the state of Pennsylvania was prepared to trust to the ordinary enforcement of order through criminal prosecutions in the state courts. On the other hand, the federal government acted much more forcefully when posed with its first real threat to internal order, sending troops and instituting prosecutions for treason in the federal circuit court against the insurgents.

This divergent treatment illustrates the tension between state and federal judicial systems that existed during the Federalist Era. States and state courts jealously guarded their authority against federal intrusions made possible by the broad powers granted the federal government by the Constitution. The federal judiciary was perhaps the most suspect branch of the new government because of the power it could potentially exercise to the derogation of state judicial authority. The Framers themselves recognized the potential danger posed by a strong national judiciary by limiting the ability of the federal courts to define the crime of treason. Before the enactment of the Bill of Rights, the treason clause in article III, explicitly defining treason as "levying war" against the United States,[3] was the only constitutional safeguard against abusive criminal

The author would like to thank Dr. Maeva Marcus and her colleagues at the Supreme Court Documentary History Project for allowing access to their collection of documents on the period and for invaluable comments and assistance on an earlier draft of the manuscript.

prosecutions by the federal government. Even with this limited definition, however, the background of the Framers' conception of the crime of treason was
the expansive judicial constructions of treason statutes in England. As understood
by the Framers, the phrase "to levy war" not only meant an actual waging of
war against the government, but any general rioting or violent opposition to the
laws of the United States.[4] Thus, when hostilities flared in 1794, it did not take
long before federal officials began to view the whiskey rebels as traitors in their
resistance to the excise.

In assessing the impact of the Whiskey Insurrection on the development of
the federal system, one must remember that the significance of this federal
response is not in its setting a precedent regarding the American law of treason,
but in its juxtaposition to the reaction of Pennsylvania. Although naturally concerned about the serious turn of events during the summer of 1794, state authorities resented the strong show of federal authority orchestrated by Alexander
Hamilton. For state officials, federal troops and treason prosecutions in the federal
courts posed much the same threat to state authority as did the actions of the
rioters themselves. Thus, although the federal government overshadowed its
efforts to restore order, Pennsylvania followed its own course through the ordinary state criminal process to vindicate state and federal authority in the west.
The prosecutions of the whiskey rebels in 1795 not only mark the culmination
of federal and state responses to the insurrection, but also shed light on the status
of Federalism in the early republic.

Even before 1794, collection of the excise was a hazardous occupation, to
which the excise men who had been tarred and feathered could testify. An
examination of the opposition to the excise before 1794 reveals that one aspect
of the federal excise tax rendered it even more odious to the western farmers
than previous state taxes on the production of distilled spirits. Under the 1791
act, the federal government prosecuted excise violations in the federal district
court. The District Court for the District of Pennsylvania, however, sat only in
Philadelphia or York, some 300 miles away from the western counties. Thus,
delinquent distillers were forced by statute to defend suits in a distant and
unfamiliar forum, instead of the more convenient—and favorable—local state
courts.[5]

This burden was not taken lightly by the western Pennsylvanians. Even during
the state ratifying convention for the Constitution, delegates from the western
counties expressed concern over the extensive jurisdiction and powers given the
federal judiciary by the Constitution. In a convention held in Harrisburg in 1788
to suggest revisions to the Constitution, the delegates, largely from the west,
concluded that Congress should not establish any inferior federal courts except
for the trial of admiralty cases.[6] The introduction of the federal judicial system
in 1789 confirmed the worst fears of those who had misgivings about article III.
To the citizens of Pittsburgh, far from the seat of the federal court, the new
federal judiciary would

work an important change on the situation of the inhabitants of Pennsylvania, whose power and commodious judicature secured us from being summoned to a distant court, or tried by a distant country. . . . The theory is now otherwise; and a citizen of Pittsburgh may be summoned to Philadelphia, and tried by a jury of that city.

With the multiplication of federal laws, such as the excise, Congress would similarly "increase the authority of their courts," or "the courts themselves must usurp jurisdiction from the state court." For the westerners, the system of federal courts not only threatened their rights to trial by a jury of the vicinage and the sovereignty of their state courts, but seemingly branded them as "lawless banditti, as that, to get justice on them, you must go beyond them."[7]

These popular sentiments were echoed by the Pennsylvania judiciary, whose power was threatened by the federal courts. Alexander Addison, president of the Pennsylvania Circuit Court for the four western counties, was perhaps the most vocal opponent of federal jurisdiction among the state judges. Writing to Governor Thomas Mifflin in response to an inquiry regarding state prosecutions brought against the first acts of opposition to collection of the federal excise in 1792, Addison assured the governor that he would be diligent in his efforts to support the excise. The reason for his enthusiasm is illuminating:

I have long entertained an opinion which the most serious reflection, (and I have given it a serious reflection,) has not altered but confirmed, that the powers of the federal courts in the extent given them by the judicial laws of the Union are useless or dangerous. Useless, because the State courts are capable in a proper manner of discharging almost all their duties. Dangerous, because if they exercise their powers they must either destroy the essence of the trial by Jury, or swallow up the State courts. It is better to have them useless than dangerous. If therefore, the State courts should punish and suppress these riots, the federal courts would have less or no inducement to interfere in them. If the State courts should not, the interference of the federal courts would be necessary; necessity would render this interference not unacceptable; habit would render the increasing interference pass without observation, and their power in all its dangerous extent would be fixed. My wish, therefore was that our State courts should suppress these riots and leave no reasonable desire in the federal courts to take notice of them.

Addison's opinion is also reflected in his response to George Clymer, the federal supervisor of the revenue for Pennsylvania, who requested his aid in the taking of depositions for prosecutions to be brought in the federal courts. Declining to help, Addison explained,

I consider the Laws of Congress as the rules of judgment in the state Courts and the citizens as punishable in the state courts for their infraction, as much as the respective state laws. I have taken and shall continue to take all measures as appear to me proper to bring to justice in the proper Courts of Pennsylvania those persons of whose violence it is the object of your mission to enquire. But this is all that is to be expected of me until I am convinced that it is my duty to do more.[8]

Addison's views suggest that the state courts were just as concerned about punishing violent resistance to the collection of the excise as was the federal government, albeit for a vastly different reason. The state courts hoped to preserve their own power within the federal system by punishing resistance to the laws of the United States, while the federal government required punishment of disobedience to a law of Congress to affirm the sovereignty of the United States.

As could be expected, however, federal officials were not particularly enamored with Addison's theory of enforcing federal law. Nor were they to be satisfied with his efforts. Early opposition to the excise consisted primarily of petitions to the government, attacks on the revenue collectors, and refusal by the distillers to comply with the law by entering their stills on the tax collector's register. On his circuit, Addison charged the grand jury respecting "the rioters in Allegheny County"; although indictments were returned, the prosecutions were eventually abandoned by the state prosecutor. However, Addison reports that several of the rioters, who kidnapped a witness to an attack on an excise collector, "were also indicted, [and] some of them have been taken and fined." In reference to a nighttime visitation by an antiexcise mob to the house of William Faulkner, the collector for Washington County, Addison charged the grand jury but upon further investigation found that "no such clear evidence could have been produced to give us reason to expect the finding of a Bill."[9]

These inconclusive proceedings, combined with suspicions of state enforcement of the law as advocated by Addison,[10] led federal officials to demand a stronger response. Hamilton, who as secretary of the treasury was ultimately in charge of collecting the excise, began to mobilize the Washington administration against opponents of the excise. His first efforts were directed toward punishing the more restrained protests of the westerners—the assembly of citizens in opposition to the excise. Informed of a meeting in Pittsburgh where the members resolved "to persist in [their] remonstrances to Congress, and in every other legal measure that may obstruct the operation of the Law," Hamilton concluded that legal opposition to a valid law was "a contradiction in terms" and that the members of the meeting were guilty of a "high misdemeanor."[11] Despite Attorney General Edmund Randolph's advice to Hamilton that "the law will not reach" the resolutions made in Pittsburgh, indictments were brought against some of the men present at the meeting. The federal grand jury, however, failed to return true bills against any of the members of the meeting.[12] Hamilton also pressed the prosecution of two men supposedly involved in the incident at Faulkner's house. However, Hamilton and the federal prosecutor had no more luck than did Addison; although two indictments for common law riot were returned by the federal grand jury and prosecutions were instituted before the federal circuit court, the government dropped the cases when it was learned that the men were not involved in the incident.[13]

Thus, federal efforts to punish resistance to the collection of the excise proved no more effective than those of the state of Pennsylvania. In both judicial systems, prosecutions were instituted and indictments returned against persons suspected of intimidating the excise collectors and fomenting general resistance to the excise. However, few cases proceeded to trial, and fewer still to a judgment of guilty. In fact, the state prosecutions seem to have been more successful than those brought in the federal courts, as a few convictions were obtained in the state courts in the western counties.

Of greater interest is the fact that the state and federal response to the crimes of the antiexcise men was identical at this time. In both judicial forums indictments were brought for rioting against collection of the excise. There was no mention of treason in either the state or federal courts. Even Washington's proclamation against opposition to the excise, drafted by Hamilton, merely warned against "all unlawful combinations and proceedings whatsoever having for object or tending to obstruct the operation of the laws."[14] Although the federal government was clearly not satisfied with the record of prosecutions against the offenders, the consensus seemed to be that such process, for the time being, was sufficient to vindicate federal and state authority.

Not everything was peaceful on the Pennsylvania frontier from 1792 until the summer of 1794. During 1793 antiexcise mobs twice broke into Fayette County Collector Benjamin Wells's house. After the first attack, in April, state warrants were issued against some of the men involved, although the sheriff of the county refused to execute them. The sheriff, Joseph Huston, was subsequently indicted in federal circuit court for his failure to execute the warrants "in contempt of the . . . United States and against the peace and dignity of the same."[15] In November, a party of six men broke into Wells's house, where they conveyed the threat to Wells that he resign his commission or "they would instantly put him to death." Indictments against two of these men for disturbing "the peace of the . . . United States" were brought directly before the federal circuit court in Philadelphia in July 1794, although only one was returned by the grand jury.[16]

The storm that burst shortly afterward was violent, although short-lived. Not surprisingly, the outbreak of hostilities seems to have been occasioned by the method of enforcing the excise that was particularly distasteful to the western farmers—the prosecution of suits against delinquent distillers in the federal district court. As a concession to the distillers, Congress amended the excise act in 1794 to allow suits for delinquencies to be brought in the more convenient state court forum.[17] Shortly before this conciliatory act, however, the federal prosecutor aggravated the situation by bringing seventy-five indictments for past violations to be prosecuted under the old act in the federal court. That the bringing of these indictments was the immediate cause of hostilities in the western counties is suggested by the fact that the government instituted very few prosecutions against delinquent distillers before 1794. Indeed, federal enforcement of the excise law was at such a low ebb in Pennsylvania that the federal prosecutor was still asking the federal circuit court in 1793 for legal instructions as to "the premises and due process of law" to be used against a distiller upon whom a delinquency had been assessed.[18]

Although the violations for which the indictments were brought had been under investigation before Congress passed the act allowing for state court prosecutions, westerners found the timing of the prosecutions brought under the old law obnoxious. When the federal marshal, David Lenox, accompanied by General John Neville, the excise inspector for the entire western region, attempted to serve process on the delinquent distillers in July, popular passions erupted. Mobilized by the cry, "The Federal Sheriff was taking away people to Philadelphia," local militia companies then being organized against the Indians formed in opposition. In the course of a two-day attack, some 500 insurgents burned General Neville's house to the ground.[19] After several meetings by delegates from the four counties, the insurgents held a general rendezvous on August 1 at Braddock's Field, the site of the annual militia brigade muster. There was talk at the rendezvous of burning General Neville's house in Pittsburgh, but calmer heads prevailed. On the march to Pittsburgh, the insurgents only burned the barn of Major Kirkpatrick, who had helped defend Neville's house during the July attack.[20]

The civil and military authorities in the western counties of Pennsylvania were concerned that opposition to the federal excise had reached such violent proportions. After the attack on General Neville's house, Judge Addison recommended to Pennsylvania's secretary of state, Alexander Dallas, that "the most pressing instructions be forwarded to the Attorneys for the state in the Western Counties, to procure testimony by subpoenaing & recognizing witnesses, &c., & to prefer indictments against those who may be discovered as engaged in the riots." In his report to Governor Thomas Mifflin, Major General John Gibson of the Pennsylvania militia minced no words in announcing, "I am sorry to have to inform your Excellency that a civil War has taken place in this County."[21]

Governor Mifflin and other state officials conferred with Washington and his cabinet to determine what to do about the late uprisings in the west. The federal authorities made it clear from the outset that they believed a resort to military force would be necessary to quell the riots. Although Mifflin and the state officials agreed that the riots must end, they did not believe that military intervention, by the state or federal government, was either necessary or proper, since "the judiciary power was equal to the task of quelling and punishing the riots, and that the employment of a military force, at this period, would be as bad as anything the Rioters had done—equally unconstitutional and illegal." In any event, the state officials expressed some doubt as to their authority to call out the state militia against the rioters.[22]

The state authorities, however, were not to take the lead in suppressing the insurgents. Frustrated by the ineffectiveness of prosecutions in the past, and concerned about the apparent seriousness of the present uprisings, along with other recent challenges to federal sovereignty,[23] the federal government opted for a strong show of authority. Pursuant to an act of Congress regulating the calling out of the militia,[24] the Washington administration presented evidence of the insurrection to James Wilson, the probable drafter of the treason clause in the Constitutional Convention and now an associate justice of the Supreme

Court. On August 4, after reviewing the evidence, Wilson certified that in the western counties "the laws of the United States were opposed . . . by combinations too powerful to be suppressed by the ordinary course of judicial proceedings, or by the powers vested in the marshal of that district." Washington's proclamation of August 7 warned "all persons being insurgents, on or before the first day of September, to disperse and retire peaceably to their respective abodes" and directed the raising of troops.[25]

As a last resort, commissioners from the federal government met with the insurgents late in the summer of 1794, but came away unsatisfied with the assurances they received of future compliance with the laws of the United States.[26] After receiving the report of the commissioners, President Washington ordered the militia into the western counties of Pennsylvania. By this time, however, the "rebellion" was over; the size of the federal force overawed the insurgents and when the soldiers reached the western counties they found "no body in arms to oppose them." The army rounded up the supposed ringleaders of opposition to the excise who were involved in the disturbances, and took some sixteen prisoners back to Philadelphia to be tried at the next session of the federal circuit court.[27]

As in 1792, tension had developed between Pennsylvania and the federal government in their efforts to end and punish opposition to the excise. An important difference, however, marks the relationship between the state and federal response in 1794. In 1792, both state and federal officials conceived of the insurgents as mere rioters who could be brought to justice in the courts, be they state or federal. In 1794, Pennsylvania officials still held this view. Although more extensive than in 1792, the disturbances in the west in 1794 were still riots for which the rioters would be indicted, tried, and punished in the courts of the state for disturbing the public peace of Pennsylvania.[28] For the federal government, however, the widespread rioting in western Pennsylvania had taken on a more ominous tone.

After several years of ineffective proceedings in the state courts and continued resistance to the excise, the federal government no longer trusted Pennsylvania to execute the laws of the United States. As secretary of state, Edmund Randolph noted to Governor Mifflin, further reliance on "a process so indeterminate in its duration" as state enforcement was no longer possible.[29] Indeed, by the summer of 1794 the federal government felt that the insurgents' activities justified the use of the ultimate prosecutorial weapon. Thus, William Bradford, Washington's attorney general in 1794, advised the president in August that the "offense which has already been committed and, which the Insurgents beyond the Allegheny Mountains still persist in, appears to the Attorney General so far as respects the Government of the United States, to be an act of High Treason by levying war against them." Bradford went on to outline the theory from English precedent, complete with citations to the English authorities:

It has been settled by uniform judicial construction, that all insurrections, risings or armed combinations to withstand the authority or alter the lawful measures of government,—

to change the established law—to redress a real or pretended grievance of a *public* nature,—and to effect other innovations of a *general* concern by their own authority and *with force*—are in construction of law high Treason within the clause of levying war "for such violences have a direct tendency to dissolve all the bonds of society and to destroy all property and all government too by numbers and an armed force."[30]

The federal government's efforts to brand the whiskey rebels as traitors to the union are seen in the trials of the insurgents at Philadelphia.

Punishment of the insurgents in the federal courts was not merely an after-thought to the sending of troops. Rather, the federal judiciary worked hand in hand with the federal troops in the west to prepare for the prosecutions that would follow. Judge Richard Peters, the federal district judge for the District of Pennsylvania, accompanied the militia to the western counties. Peters did not spend much time in Pittsburgh, but he was kept busy examining witnesses about the rebellion. Federal prosecutor William Rawle remained in the western counties after Peters's departure, despite his fears of not being able to obtain sufficient judicial assistance from state judges in the west. Rawle was aided in his investigations by Judge Addison, who with the arrival of federal troops seems to have become more tolerant of the exercise of federal jurisdiction. Chief Justice McKean of the Pennsylvania Supreme Court, who was a commissioner for the state of Pennsylvania, also aided in the admission of prisoners to bail.[31]

The insurgents brought back to Philadelphia for trial before the federal circuit court remained some five months in jail before the trials began in May. When the session of the court did begin, the attorney general brought indictments for treason against thirty-five of the insurgents for "levying war against the United States."[32] Of these thirty-five bills, the grand jury only returned twenty-four indictments for high treason. Of the twenty-four persons indicted, thirteen had never been apprehended, and one was later found to be protected by the general amnesty, so only ten of the insurgents actually stood trial for treason.[33]

The chief objection of the insurgents prior to the opening of the circuit court session was that they were forced to stand trial in Philadelphia at all. Relying on section 29 of the Judiciary Act, which provided that "in cases punishable with death, the trial shall be had in the county where the offense was committed" unless "that cannot be done without great inconvenience," defense counsel William Lewis moved before the Supreme Court for the creation of special circuit courts in the western counties for the trials of the insurgents. Despite the "general inclination of the Judges" to grant the request, "the peculiar difficulties of the case" led the Court to deny the motion. Philadelphia was to remain the venue for the treason trials.[34]

Undaunted, Lewis opened the trials in May by objecting to procedural defects in the selection of the jury venire. As the insurgents were to be tried in Philadelphia, the Judiciary Act required that at least twelve jurors be summoned from the jurisdiction where the crime was alleged to have been committed. This had been done, so that there were forty-eight jurors from the western counties, but to complete the venire for the treason trials the marshal had summoned sixty additional jurors from the Philadelphia area for a total of 108. Again echoing the long-standing complaint of the westerners that trial in the distant federal courts deprived them of their rights to trial by jury, Lewis pointed out that section 29 of the Judiciary Act also directed the federal courts to look to state law in "the mode of forming juries . . . so far as the laws of the same shall render such designation practicable" in the courts of the United States. In Pennsylvania, the venire for any particular session of court was limited in number to no more than sixty. Because sixty jurors was the maximum under Pennsylvania law, Lewis argued, only twelve jurors in addition to the forty-eight from the west could be selected to complete the venire.[35] This would, of course, produce individual trial juries with a much more western viewpoint.

Unfortunately for Lewis, the federal circuit court in Philadelphia, consisting of District Judge Peters and Associate Justice William Paterson of the Supreme Court, were not receptive to his argument that the Judiciary Act required strict adherence to state procedure. According to Peters, "The judiciary of the United States should not be fettered and controlled in its operations, by a strict adherence to state regulations and practice." Paterson argued that the issue was really one for the common law, and that he saw no irregularity in the formation of a venire for each case of treason, whereby the rule of the state against more than sixty jurors per venire would be satisfied.[36] Thus, the trials proceeded with a majority of the jurors from the eastern half of Pennsylvania.

Despite the advantages of a Philadelphia forum and eastern juries, the government had difficulty in obtaining convictions for treason. As William Rawle later wrote to Judge Addison, the trials were marked by "a great unwillingness to say too much against . . . fellow citizens, a reluctance in the jury to convict the smaller engine on the testimony of their ringleaders [some of whom had been pardoned under a general amnesty], and a natural repugnance to capital convictions."[37] The court did not conduct a bloody assize; when the evidence was obviously insufficient to convict for treason, under any definition of the term, the court was careful to direct the jury not to convict.[38] When the trials were finished, only two defendants among those indicted, John Mitchell and Philip Vigol, stood convicted of high treason.

Mitchell was charged with high treason for his involvement in the burning of General Neville's house and the rendezvous at Braddock's Field. After the close of the evidence, Rawle stated the law in support of the prosecution. His reliance on the English authorities was explicit:

By the English authorities, it is uniformly and clearly declared, that raising a body of men to obtain, by intimidation or violence, the repeal of a law, or to oppose and prevent by force and terror, the execution of a law, is an act of levying war. Again:—an insurrection with an avowed design to suppress public offices, is an act of levying war.

Rawle closed for the government after arguing that Mitchell's conduct was not excused by extenuating circumstances.[39]

Edward Tilghman and Joseph Thomas, Mitchell's defense counsel, argued forcefully that the doctrine of constructive levying of war espoused by Rawle was a dangerous one. Directed by the court to consider whether Mitchell's actions amounted to a levying of war, Tilghman pointed out the ultimate effect of the prosecutor's interpretation:

Take, then, the distinction of treason by levying war, as laid down by the attorney of the district, and it is a constructive or interpretative weapon, which is calculated to annul all distinctions heretofore wisely established in the grades and punishments of crimes; and by whose magic power a mob may easily be converted into a conspiracy; and a riot aggravated into high treason.

Tilghman also argued that Congress could not have intended the constructive levying of war by the excise insurgents to amount to treason, as it had provided for separate punishment for acts amounting to a resistance of the laws, such as the obstruction of judicial process. Tilghman concluded by asserting that the factual evidence did not demonstrate a plan by the insurgents for a levying of war, and that even though Mitchell was "notoriously drunk" during the rendezvous at Braddock's Field and his conduct might "prove him to be a very bad man, . . . [it] will not be sufficient to maintain a charge of high treason."[40]

In rebuttal, Attorney General Bradford reiterated the distinction between a private and a general, public uprising, the latter being "unquestionably, high treason." The burning of General Neville's house was an overt act of treason, not directed against Neville in particular, but "actuated by one single, traiterous, motive, a determination, if practicable, to frustrate and prevent the execution of the excise law."[41]

Not only did Justice Paterson accept the doctrine of constructive levying of war, but charged the jury that they were to accept it also. Reviewing the testimony, Paterson concluded that the riots were "of a general nature, and of national concern." The martial spirit and manner of the rioters indicated a levying of war, and not a "spirit of revenge against [Neville] as a private citizen." More ominously for Mitchell, Paterson also found that Mitchell's involvement in the insurrection was treason, and advised the jury to do its duty accordingly. Indeed, the only thing seemingly left to the jury to do was to pronounce the verdict of guilt; the facts and law as analyzed by Paterson directed the decision. Not surprisingly, the jury returned a verdict of guilty in fifteen minutes.[42]

Philip Vigol (or Weigle) was indicted for his participation in the attacks on two excise offices, one of which was on the house of the hapless Benjamin Wells of Fayette County. As the report of the case notes that "no question of law arose upon the trial,"[43] it seems that court and counsel assumed that Vigol's participation in the activities of the antiexcise mob constituted a constructive levying of war against the United States after the decision in the *Mitchell* case. This is supported by Gallatin, who observed of the case:

There is no doubt of the man being guilty in a legal sense of levying war against the United States, which was the crime charged to him. But he is certainly an object of pity more than of punishment, at least when we consider that death is the punishment—for he is a rough ignorant German who knew very well he was committing a riot and he ought to have been punished for it, but who had certainly no idea that it amounted a levying war and high treason.[44]

Paterson stated in his charge to the jury that the actions of the prisoner indicated an intention "to suppress the office of excise in the Fourth survey of this state" and that this intention, coupled with the acts proved by the evidence, constituted "the crime of high treason . . . [as] consummate in the contemplation of the constitution and law of the United States." Again, the jury found the defendant guilty.[45]

Juxtaposed with the prosecutions in the federal courts were those cases that found their way into the state courts of the four western counties. The defendants in the state courts, who were certainly less notorious than the men who were indicted in the federal court, were nonetheless tried for substantially equivalent offenses—resistance to federal authority and the collection of the excise. Although the insurgents were charged with nothing more than riot or simple assault in the state courts, the state court prosecutions seem to have been more effective in bringing the rioters to justice than were the federal prosecutions.

Judge Addison's charge to the grand juries of the four counties during the September term in 1794 was clearly aimed at overcoming resistance to federal authority. Addison elaborated on the consequences of violent resistance to the federal government, warning that war with the United States was the ultimate result of violent opposition to the excise.[46] During the December term, however, Addison turned to the punishment of the insurgents. Again lecturing the grand jury that resistance to the excise by violent measures was illegal and contrary to the principles of democratic government, the judge observed that "riots and terror" would not in any event lead to a repeal of the excise. After pointing out these political realities to the grand jury, Addison admonished the jurors

to deal faithfully and make true presentments in all cases of any breach of the peace or other offence especially respecting the late troubles. This will be the true test of our integrity and will determine how far government ought to trust us with the management of ourselves.[47]

Nowhere in the charges, forceful statements of law and order as they are, does Addison mention the possibility that the insurgents are traitors to the United States. Given his view that the state courts should enforce the federal law as a means of protecting their own authority against the federal courts, this at least suggests that Addison did not believe the insurgents to be guilty of treason. The charge also indicates that Judge Addison still believed the state courts to be fully competent to enforce the law, both for the state and federal government.

There were numerous prosecutions for riot in the western counties in 1795, perhaps the most celebrated being that of the mob that attacked the tavern where the federal commissioners stayed while they negotiated with the insurgents. Indeed, the indictment of these men was cited as an example that the westerners were fully capable of resolving the insurrection on their own:

Many persons have been indicted in the Courts here for offenses in the late troubles. I shall only mention, particularly, the persons who insulted the Commissioners at Greens-burgh. I will further observe that the Grand Juries in the several counties have given such specimens of their sense of duty, as will justify at any future occasion, a confidence in the juries of this country in the most popular cases; and will justify the opinions of the friends to the exercise of the state jurisdiction.[48]

In Westmoreland County during the 1795 December term, at least thirty-six of the insurgents were indicted for riot, and only one bill was returned *ignoramus* by the grand jury. Of those indicted, thirteen were convicted of riot, six were convicted of assault in lieu of riot, eight prosecutions were dropped by the state, and only nine were acquitted of all charges.[49] In Allegheny County, there was a conviction for raising a liberty pole, on an unspecified charge, as an insult to the federal commissioners.[50] Although the evidence is by no means complete or conclusive, the state courts seem to have recognized their responsibility to enforce the laws against the insurgents, and the successful record of state prosecutions casts some doubt on the necessity or justification for the stringent legal response of the federal government to the insurrection. It remains unclear whether or not western Pennsylvania was in such a state of anarchy that the unrest, if left solely to "the ordinary course of judicial proceedings" in the state courts, could not have been suppressed.

Even with two convictions for treason, no blood was shed by the federal government in punishing the excise insurgents. After the trials were over, Washington pardoned the two defendants that had been convicted and sentenced to death, characterizing one as a "simpleton" and the other as "insane."[51] Nonetheless, significant legal precedents had been established. Constructive levying of war against the United States was now punishable as treason, just as it had been in England. The federal government's purposes in seeking this result, as well as Pennsylvania's reasons for opposing it, are less clear than the effect of the trials on the law of treason.

Constructive treason prosecutions did not flourish during the Whiskey Insurrection because of some perceived limitation on the ability of the government to prosecute only statutory crimes. While treason was one of the few federal crimes established by statute, the federal courts during the 1790s sanctioned the federal prosecution of common law crimes against the United States.[52] The Whiskey Insurrection itself is evidence that the federal government and courts recognized the ability of the United States to prosecute lesser crimes under the common law. As discussed earlier, the first federal prosecutions against opponents of the excise were brought as common law misdemeanors for breaching the peace of the United States.[53] During the April 1795 term of the circuit court, both treason and misdemeanor indictments were brought against a number of the insurgents, and while the grand jury was often reluctant to return treason indictments, it did return true bills for misdemeanors against most of those charged in the alternative.[54] In addition, all of those defendants indicted for rioting and sedition in other counties in support of the insurgents were charged with common law misdemeanors.[55] The course of proceedings in the federal courts indicates that the constructive treason prosecution arose in 1794 not because treason was the only crime available, but because it was the one the federal government thought was most appropriate.

Political conflicts certainly played some part in Pennsylvania's resistance to the exercise of federal authority. The state's administration was staunchly Republican, and Governor Mifflin had been Washington's political enemy since the days of the Revolution.[56] However, the rhetoric of state and federal officials over how to suppress the insurgents, along with their mutual mistrust, suggests that more than partisan political differences were at the heart of the conflict. Commenting on his thwarted expectations during the trials of the insurgents, William Rawle noted, "Something . . . must, I think, be attributed to the difficult distinction necessary to be made between the different jurisdictions."[57] Indeed, jurisdictional differences are perhaps the best explanation for the Whiskey Insurrection.

Federalism was still a new phenomenon to the United States and its component parts. As the Whiskey Insurrection indicates, the interrelationships between state and federal authority were unclear. Courts battled for jurisdiction, executive officials argued over the sovereignty of the state versus the general government, and legislatures debated difficult questions as to what the federal government was to do when a state failed to enforce the laws or suppress an insurrection. The entire course of the insurrection is marked with these conflicts. Judge Addison's views on the necessity of the federal courts, Hamilton's fear of a general revolt against federal authority, and Justice Wilson's certification that state authority was no longer sufficient to maintain order in the west all demonstrate the tension between state and federal jurisdiction. Even the protests of the insurgents, against a federal tax enforced in the federal courts, reflect the growing pains of federalism. In the final analysis, the treason trials of the whiskey rebels are the response of the federal courts to both the "storm in the west" and this conflict between state and federal authority under the Constitution.

NOTES

1. St. George Tucker to James Monroe, Mar. 8, 1795, in James Monroe Papers, College of William and Mary.

2. Congress established the excise tax in "An Act repealing, after the last day of June next, the duties heretofore laid upon Distilled Spirits imported from abroad, and laying others in their stead, and also upon Spirits distilled within the United States, and

for appropriating the same," ch. 15, sec. 15, *The Public Statutes at Large of the United States of America, from the Organization of the Government in 1789* (Boston: Little & Brown, 1845), 1:199, 203 (1791) [hereinafter cited as "1 *Stat.*"].

3. U.S. Const. art. III, sec. 3.

4. For a discussion of the development of the English law of constructive treason with regard to the clause "to levy war," see W. S. Holdsworth, *A History of English Law*, 12 vols. (Boston: Little, Brown, & Co., 1922-38), 8:318-21. The Framers narrowed significantly the English statutory definition of treason, and the ability of courts to expand upon it, by eliminating from the constitutional definition of treason the clause which defined as treason actions that did "compass or imagine the Death of our Lord the King." Nonetheless, the Framers recognized that by borrowing some "operative" language from the English statutes, English meanings would govern. Thus, Edmund Randolph, considering the clause regarding adherence to the enemy during the Constitutional Convention, "thought the clause defective in adopting the words 'in adhering' only. The British Stat: adds, 'giving them aid and comfort' *which had a more extensive meaning." Notes of Debates in the Federal Convention of 1787 Reported by James Madison* (New York: W. W. Norton & Co., 1966), p. 490 (emphasis added). The law lectures of James Wilson, a delegate at the Constitutional Convention and later Associate Justice of the Supreme Court, illustrate the Framers' assumption that English precedent would define the phrase "to levy war," borrowed directly from the English treason statutes. Wilson's lecture on treason is contained in *The Works of James Wilson*, ed. R. G. McCloskey, 2 vols. (Cambridge, Mass.: Belknap Press, 1967), 2:663-69.

5. Excise Act, ch. 15, sec. 42, 1 *Stat.*, p. 209; "An Act to establish the Judicial Courts of the United States," ch. 20, sec. 3, 1 *Stat.* pp. 73, 74 (1789).

6. Jonathan Elliott, ed., *Debates in the Several State Conventions on the Adoption of the Federal Constitution* (Philadelphia: J. B. Lippincott Co., 1836), 3:469 (statement of William Findley); Proceedings of the Meeting at Harrisburg, in Pennsylvania, *ibid.* 3:546.

7. *Pittsburgh Gazette,* Dec. 10, 1791.

8. Alexander Addison to Thomas Mifflin, Nov. 4, 1792, in John B. Linn and William H. Egle, eds., *Pennsylvania Archives*, 2d ser. (Harrisburg: Clarence M. Busch, State Printer, 1896), 4:32; Alexander Addison to George Clymer, Sept. 29, 1792, in Harold C. Syrett et. al., eds., *The Papers of Alexander Hamilton* (New York: Columbia University Press, 1961-1979), 12:519, n.5, emphasis added.

9. Alexander Addison to Thomas Mifflin, Nov. 4, 1792, *Pennsylvania Archives*, 2d ser., 4:31-32.

10. See, for example, George Clymer to Alexander Hamilton, Oct. 4, 1792, in *Hamilton Papers* 12:518-19; Alexander Hamilton to Thomas Mifflin, Dec. 3, 1792, in *ibid.* 13:277.

11. Alexander Hamilton to Tench Coxe, Sept. 1, 1792, in *ibid.* 12:305; Alexander Hamilton to George Washington, Sept. 1, 1792, in *ibid.* 12:312; Alexander Hamilton to John Jay, Sept. 3, 1792, in *ibid.* 12:316. The proceedings of the meeting are reprinted in "At a Meeting of sundry Inhabitants of the Western Counties of Pennsylvania, held at Pittsburgh, on the 21st day of August, 1792," in *ibid.*, 12:308, n.5.

12. Edmund Randolph to Alexander Hamilton, Sept. 8, 1792, in *ibid.*, 12:337; George Washington to Alexander Hamilton, Sept. 7, 1792, in *ibid.* 12:332-33. Gallatin notes that the fact that "no bill having been even found at York against the members of the

Committee must convince everybody that our measures were innocent" (Albert Gallatin to Thomas Clare, Dec. 18, 1792, in Albert Gallatin Papers, New York Historical Society).

13. George Clymer to Alexander Hamilton, Oct. 4, 1792, *Hamilton Papers* 12:520; George Washington to William Rawle, Mar. 13, 1793, Miscellaneous Letters (M-179, reel 9), RG 59, National Archives.

14. "A Proclamation Concerning Opposition to the Excise Law," *Federal Gazette and Philadelphia General Advertiser*, Sept. 25, 1792.

15. Hamilton cited Huston's failure to execute the warrants as an example of the state officials' sympathy with the excise insurgents. Alexander Hamilton to George Washington, Aug. 5, 1794, in *Hamilton Papers* 17:45; *United States* v. *Huston*, October sess. 1793 (indictment), Criminal Case Files of the United States Circuit Court for the Eastern District of Pennsylvania 1791–1840 (M-986, reel 1), RG 21, National Archives [hereafter cited as *"Circuit Court Records"*].

16. Deposition of Benjamin Wells, Jan. 29, 1794, Oliver Wolcott Papers, Connecticut Historical Society; *United States* v. *Smilie*, July sess. 1794 (indictment), *Circuit Court Records*.

17. "An Act for making further provision for securing and collecting the Duties on foreign and domestic distilled Spirits, Stills, Wines and Teas," ch. 49, sec. 18, 1 *Stat.*, pp. 378, 381 (1794).

18. Stephen B. Presser, "A Tale of Two Judges: Richard Peters, Samuel Chase, and the Broken Promise of Federalist Jurisprudence," *Northwestern University Law Review* 73 (March-April 1978), 26, 75; *United States* v. *Lang*, October sess. 1793, *Circuit Court Records*.

19. George Clymer to Robert Johnson, Mar. 8, 1794, in Historical Collections, Washington and Jefferson College; Declaration of Fayette County Representatives, Sept. 10, 1794, in Whiskey Rebellion Papers (container 1), Library of Congress; William Irvine to Alexander Dallas, Aug. 20, 1794, *Pennsylvania Archives*, 2d ser., 4:154; John Neville to Tench Coxe, July 18, 1794, in *Hamilton Papers* 17:4, n.2.

20. "Circular of the Western Insurgents to the Militia Officers," July 28, 1794, *Pennsylvania Archives*, 2d ser., 4:67. For a general account of the insurgents' activities arising out of the Braddock's Field rendezvous, see Leland D. Baldwin, *Whiskey Rebels: The Story of a Frontier Uprising* (Pittsburgh, Penn.: University of Pittsburgh Press, 1939), pp. 146–64.

21. Alexander Addison to Alexander Dallas, July 24, 1794, *Pennsylvania Archives*, 2d ser., 4:62; John Gibson to Thomas Mifflin, July 18, 1794, in *ibid.* 4:58.

22. "Conference Concerning the Insurrection in Western Pennsylvania," Aug. 2, 1794, in *Hamilton Papers* 17:9, 10–12, and nn. 11–12. Nonetheless, Dallas suggested to Major General Gibson of the Pennsylvania Militia in Pittsburgh that "if the Civil authority can be supported by the assistance of the Militia, the exercise of your discretion for that purpose, upon the request of the Magistrates, must be highly agreeable to the Governor" (Alexander Dallas to Henry Knox, July 18, 1794 [transmitting his instructions to Gibson], in Oliver Wolcott Papers, Connecticut Historical Society).

23. Hamilton believed that the Whiskey Insurrection was but one instance of a general and growing opposition to federal authority, which included Georgia's attempt to void the effect of the Supreme Court's judgment in *Chisholm* v. *Georgia* and the disaffection of Kentuckians with the federal government's efforts to negotiate with Spain for navigation rights on the Mississippi ("Conference Concerning the Insurrection in Western Pennsylvania," Aug. 2, 1794, in *Hamilton Papers*, 17:12, and nn. 13, 15).

24. "An Act to provide for calling forth the Militia to execute the laws of the Union, suppress insurrections and repel invasions," ch. 28, 1 *Stat.* p. 264 (1792).

25. *American State Papers: Miscellaneous* (Washington: Gales and Seaton, 1834), 1:85; "Proclamation of President Washington," Aug. 7, 1794, *Pennsylvania Archives*, 2d ser., 4:108.

26. One of the commissioners' bargaining chips was the promise that future suits against the distillers would be brought in the state courts, so long as this would cause no "danger of . . . [the United States] being frustrated in the object of the suits and prosecutions" (Edmund Randolph to James Ross, Jasper Yeats, and William Bradford, Aug. 7, 1794, in Gratz Collection, Historical Society of Pennsylvania).

27. "Second Proclamation of President Washington," Sept. 25, 1794, *Pennsylvania Archives*, 2d ser., 4:304–05; St. George Tucker to James Monroe, Mar. 8, 1795, in James Monroe Papers, College of William and Mary; *Philadelphia Gazette*, Dec. 5, 1794. Not surprisingly, Pennsylvania had the most difficulty in meeting the militia quota imposed by the federal government. See Harry M. Tinkcom, *The Republicans and Federalists in Pennsylvania, 1790–1801: A Study in National Stimulus and Local Response* (Philadelphia: Pennsylvania Historical and Museum Commission, 1950), pp. 101–03. For an insightful analysis of the federal government's decision first to negotiate with the insurgents before resorting to military force, see Richard H. Kohn, "The Washington Administration's Decision to Crush the Whiskey Rebellion," *Journal of American History* 59 (Dec. 1972), 567–84.

28. This view is expressed by Governor Mifflin in his letter to George Washington, Aug. 5, 1794, in *Pennsylvania Archives*, 2d ser., 4:89–90. In a message to the Assembly after the Washington administration's decision to send troops, however, Mifflin did acknowledge that the riots against "the system of Federal policy" would require the use of military force ("Governor Mifflin's Message to the Assembly," Sept. 2, 1794, in *ibid.*, 4:209–18). The Mifflin administration's maneuvering with the federal government over the suppression of the insurrection and ultimate acquiescence to the federal plan is set forth in more detail in Kenneth R. Rossman, *Thomas Mifflin and the Politics of the American Revolution* (Chapel Hill: University of North Carolina Press, 1952), pp. 249–67; and Tinkcom, *Republicans and Federalists in Pennsylvania*, pp. 91–112.

29. Edmund Randolph to Thomas Mifflin, Aug. 7, 1794, in *Hamilton Papers* 17:67, 69.

30. William Bradford to George Washington, Aug. 2, 1794, in George Washington Papers, Library of Congress (emphasis in original; citations omitted).

31. Alexander Hamilton to Henry Lee, Oct. 20, 1794, in *Hamilton Papers*, 17:332; William Rawle to Edmund Randolph, Oct. 2, 1794, in Richard Peters Papers, vol. 10, Historical Society of Pennsylvania; William Rawle to Alexander Addison, Nov. 24, 1794, in *Pennsylvania Archives*, 2d ser., 4:397; William Rawle to Alexander Addison, Nov. 26, 1794, in *ibid.*, 4:398; Deposition of Daniel Depew, Dec. 23, 1794, in Richard Peters Papers, vol. 1, Historical Society of Pennsylvania (deposition taken by Judge Addison for federal prosecution); *Circuit Court Records*, Nov. 6, 1794 (admission of Edward Cooke to bail by Justice McKean).

32. Baltimore *Federal Intelligencer*, Jan. 2, 1795; William Bradford to Samuel Bayard, Mar. 30, 1795, Gratz Collection, Historical Society of Pennsylvania. The Judiciary Act of 1789 required that prosecutions punishable by death be brought in the federal circuit court (Judiciary Act, ch. 20, secs. 9, 11, 1 *Stat.*, pp. 76–77, 79). Congress restated the prohibition against levying war from the treason clause of the Constitution when it set

forth the death penalty for treason in "An Act for the Punishment of certain Crimes against the United States," ch. 9, sec. 1, 1 *Stat.*, p. 112.

33. Appendix A; Albert Gallatin to Thomas Clare, May 30, 1795, in Albert Gallatin Papers, New York Historical Society; William Bradford to William Rawle, June 4, 1795, in *Circuit Court Records*. Some of the insurgents were indicted for lesser crimes, such as misprison of treason and misdemeanor. See Appendix A (six misdemeanor indictments and two misprison of treason indictments). Appendix B records those indictments for misdemeanors against citizens of other counties for pole raisings and seditious statements in support of the insurgents.

34. *United States* v. *Stewart et al.*, 2 Dall., pp. 343, (C.C.D. Pa. 1795). The record of Lewis's motion before the Supreme Court is in Maeva Marcus et al., ed., *The Documentary History of the Supreme Court of the United States, 1789-1800.*

35. *United States* v. *The Insurgents*, 2 Dall., pp. 335, 336–37 (C.C.D. Pa. 1795); Judiciary Act, ch. 20, sec. 29, 1 *Stat.*, p. 88. Lewis also objected that the defendants had not received copies of the captions of the indictments before trial, and the Court accordingly postponed the trials for three days to allow for compliance (*United States* v. *The Insurgents*, 2 Dall., pp. 337–38, 342).

36. *United States* v. *The Insurgents*, 2 Dall., pp. 341–42.

37. William Rawle to Alexander Addison, Aug. 15, 1795, in *Pennsylvania Archives*, 2d ser., 4:450.

38. In the trial of Robert Porter, 2 Dall. p. 345 (C.C.D. Pa. 1795), Attorney General Bradford admitted that "the evidence did not amount to what he had expected," and the court "directed the jury to find a verdict in favor of the prisoner" (Albert Gallatin to Hannah Gallatin, May 18–19, 1795, in Albert Gallatin Papers, New York Historical Society).

39. *United States* v. *Mitchell*, 2 Dall. pp. 348, 348–50 (C.C.D. Pa. 1795).

40. *Ibid.*, pp. 350–52. In "An Act for the Punishment of certain Crimes against the United States," ch. 9, sec. 22, 1 *Stat.* p. 117, Congress established the obstruction of judicial process as a specific statutory crime.

41. *United States* v. *Mitchell*, 2 Dall., pp. 353–54. Jacob E. Cooke has suggested that the attack on Neville's house may have been motivated by not only hatred for the excise, but by personal animosity against Neville based upon political intrigues in the region ("The Whiskey Insurrection: A Re-Evaluation," *Pennsylvania History* 30 [July 1963], 316, 336–39).

42. *United States* v. *Mitchell*, 2 Dall., pp. 355–56. Although Gallatin, who was a witness at some of the treason trials, opined that the evidence against Mitchell was no more damning than that against the other insurgents tried for the attack on Neville's house, he concluded that the differences in verdict resulted from the inexperience of defense counsel Thomas, who used his peremptory challenges to obtain a jury of twelve Quakers in the mistaken belief that Quakers would never sentence Mitchell to death (Albert Gallatin to Hannah Gallatin, June 1, 1795, in Albert Gallatin Papers, New York Historical Society). Gallatin noted that the Quakers, while perhaps more lenient in cases of murder and rape, did not look with sympathy on cases of "insurrection, rebellion & treason."

43. *United States* v. *Vigol*, 2 Dall., pp. 346 (C.C.D. Pa. 1795).

44. Albert Gallatin to Hannah Gallatin, May 25, 1795, in Albert Gallatin Papers, New York Historical Society.

45. *United States* v. *Vigol*, 2 Dall., p. 347.

46. Grand Jury Charge No. 12 ("Necessity of Submission to the Excise Law"), Alexander Addison, *Charges to the Grand Juries of the Counties of the Fifth Circuit, in the State of Pennsylvania* (Philadelphia: Kay and Brother, 1883), pp. 100–12.

47. Grand Jury Charge No. 13 ("Remarks on the Late Insurrection"), *ibid.*, pp. 116–17, 121, 126.

48. *Pennsylvania* v. *Cribs*, 1 Add. 277 (Westmoreland Co. Ct. 1795), "Extract of a letter from Washington county, dated 25th December 1794," Philadelphia *Aurora*, Jan. 28, 1795.

49. Westmoreland County Court of Common Pleas Docket Records, December term 1795.

50. *Pennsylvania* v. *Morrison*, 1 Add. 274 (Allegheny Co. Ct. 1795). Addison's concern over the seditious effects of the raising of liberty poles during the insurrection is exhibited in Grand Jury Charge No. 13 ("Remarks on the Late Insurrection"), Addison, *Grand Jury Charges*, pp. 126–27.

51. John C. Miller, *The Federalist Era* (New York: Harper and Row, 1960), p. 159.

52. Presser, "A Tale of Two Judges," pp. 48–58. The Supreme Court did not expressly reject the notion of federal common law crimes until 1812 in *United States* v. *Hudson and Goodwin*, 11 U.S. (7 Cranch) 32 (1812).

53. Washington, in instructing Hamilton to proceed against the insurgents in 1792, noted that reference was to be made to state law in prosecuting opponents of the excise in the federal courts. George Washington to Alexander Hamilton, Sept. 7, 1792, in *Hamilton Papers* 12:332.

54. See Appendix A (cases of John Corbley, Thomas Geddes, Harmon Husbands, Caleb Mountz, and Robert Philson).

55. See Appendix B.

56. Kohn, "The Washington Administration's Decision," pp. 572–73.

57. William Rawle to Alexander Addison, Aug. 15, 1795, in *Pennsylvania Archives*, 2d ser., 4:450.

STEVEN R. BOYD

Afterword

I have assumed, throughout the process of preparing this volume, that it could serve two purposes. First, it could enliven student interest in history and the historical process. Second, it could stimulate further research on the Whiskey Rebellion even as it made those currently active in the field aware of other research in progress. The first is out of my hands. If others find the mix of primary and secondary sources herein a useful combination for introducing students to a more sophisticated understanding of the Whiskey Rebellion and history in general, then the volume will have accomplished a major objective.

I can do more with regard to research on the Whiskey Rebellion. I have, in preparing this volume, read and discussed the rebellion with a variety of historians, some whose work is represented in this volume, others whose work is still in progress. What emerges from that is a sense of the future directions our research will take us as we continue to examine the Whiskey Rebellion.

There are several focal points that seem most likely to attract further attention. One is geographic in nature. As several of the essays in this volume suggest, historians now are more aware of the breadth of resistance to the excise program of the Washington administration. Noncompliance with the tax was epidemic not only in Western Pennsylvania, but also in Kentucky, and parts of Maryland, Virginia, and the Carolinas at least. Historians will continue in all likelihood to expand the geographic perimeters of their research, as Mary K. Bonsteel Tachau and Roland M. Baumann have done, in order to better understand the similarities and differences in the responses of western Pennsylvanians and others to the tax, and the reactions of the administration to the noncompliance of those different regions.

If we recognize that the resistance to the excise tax was widespread, then we need to ask why did it escalate into a so-called rebellion in only one region. A partial answer is that the resistance to the excise tax was based on its perceived inequity by people who believed they had a constitutional right to resist unjust laws. The argument that the tax on whiskey was unfair to westerners was a common one. Hamilton responded that the tax could of course be passed on to consumers. Historians have tended to agree with Hamilton. Dodee Fennell, in an essay originally intended to be included in this volume, suggests that the situation was more complex than that. She has found that the tax on whiskey posed a disproportionately heavier burden for small producers who paid the tax-per-gallon rate while large producers, who owned and operated their own stills, could pay a flat fee that cut the tax per gallon in half. She also notes that those who did not own a still, but paid a share of their grain to a still operator to convert it to whiskey, were further disadvantaged by having to pay the tax on the entire product, although the transaction in which they were involved generated no cash. Finally, she shows that this inequity was further exacerbated by the federal governments decision to purchase whiskey in the west only from those who had paid the tax (the army was the largest single purchaser of whiskey) and at the lowest possible price. This, in effect, negated Hamilton's claim that the tax could be passed on to the consumer. The inequity of the tax was of course a common denominator effecting producers in all regions. It remains to be seen if the situation in Pennsylvania was materially different from that in other regions. Were there more large producers in Western Pennsylvania who could take advantage of the alternative tax schedule available to them? Or was the shift to a more capitalistic stage of agriculture still at an early stage in those counties, and the impact of the excise therefore resented more by the smaller, least capitalistic producers?

It also remains to be seen if the policy of the government in purchasing whiskey was uniform across the frontier, or if in fact, if the manner in which whiskey was purchased in Pennsylvania was distinct from the mode applied in other areas. If there are differences in these areas, they too may have been contributing factors in the outbreak of the rebellion.

A second factor to be considered in evaluating the causes of the rebellion is the political values of the people involved. In Pennsylvania there was long-standing enmity toward excise taxes among the Scots-Irish and a belief that resistance to unjust taxes was legitimate. The Revolution reinforced this attitude with its appeal to higher law and its legitimization of resistance to tyranny. Pauline Maier argues that this tradition was undercut by events in the postwar period and delegitimized by the Constitution. Yet this process was not uniform across the nation. Findley and Brackenridge, in their respective histories, both explain that the whiskey rebels believed that they had a constitutional right to resist, ultimately with force, the unjust taxes of the federal government. After all, Brackenridge notes, they had been promised that there would be no excise under the new government. And despite their best efforts to obtain its repeal, the government proved unresponsive to westerners' complaints. The rebellion became in their eyes, therefore, a legitimate response to tyrannical power.

This perception of the law was heightened by the specific circumstances that led to the assault upon General Neville's house. On June 5, 1794, the president signed a bill which provided for violators of the excise act to be tried in state courts if no federal court were within fifty miles. Yet on May 30, federal Judge Richard Peters issued processes requiring those accused of violations of the excise act to appear in federal district court in Philadelphia. These processes were not served until July, and it was the serving of these processes, after the effective date of the new law, that triggered armed resistance to the federal marshall serving them and consequently to the rebellion. Judge Peters was of course perfectly correct in issuing the processes and Federal Marshall Lenox also acted properly. But, if the attack upon General Neville's house was spontaneous (he was shielding Marshall Lenox whom the rebels wished to deprive of his processes), it was an explicable action in light of the constitutional beliefs of the westerners.

Those constitutional views in turn also suggest one of the major consequences of the suppression of the rebellion. The right to resist unjust laws faced increasing opposition following independence. Federalists indeed made the argument against such violence a major weapon in their arsenal of arguments for ratification of the new Constitution. Ratification did not, however, eliminate political violence. Quite the contrary, it increased it as both Federalists and anti-Federalists used physical force and the threat of force in their efforts to secure the ratification or defeat of the Constitution. Once ratified, however, the pressure to accept a narrower definition of the legitimate modes of political participation drove increasing numbers of anti-Federalists into the electoral process. The suppression of those who remained outside of that process until 1794 signaled a major step in the implementation of the Constitution.

In suppressing the rebels, then, the federal and state governments moved to define more narrowly than the existing tradition, but well within the guidelines of the Constitution, the rights of its citizens. If before 1787 they had a right to resist unjust laws, that right was restricted in theory by the adoption of the Constitution. But it took the rebellion and its suppression to persuade westerners to accept that new limit. That most westerners did so was clear to Brackenridge and Findley. Both acknowledged in their respective histories that the rebels' presuppression understanding of their constitutional rights was indeed in error, and that under this republican government the citizens had the right to resort only to the electoral process to secure a redress of their grievances.

This is, of course, only one of a number of areas of research still open. Richard A. Ifft, in his chapter, breaks additional new ground in examining the state prosecutions of the rebels and the meaning of those prosecutions in the larger arena of federal state relations. Ifft has not, however, exhausted even the Pennsylvania record on this matter. Mary K. Bonsteel Tachau has initiated a study of Pennsylvania that will parallel her earlier work on Kentucky and investigate further some of the questions Ifft raises. But court and other institutional records for other states remain an untapped resource.

As one example, we tend to assume that in the aftermath of the rebellion the excise ceased to be a controversial matter and that collections were made. Again, Tachau has suggested that was not the case, in either Kentucky or Pennsylvania. But what of the other jurisdictions? Did other forms of noncompliance, less violent or overt, prevail between the end of the rebellion and the repeal of the tax in 1801? Or did collections increase over time? And, if they did, was the suppression a factor in encouraging such compliance?

Similarly, we assume that when the administration called for troops to suppress the rebellion, the muster proceeded routinely. But was that the case? The administration, at the outset, was uncertain if troops could be mobilized. Although they were able to raise the requisite number, we know very little about that process. Was it orderly? Were there degrees of resistance to it? What was the attitude of the troops?

Finally, we know very little about how those outside the administration or organized groups, e.g., the Democratic-Republican Societies, reacted to the rebellion. We tend to think in monoliths—the western country and the administration, the rebels and the militia. Yet the lines of demarcation were not so clearly drawn. Certainly the entire western country did not revolt and elements in the east sided with the rebels. For an agrarian protest by beleaguered small farmers, we know far too little about those farmers, and their counterparts across the country (who were after all the majority of the population). How did they perceive the rebellion and its suppression? And again, research is in progress on aspects of these questions, but the field is a broad one and the questions far more than I have indicated here.

These brief remarks, then, do not exhaust the questions that lie before us. They, with the essays that precede them, merely suggest what the future perspectives on the Whiskey Rebellion may be.

Note on Sources

The major secondary sources for the Whiskey Rebellion are identified in Thomas P. Slaughter's "The Friends of Liberty, The Friends of Order, and the Whiskey Rebellion," chapter 1 in this volume. For those interested in reading further on the rebellion, that chapter constitutes a superior guide. For those inclined to do additional research among the primary sources, there is no comparable chapter. This note will identify the major primary sources, published and manuscript, as a further aid to students interested in examining for themselves additional parts of the original record and researchers intent on investigating anew the complexities of the Whiskey Rebellion.

A convenient compilation of some of the primary sources of the rebellion is contained in volume four of the second series of *The Pennsylvania Archives*, ed. John B. Linn and William H. Egle (Harrisburg, 1876). The volume is the most extensive collection of documents on the Whiskey Rebellion to date. It is of course far from complete, and inadequately edited. One must, therefore, eventually turn to other sources. The most revealing of those are the private papers of the principal actors. Thus the Washington Papers and the Alexander Hamilton Papers, both at the Library of Congress, are crucial. The former are available on microfilm, the latter are printed in Harold C. Syrett, et al. eds., *The Papers of Alexander Hamilton* (New York, 1961–1979). Also useful are the Tench Coxe Papers at the Pennsylvania Historical Society, and available on microfilm. Coxe served as Hamilton's commissioner of the revenue and his private correspondence, which has been available only for the last decade, sheds much light on the rebellion. Finally, among the federal actors in the drama are the papers of Issac Craig, Carnegie Library, Pittsburgh; the papers of John Neville, also at the Carnegie Library, Pittsburgh, and in the Oliver Wolcott Papers, Connecticut Historical Society; and the John William Wallace papers at the Pennsylvania Historical Society.

The records of the Department of the Treasury complement these private papers. See in particular Walter Lowrie and Walter S. Franklin, eds., *American State Papers, Finance: Documents, Legislative and Executive of the Congress of the United States*, 5 vols., (Washington, 1834), which contains much information concerning the collection of the excise tax. Also important are the Whiskey Rebellion Papers, and the Letters Sent by the Commissioner of the Revenue and the Revenue Office, 1792–1807, both in RG 58, Records of the Internal Revenue Service, National Archives.

The official court records of the trials of several of the rebels are printed in Alexander Dallas, *Reports of Cases Ruled and Adjudged in the Several Courts of the United States, and of Pennsylvania, Held at the Seat of the Federal Government*, 4 vols., (Philadelphia, 1798–1807). Additional material is available in the criminal case files of the United States Circuit Court for the Eastern District of Pennsylvania, 1791–1840, National Archives, and in the papers of Judges William Bradford at the Pennsylvania Historical Society and James Iredell at the North Carolina Department of History and Archives, Chapel Hill. These and other relevant documents have also been collected by the staff of the Documentary History of the Supreme Court and will be published, starting in 1985, in Maeva Marcus et al., eds., *The Documentary History of the Supreme Court of the United States, 1789–1800*.

The points of view of those outside of the Washington administration are not as well represented in the traditional sources. The most comprehensive statements are the histories of Brackenridge and Findley, excerpted above, and available on microcard in Clifford K. Shipton, ed., *Early American Imprints*. Other important contemporary comments were made by Albert Gallatin, whose papers are available at the New York Historical Society and on microfilm. See also *The Speech of Albert Gallatin . . . Relative to the Western Insurrection* (Philadelphia, 1795). Alexander Addison also left considerable material relevant to the rebellion which is housed in the Addison papers, University of Pittsburgh. See also his *Charges to Grand Juries of the Counties of the Fifth Circuit in the State of Pennsylvania* (Philadelphia, 1800). Both the Gallatin speech and Addison volume are available in Shipton's *Early American Imprints*. There are also miscellaneous "Whiskey Rebellion" manuscript collections at the Pennsylvania Historical Society, the Library of Congress, and the National Archives.

The Debates and Proceedings in the Congress of the United States, 1789–1824, comp. Joseph Gales (Washington, D.C., 1834–56) [The Annals of Congress], shed additional light on the rebellion. Further insight into the diverse responses of the nation to the rebellion can be gleaned from newspapers. See in particular the Philadelphia *Gazette of the United States*, the Philadelphia *Independent Gazetteer*, and the Philadelphia *General Advertiser*, as well as the *Carlisle Gazette* and the *Pittsburgh Gazette*.

The other principal "actors" in the Whiskey Rebellion were of course the state governments. The records of the state of Pennsylvania that pertain to the rebellion include the printed journals of the house of representatives and senate and the miscellaneous executive and legislative material printed in the *Pennsylvania Archives*. Additional material, including executive minutes, correspondence, and petitions, are in RG 26, Pennsylvania State Archives, Harrisburg. For a guide to those records, see Frank M. Suran, comp., *Guide to the Record Groups in the Pennsylvania State Archives* (Harrisburg, 1980).

Also important are the county court records. The principal published source is Alexander Addison, *Reports of Cases in the County Courts of the Fifth Circuit, and in the High Court of Appeals, of the State of Pennsylvania* (Washington, Pa., 1800). The bulk of these records, including the records of the trials of various rebels for violations of state law are still stored in their respective county courthouses, while the petitions for clemency from those convicted of state crimes are in RG 26, Pennsylvania State Archives, Harrisburg.

Comparable material is also available for the other state governments which faced a similar, if less explosive situation. Those sources are identified for Kentucky in Mary K. Bonsteel Tachau's bibliographic essay in *Federal Courts in the Early Republic: Kentucky, 1789–1816* (Princeton, 1978). Similar records presumably exist for Maryland, Virginia, and the Carolinas among the official records of the state governments and the private papers of their prominent political leaders.

In addition to these traditional sources, the records of economic development and social change in western Pennsylvania are also important. Particularly useful in that regard are the tax data printed in the *Pennsylvania Archives*. The extant original records remain in the various county courthouses. This material supplements the demographic data available in the 1790 census and can provide considerable insight into the nature of social and economic change in the western counties.

This does not complete the list of sources available for further study of the Whiskey Rebellion. Indeed, no such list is feasible, for the sources for such a study are as diverse as the questions asked. This note identifies principally the sources utilized by the authors in this volume. Historians can use these sources as a starting point as they continue to develop new perspectives on the Whiskey Rebellion.

Appendix A

Indictments in the Circuit Court for the District of Pennsylvania
May 1975 Term—the Western Counties

Source: Criminal Case Files of the United States Circuit Court for the Eastern
District of Pennsylvania 1791–1840 (M-986, reel 1), RG 21, National Archives

Name	County of Origin	Charge
John Barnet	Washington	Treason
John Black	Washington	Treason
David Bolton	Washington	Treason
David Bradford	Washington	Treason
Thomas Burney	Allegheny	Treason
John Corbley	Washington	Treason
John Corbley	Washington	Misdemeanor
William Crawford	Washington	Treason
Marmaduke Curtis	Allegheny	Treason
Alexander Fulton	Washington	Treason
Ebenezer Gallagher	Allegheny	Treason
Thomas Geddes	Fayette	Treason
Thomas Geddes	Fayette	Misdemeanor
Daniel Hamilton	Washington	Treason
John Hamilton	Washington	Misprison of Treason

Disposition	Date	Offense	At Trial
True Bill (Not guilty)	May 4, 1795	Neville's House	Yes
Ignoramus	May 6, 1795	Neville's House	Yes
True Bill (Later found not guilty)	May 6, 1795	Neville's House	No
True Bill	May 5, 1795	Braddock's Field	No
Ignoramus	May 11, 1795	Neville's House	Yes
Ignoramus	May 7, 1795	Braddock's Field	Yes
True Bill (Prosecution dropped on Apr. 4, 1796)	May 11, 1795	Conspiring to levy war against the United States	Yes
Ignoramus	May 11, 1795	Braddock's Field	Yes
True Bill (Not guilty)	May 5, 1795	Neville's House	Yes
True Bill	May 11, 1795	Meeting on July 28, 1794 at Cannonsburg to organize the Braddock's Field rendezvous	No
True Bill	May 6, 1795	Neville's House	No
Ignoramus	May 9, 1795	Pole raising in Uniontown on Aug. 10, 1794	Yes
True Bill	May 9, 1795	Same	Yes
True Bill	May 4, 1795	Neville's House	No
Ignoramus	May 9, 1795	Failure to disclose treasonous activities	Yes

Name	County of Origin	Charge
William Hanna	Allegheny	Treason
Samuel Hanna	Allegheny	Treason
John Holcroft	Allegheny	Treason
Richard Holcroft	Allegheny	Treason
Harmon Husbands	Bedford	Treason
Harmon Husbands	Bedford	Misdemeanor
Peter Lisle	Allegheny	Treason
David Lock	Washington	Treason
John Lockery	Washington	Treason
Thomas Miller	Allegheny	Treason
William Miller	Allegheny	Treason
John Mitchell	Washington	Treason (Guilty)
John Mitchell	Washington	Felony
William Bradford	Washington	Felony
Caleb Mountz	Fayette	Treason
Caleb Mountz	Fayette	Misdemeanor
Benjamin Parkinson	Washington	Treason
Robert Philson	Bedford	Treason
Robert Philson	Bedford	Misdemeanor
Robert Porter	Washington	Treason
Joseph Posey	Westmoreland	Treason

Disposition	Date	Offense	At Trial
True Bill	May 8, 1795	Neville's House	No
True Bill	May 11, 1795	Neville's House	No
True Bill (Case dismissed under amnesty)	May 6, 1795	Neville' House	Yes
True Bill	May 8, 1795	Neville's House	No
Ignoramus	May 11, 1795	Inciting insurrection in Washington County	Yes
True Bill	May 11, 1795	Same	Yes
True Bill	May 11, 1795	Neville's House	No
True Bill	May 8, 1795	Braddock's Field	No
True Bill (Not guilty)	May 4, 1795	Meeting on July 28, 1794 at Cannonsburg to organize the Braddock's Field rendezvous	Yes
True Bill (Not guilty)	May 6, 1795	Neville's House	Yes
True Bill	May 5, 1795	Neville's House	No
True Bill	May 11, 1795	Neville's House	Yes
True Bill	May 7, 1795	Robbing the Mail	Yes
True Bill	May 7, 1795	Same	Yes
Ignoramus	May 11, 1795	Pole raising in Franklin on Aug. 10, 1794	Yes
Ignoramus	May 11, 1795	Same	Yes
True Bill	May 5, 1795	Neville's House	No
True Bill	May 11, 1795	Inciting insurrection in Washington County	Yes
True Bill	May 11, 1795	Same	Yes
True Bill (Not guilty)	May 7, 1795	Neville's House	Yes
Ignoramus	May 6, 1795	July 24, 1794 attack on Fayette County revenue office	Yes

Name	County of Origin	Charge
Joseph Scott	Allegheny	Treason
Thomas Sedgewick	Washington	Misprison of Treason & Misdemeanor
Thomas Spiers	Washington	Treason
James Stewart	Allegheny	Treason
Philip Vigol	Westmoreland	Treason
Gabriel Walker	Allegheny	Treason
Isaac Walker	Allegheny	Treason
Edward Wright	Allegheny	Treason

Disposition	Date	Offense	At Trial
Ignoramus	May 7, 1795	Braddock's Field	Yes
Ignoramus	May 8, 1795	Failure to disclose treasonous activities	Yes
True Bill	May 12, 1795	Meeting on July 28, 1794 at Cannonsburg to organize the Braddock's Field rendezvous	No
True Bill (Not guilty)	May 6, 1795	Neville's House	Yes
True Bill (Guilty)	May 6, 1795	July 24, 1794 attack on Fayette County revenue office	Yes
Ignoramus	May 12, 1795	Braddock's Field	Yes
Ignoramus	May 12, 1795	Braddock's Field	Yes
True Bill (Not guilty)	--	-- 1/	Yes

1/ See Albert Gallatin to Thomas Clare, May 30, 1795, Albert Gallatin Papers, New York Historical Society.

Appendix B

Indictments in the Circuit Court for the District of Pennsylvania
May 1975 Term—other Counties

Source: Criminal Case Files of the United States Circuit Court for the Eastern
District of Pennsylvania 1791–1840 (M-986, reel 1), RG 21, National Archives

Name	County of Origin	Charge
Andrew Bellsmeyer	Northumberland	Misdemeanor
William Bonham	Northumberland	Misdemeanor
William Bonham	Northumberland	Treason
Thomas Caldwell	Northumberland	Misprison of Treason and Misdemeanor
George Langs	Northumberland	Same
John Macky	Northumberland	Same
Robert Lusk	Cumberland	Misdemeanor
Daniel Montgomery	Northumberland	Misdemeanor
William Montgomery	Northumberland	Misdemeanor
Frederic Reamer	Franklin	Misdemeanor
Nathan Stockman	Northumberland	Misdemeanor
George Weiscarver	Bedford	Misdemeanor
George Lucas	Bedford	Misdemeanor
Thomas Wilson	Franklin	Misdemeanor

Disposition	Date	Offense
Ignoramus	May 11, 1795	Pole raising in Sept. 1794
True Bill	May 8, 1795	Same
Ignoramus	May 8, 1795	Same
True Bill as to Misprison of Treason; Ignoramus as to Misdemeanor	May 9, 1795	Same
Same	May 9, 1795	Same
Same	May 9, 1795	Same
True Bill	Oct. 1, 1795	Seditious Letter
True Bill	May 9, 1795	Pole raising in Sept. 1794
True Bill	May 9, 1795	Same
Ignoramus	May 9, 1795	Pole raising on Sept. 13, 1794
True Bill	May 12, 1795	Pole raising in Sept. 1794
Ignoramus	May 11, 1795	Pole raising on Sept. 1, 1794
Ignoramus	May 11, 1795	Same
True Bill	May 9, 1795	Sedition for saying "any man who supports the Excise is a damned rascal" on Sept. 15, 1794

Index

Adams, John, 149

Addison, Alexander: biography, 49–51; his letter to Lee describing the rebellion, 51–56; Brackenridge on, 63, 64, 66, 74n.11; on compliance and removal of tax collectors, 94n.30; prefers state courts to federal, 167–68; and prosecution of rebels, 170, 172; emphasizes resistance to federal authority, rather than treason, in state court, 175

American Revolution, influence on rebels, 13, 124, 130

American State Papers, Finance, 100, 188

Ames, Fisher, on Philadelphia tax protest, 127–28, 147, 154

Anti-Constitutionalist party, 65, 72

Anti-Federalists, 66, 73; vs. Federalists as cause of rebellion, 21, 29n.29, 67; on proposed Constitution and excise tax, 93n.12; questions about representation, 120; fear of taxing powers, 121

arrearages in taxes forgiven, 102, 114n.39

Bache, Franklin, 151

Baldwin, Leland D., on causes of rebellion, 15

barter economy, and whiskey production, 12, 15, 121

Battle of Fallen Timbers (1794), 110

Bell, Rudolph, and external restraints on government, 130

Berr, Alexander, 38, 89

Biddle, Clement, describes danger to tax collectors, 34

Black, John, 45

Boston Tea Party of 1773, 13

Brackenridge, Henry Marie, 15; his defense of rebels, 11; feud with Craig, 11, 51; on causes of rebellion, 13

Brackenridge, Hugh Henry, 15, 16, 184; on his participation in and causes of the rebellion, 11, 12, 62–73; biography of, 61–62; on Tom Tinker's letters, 84–85

Braddock's Fields, insurgents call militia to, 59n.27, 148, 170, 173

Bradford, David, 32, 33, 59n.22; Addison claims he would not prosecute rebels, 53; opposed excise, 63; Brackenridge on, 66, 69, 72

Bradford, William, 149; calls resistance treasonous, 171–72, 174

Breaden, Nathaniel, 33

Brooks, Collector, attacked 101

Brownsville meeting (July 27, 1791): described by Hamilton, 32–33; Findley on, 46n.2, 80, 92n.10; Brackenridge on, 67–68

Bush, Ambrose, 106, 107

Contributors

ROLAND M. BAUMANN, Chief of the Division of Archives and Manuscripts, Pennsylvania Historical and Museum Commission, is the author of numerous articles in *The Pennsylvania Magazine of History and Biography* and *Pennsylvania History*. He is currently engaged in a study of the 1788 Harrisburg Convention.

STEVEN R. BOYD, an associate professor of history at the University of Texas at San Antonio, specializes in the constitutional history of the Revolution and Early National periods. His earlier publications include *The Politics of Opposition: Antifederalists and the Acceptance of the Constitution* (New York, 1978). He is currently working on an impact study of the Constitution in the early national period.

RICHARD A. IFFT, a graduate of Georgetown School of Law, is an attorney with the firm of Hamel and Park in Washington D.C. He was recently the managing editor of and a contributor to the *Georgetown Law Journal*. He is currently working on an article on St. Clair's defeat on the Wabash in 1791.

RICHARD H. KOHN is Chief of Air Force History, Department of the Air Force. His earlier publications include *Eagle and the Sword: The Federalists and the Creation of the Military Establishment in America, 1783–1802* (New York, 1975) and "The Washington Administration's Decision to Crush the Whiskey Rebellion," which won the Binkley-Stephenson prize of the Organization of American Historians for the best essay published in the *Journal of American History* in 1973.

JAMES KIRBY MARTIN is a professor of history at the University of Houston who specializes in early American social, political, and military history. He is the author of numerous books and articles, including most recently with Mark E. Lender, *Drinking in America: A History* (New York, 1982). He is currently completing a biography of Benedict Arnold.

JAMES ROGER SHARP is a professor of history at Syracuse University. He is the author of *The Jacksonians Versus the Banks: Politics in the States After the Panic of 1837* (New York, 1970). He is completing a book tentatively entitled "The Jeffersonians' Conception of Party: The Development of the Idea of a Loyal Opposition," and coediting for Greenwood Press "American Legislative Leaders," a biographical directory of state speakers of the house of representatives.

THOMAS P. SLAUGHTER is an assistant professor of history at Rutgers University, specializing in Anglo-American political and legal history. His earlier publications include "The Tax Man Cometh: Ideological Opposition to Internal Taxes, 1760–1790," in *The William and Mary Quarterly*, 3d ser., 41 (October, 1984). He is now completing a monograph on the Whiskey Rebellion to be published by Oxford University Press.

MARY K. BONSTEEL TACHAU is a professor of history at the University of Louisville. Her earlier publications include *Federal Courts in the Early Republic: Kentucky, 1789–1816* (Princeton, 1978) which received the first Governor's Award of the Kentucky Historical Society. She also received the award for the best article published in volume two of the *Journal of the Early Republic* for her essay, "The Whiskey Rebellion, A Forgotten Episode of Civil Disobedience."